D0175331

Advance Praise for *Reverse Innovation*

Leaders of Developed-World Multinationals

"Innovation knows no geographic boundaries. This book is a defining work on how we invest and engage the future."

—William D. Green
Executive Chairman
Accenture

"The global community is now so networked that innovation can come from just about anywhere and make an impact everywhere."

—John T. Chambers
Chairman and CEO
Cisco Systems, Inc.

"Unique and important work, hard-hitting examples, detailed and actionable steps, and clear explanations."

—Omar Ishrak
Chairman and CEO
Medtronic, Inc.

"As the world's economic center of gravity continues to shift—and as new consumers continue to emerge—it's clear that the logic and business practices that drove yesterday's success won't drive tomorrow's."

—Ajay Banga
President and CEO
MasterCard

"I wish I had this book ten years ago."

—Peter F. Volanakis
Former President and COO
Corning Incorporated

"More than anything, this book inspires true hope that reverse innovation can be a force for good for all."

—Christopher R. Hyman
CEO
Serco Group plc, London

"Reverse Innovation can improve the lives of billions."

—Gururaj (Desh) Deshpande
Cofounder and Chairman
Sycamore Networks

"Reverse Innovation concisely expresses both the challenges and the opportunities in the rapidly developing high-growth areas of the world."

—Samuel R. Allen
Chairman and CEO
Deere & Company

"Govindarajan and Trimble offer a framework for the next phase of globalization."

—Jeffrey R. Immelt
Chairman and CEO
General Electric

"Govindarajan and Trimble have tapped into one of the fundamental changes in global business today."

—Alexander (Sandy) M. Cutler
Chairman and CEO
Eaton Corporation

"With keen insight, Govindarajan and Trimble have put forth a powerful business case for reverse innovation."

—James H. Quigley
Former CEO
Deloitte Touche Tohmatsu Limited

"Multinational companies need to throw out the old playbook."

—Steve Pagliuca
Managing Director
Bain Capital, LLC

"This book advances compelling, fresh thinking."

—Douglas R. Conant
President and CEO
Campbell Soup Company

"The emerging economies are not only the growth markets of the next century, but they will also be a great source of idea making."

—William F. Achtmeyer
Chairman and Managing Partner
The Parthenon Group

"Growth in emerging markets requires the mind-set, organization, and discipline the authors recommend."

—Ian M. Cook
Chairman, President, and CEO
Colgate-Palmolive Company

"Govindarajan and Trimble go well beyond innovation in this book—to reverse innovation."

—Peter A. Darbee
Former CEO
Pacific Gas & Electric Company

"Steady, incremental growth in emerging markets is not enough."

—Thomas H. Glocer
Former CEO
Thomson Reuters

"This book is a must-read."

—Raj L. Gupta
Retired Chairman and CEO
Rohm and Haas

Reverse Innovation is a playbook for unlocking the growth potential of emerging markets."

—William R. Johnson
Chairman, President, and CEO
H.J. Heinz Company

"If necessity is the mother of innovation, more innovation will come from the developing world, validating this book's unique hypothesis."

—Vinod Khosla
Cofounder
Sun Microsystems

"Govindarajan and Trimble make a strong case for companies to 'learn how to operate on a different axis' in order to fully seize the opportunities in growing markets."

—Richard J. Kramer
Chairman, President, and CEO
Goodyear Tire & Rubber Company

Reverse Innovation is a playbook for leaders who want to unlock growth in emerging markets."

—Robert A. McDonald
Chairman, President, and CEO
Procter & Gamble

"I can think of a dozen times where the approaches laid out in *Reverse Innovation* would have led to a better outcome for our company as we sought growth in emerging markets."

—Donald K. Peterson
Former CEO
Avaya, Inc.

"The clarity of the authors' ideas will serve leaders of global companies well."

—Michael H. Thaman
Chairman, President, and CEO
Owens Corning

"This is a book rich with big ideas."

—Michael R. Traem
CEO
Arthur D. Little

"*Reverse Innovation* is a great playbook."

—Brian Goldner
President and CEO
Hasbro, Inc.

Leaders of Emerging Market Firms

"This book is a must-read for businesses not only in the developed world but also in the developing world."

—Adi Godrej
Chairman
Godrej Group, India

"A very lucidly articulated roadmap of business innovation for the world to embrace."

—Mukesh D. Ambani
Chairman and Managing Director
Reliance Industries Limited, India

"*Reverse Innovation* is a good compass for emerging multinationals in their endeavor to expand and achieve a prominent global presence."

—Frederico F. Curado
President and CEO
Embraer, Brazil

"A great resource to lubricate your thinking about winning solutions in the emerging world—and how to leverage these globally!"

—Piyush Gupta
CEO
DBS Bank, Singapore

"I found the summaries and 'Questions for Reflection' at the end of each case study to be particularly useful."

—Vikram S. Kirloskar
Chairman and Managing Director
Kirloskar Systems Limited, India

"The wonderful case studies in this book all highlight one thing—innovation is bred from dissatisfaction."

—TK Kurien
CEO
Wipro, India

"This book is about an idea whose time has come. An eminently practical guide to the future of corporate growth."

—Anand G. Mahindra
Managing Director
Mahindra & Mahindra Ltd., India

"This book is an essential field guide for global business leaders."

—N.R. Narayana Murthy
Chairman Emeritus
Infosys, India

"Well worth reading."

—Zhang Ruimin
CEO
Haier Group, China

"This book explains how innovations are increasingly originating in developing countries and flowing back to rich ones."

—Ratan N. Tata
Chairman
Tata Sons Limited, India

Academic Thought Leaders

"Water may not flow uphill, but innovation does! This book is both an inspiration and a cautionary tale."

—Roger L. Martin
Dean of the Rotman School of Management
University of Toronto

"A brilliant, freshly imagined view of innovation."

—Warren G. Bennis
Distinguished University Professor
University of Southern California

"Timely and relevant for any company hoping to remain competitive in this rapidly changing world."

—Jeffrey Pfeffer
Thomas D. Dee II Professor of Organizational Behavior
Stanford Graduate School of Business

"Govindarajan and Trimble make a compelling case for a fundamentally different form of innovation."

—Michael L. Tushman
Paul R. Lawrence MBA Class of 1942 Professor of
Business Administration
Harvard Business School

"A fascinating new paradigm."

—Laura D. Tyson
Chair of the President's Council of Economic Advisors
Clinton Administration

(You can read the complete endorsements on the following websites: www.vg-tuck.com, www.innovationreverse.com or at www.hbr.org)

REVERSE INNOVATION

Vijay Govindarajan
Chris Trimble

INNOVATION

CREATE FAR
FROM HOME,
WIN
EVERYWHERE

HARVARD BUSINESS REVIEW PRESS

Boston, Massachusetts

Copyright 2012 Vijay Govindarajan and Chris Trimble
All rights reserved
Printed in the United States of America

10 9 8 7 6 5 4 3 2 1

No part of this publication may be reproduced, stored in or introduced into a
retrieval system, or transmitted, in any form, or by any means (electronic, mechanical,
photocopying, recording, or otherwise), without the prior permission of the publisher.
Requests for permission should be directed to permissions@hbsp.harvard.edu, or
mailed to Permissions, Harvard Business School Publishing, 60 Harvard Way, Boston,
Massachusetts 02163.

Library of Congress Cataloging-in-Publication Data

Govindarajan, Vijay.
    Reverse innovation : create far from home, win everywhere / Vijay Govindarajan,
Chris Trimble; [foreword by] Indra K. Nooyi.
        p. cm.
    ISBN 978-1-4221-5764-0 (hardback)
    1. International business enterprises—Management—Case studies. 2. Technological
innovations—Management—Case studies.   3. Strategic planning—Case studies.   I. Trimble,
Chris.   II. Title.
    HD62.4.G683 2012
    658.4′063—dc23

                                                    2011040347

The paper used in this publication meets the requirements of the American National
Standard for Permanence of Paper for Publications and Documents in Libraries and
Archives Z39.48-1992.

To

DR. C. K. PRAHALAD

A Guiding Light

CONTENTS

FOREWORD

Years ago, in what feels now like a bygone era, large multinational businesses derived most of their revenues, and sought most of their growth, in home markets. If these firms looked abroad, it was typically to other rich countries.

But nothing in the global ecosystem is static. Home markets are mature and saturated. Most of the world's untapped buying power is in the emerging markets of Asia, South Asia, Eastern Europe, Africa, and Latin America. Multinationals now understand that a truly global strategy must include smart pathways to strong positions in emerging economies. For there is where the richest future growth is to be found.

Reverse innovation—the subject of this important book—is one of those smart pathways. It is a powerful new tool to add to your innovation capabilities. And it is certainly one of the keys to making the most of emerging-market opportunities.

As you will read in chapter 11, PepsiCo has begun to reap the benefits of reverse innovation in its snack-foods business. Like virtually every multinational business, we at PepsiCo once approached overseas markets in the conventional way: we exported! We created products in America, and then we sent them around the world. Sometimes we made small modifications in flavor and packaging for local markets, but our offerings were basically global products.

Now, however, we have the benefit of new insights. First, we have learned better to appreciate the important differences of people from place to place. Second, we have learned that a market wants to have its culture, values, and tastes reflected back to it in the products it chooses to consume. And third, we have learned that people around the world—even for all of their differences—still have *some* desires in common. It seems that everywhere, in our sector of the economy, people are demanding products made with natural, healthful ingredients and manufactured in a sustainable way. For us, that has meant offering products that are not just "Fun for You," but also "Good for You."

If you look at these three insights, you will see that they combine global vision and mission with an intense focus on local needs and preferences. This mixture is at the heart of reverse innovation. The good news is that multinational businesses—with their deep resources, broad reach, and diverse international talent base—are ideally suited to execute such a global-local juggling act. The bad news is that it's much easier to accept the wisdom of reverse innovation than it is to put it into practice.

The tremendous value of this book is that authors Vijay Govindarajan and Chris Trimble have richly stocked it with practical lessons to go along with the underlying theory. Throughout—and especially in the eight case-study chapters—they show the struggles and occasional missteps that are always an important part of any transforming journey.

For me, the key insight the book holds is one that will feel absolutely true to any multinational executive: the lessons of what the authors call *dominant logic*. Every enterprise that has enjoyed great success is both sustained *and* endangered by all that it has learned in the past. That is its dominant logic. The challenge of reverse innovation lies in its requirement that you set aside—if only for certain initiatives—the powerful logic of the past. Otherwise, it will stand in the way of the humility necessary to admit that you still have much to learn.

It is very hard for innovators in research centers in the United States to know what will appeal to—much less delight—consumers in Beijing or Mumbai, Nairobi or Mexico City. You have to roll up your sleeves in those places and learn by engaging with and listening to the customers there, by understanding your local rivals, and by empowering your own people who grew up in those places, to put their regional knowledge to work.

We are none of us infallible geniuses. Along the way to doing important things—big, valuable things—we will all make mistakes. That is not a reason to shirk from beginning. We need to accept that mistakes are inevitable and give ourselves permission in advance to make them. Happily, the authors let you look over the shoulders of PepsiCo and many other businesses as we learn how to practice reverse innovation. You will get to see the bitter with the sweet. And it may save you from making some mistakes of your own.

—Indra K. Nooyi, chairman and CEO, PepsiCo

PREFACE

Leaving Something to Chance

I wish I could say that this book is the culmination of a decades-long, well-executed plan. The truth, however, is that it is the happy result of three chance events.

Event 1: An Unexpected Book

I earned my chartered accountancy degree in India in the 1970s. My course of study included many dry texts filled with numbers and abstract concepts. There was also a reference list of books not explicitly covered in the classes. I read many of these, including one by a legendary Harvard Business School professor named Robert Anthony. In it, Anthony expressed a view of my chosen field that was a total revelation to me: accounting, he asserted, was *not* the technical subject I had thus far presumed it to be. Instead, it was a force that could be used to influence human behavior in constructive ways.

This was so different from anything I had previously learned that I became determined to go to the Harvard Business School. I wanted to be exposed to people who, like Bob Anthony, had such interesting and surprising ideas that they could make accounting come to life for me and make it suddenly seem new.

At Harvard, I saw accounting as a tool for the execution of strategy. There were relationships between numbers, human motivation, and business execution. Accounting was a crucial instrument for achieving superior execution.

Slowly, then—entirely because I stumbled upon Bob Anthony's book—my focus changed from "dry" accounting systems to the study of *all* of the administrative systems that exert a behavioral influence on an enterprise. In time I became a researcher, teacher, and consultant in the field of strategy execution.

Event 2: An Unexpected Partnership

I met my coauthor, Chris Trimble, more than a decade ago. The Tuck School of Business at Dartmouth, where I have taught since 1985, had received a large donation to establish a research center that would focus on global strategy and innovation. I was looking for a partner in the endeavor. Chris, who had been one of Tuck's top MBA graduates and had been working as a consultant, was seeking a new challenge, with an eye toward academia. He agreed to join me.

Neither of us anticipated what followed: more than a decade of happy and productive work focused on the challenges of making innovation happen inside established organizations. In addition to *Harvard Business Review* articles, one of which, "Stop the Innovation Wars," was a McKinsey Award winner, we have produced two prior books on innovation: *Ten Rules for Strategic Innovators* and *The Other Side of Innovation*. These books formed a crucial foundation for this book.

I am profoundly grateful to have met and struck up such a vibrant partnership with Chris. His contributions to this book have spanned a wide range. He developed theory, articulated key concepts in a high-impact way, served as the deep expert on innovation execution, produced many passages of hard-hitting prose, and even coined the term *reverse innovation*. In short, he has been a true partner in every aspect of our work, as well as a close friend.

Event 3: An Unexpected Assignment

Thanks to a lightning strike of good fortune, I spent two remarkable years serving as GE's first professor in residence and chief innovation consultant. Two conversations, spread out over several years, yielded the tremendous opportunity.

In 2001, I gave a talk at a conference. After my session ended, I had time to kill before my flight home, so I stayed and listened to a talk by Susan Peters. She was then GE's chief learning officer, and in her talk, she described the company's approach to leadership development. I was captivated by this glimpse into GE's thought process. After the talk, I went up and introduced myself to Susan. She asked me what I did, and I described my work at the Tuck School on innovation and execution.

A few years after that, GE CEO Jeffrey Immelt came to speak at Tuck. I requested a half hour one-on-one meeting. We talked about the challenges of combining innovation and efficiency, and I shared some ideas from our research. A year or so after that, Chris and I published *Ten Rules*. I sent a copy to Immelt, and he responded with a handwritten letter.

In 2007, Immelt discussed with Peters a plan for bringing an academic into GE to advise the company on innovation. He asked her to assemble a list of possible candidates with innovation expertise. When my name came up, it clicked with both of them.

GE as a Reverse Innovation Laboratory

I started my two-year adventure at GE in January 2008. Jeff Immelt had asked me to consult to two business units: GE Healthcare and GE Energy. Both were seeking ways of competing more effectively in the emerging markets of India and China. Immelt saw clearly that GE's future as a company was tied to its performance in the developing world and, in particular, its skill at *reverse innovation*—that is, its ability to innovate specifically for emerging markets. "For GE to win in the U.S.," he said, "it *must* win in India and China." Or, as our book's subtitle exhorts, to win everywhere, you must learn to create far from home.

Once I investigated the health-care and energy markets of the developing world, I saw exactly the same sets of opportunities and constraints. In both markets, there were deficient infrastructures that struggled to meet growing demand.

For example, health care in India faced an urgent shortage of hospital beds. This deficiency coincided with a rapidly growing and more-prosperous middle class that was beginning to experience higher rates of so-called lifestyle ailments such as diabetes and obesity. There was also a shortage of physicians and other health professionals. And India had a grossly underserved rural population with little or no access to basic care or to the sorts of diagnostic technologies that could catch illnesses at an early, easily treatable stage.

Furthermore, the underdeveloped and unreliable electric grid in India made it impossible for small local clinics to rely on traditional ultrasound or electrocardiogram machines that ran on house current. Moreover, existing versions of these typically high-performance machines were cost-prohibitive in a predominantly poor country.

These were daunting barriers. However, I also saw that both health care and energy presented opportunities that exceeded a trillion dollars over the next two decades. GE urgently needed creative solutions. At that time, however, GE was playing a traditional market-share game in India, China, and other developing nations. The company was trying to sell lightly modified global products into markets that instead needed fresh ideas—breakthrough innovations engineered for local realities. Consequently, I believed that if GE expected to tap into these trillion-dollar opportunities in a significant way, it needed to play a *market-development* game, not a *market-share* game.

My time at GE was invaluable in helping to formulate the concepts, methods, and requirements for practicing reverse innovation. Critically, I was exposed to a fascinating and ultimately quite successful project under the leadership of Omar Ishrak, the head of GE's ultrasound business, to create a portable, low-cost ultrasound machine in China. The project demonstrated, in so many ways, what GE needed to be doing in almost every business unit to win in emerging markets. In October 2009, I coauthored a *Harvard Business Review* article on reverse innovation (with Jeff Immelt and Chris Trimble). "How GE Is Disrupting Itself" chronicles Ishrak's ultrasound project.

I was privileged to get a firsthand look at how a powerhouse U.S. multinational climbed the reverse innovation learning curve. It was a rich education. Suffice it to say that my debt to GE, as an inspiration for this book, is enormous.

The book is also stocked with many examples from other companies. In particular, chapters 5 through 12 in part 2 include richly detailed profiles of inspiring experiments in reverse innovation. We are indebted to the seven other organizations that generously shared their experiences with us with candor and in detail.

We regard the study of reverse innovation as an emergent field. It is a *next*-practice endeavor rather than a *best*-practice one. There is still so much yet to be learned. Nevertheless, the reverse innovation initiatives described in this book reveal a great deal about what works well—and what does not—when you are innovating for emerging markets. We hope that the concepts and evidence we have gathered here will tempt you to tackle your own reverse innovation endeavor. Perhaps, then, you will look back on the discovery of our book as an important chance event in your own business career.

Two Special Acknowledgments

In my previous books, I have gone to great lengths to acknowledge every contributor. This book is no different from my past books, in that the number of individuals involved is large. Nonetheless, I'd like to make an exception in this case, so that I may focus only on the two individuals who made, by far, the largest and most noteworthy efforts.

The first is Lew McCreary. Given his long and impressive career in journalism, including writing and editing for the *Harvard Business Review*, I was fortunate to be able to add Lew to the team for this book. Lew's contributions were broad and numerous. He participated in almost every interview, offered insights derived from a career writing about business, and drafted most chapters. Lew's deft writing brings style, originality, charm, wit, and energy to these pages, far beyond what we could otherwise have achieved.

The second is Chris Trimble, my close partner and coauthor since 2000. I often urge corporations that I advise to bring about discontinuous changes in their organizations. Chris Trimble has brought about a discontinuous change in my career. As Chris has taken on a new role at Dartmouth, this book is the culmination of our full-time partnership. He has made me a better professor—and a better person.

—Vijay Govindarajan

PART I

The Reverse Innovation Challenge

CHAPTER ONE

The Future Is Far from Home

Innovating for emerging markets, rather than simply exporting, can unlock a world of opportunities for multinationals.

GATORADE. It is as American as baseball and apple pie.

Its 1960s roots can be traced to the sun-scorched University of Florida and its football team—the Gators. Oppressive heat and humidity led the team's trainers to seek better ways than water alone to quickly rehydrate players. They turned to the school's research labs, which came back with a concoction of water, glucose, sodium, potassium, and flavorings. The tasty cocktail sped the replenishment of the electrolytes and carbohydrates that players lost through sweat and exertion.

Even before it became an actual brand, Gatorade got a nice marketing boost from the coach of Georgia Tech. Asked how his team had lost to Florida in the 1967 Orange Bowl, he lamented, "We didn't have Gatorade."

It is a great story, and it is wonderfully fitting for an American icon. But there is an interesting missing link, one that leads back to events far from Gainesville, Florida.

Earlier in the 1960s, there were epidemic outbreaks of cholera in Bangladesh and elsewhere in South Asia. The key to keeping cholera patients alive was simple: keep them hydrated.

According to Mehmood Khan, chief scientific officer of PepsiCo (which bought Gatorade in 2001), Western doctors who went to Bangladesh and elsewhere to help stem the epidemic were surprised to discover a centuries-old local treatment for the severe diarrhea caused by cholera. The concoction included ingredients such as coconut water, carrot juice, rice water, carob flour, and dehydrated bananas. At the time, Western medical opinion held that putting carbohydrates in the stomachs of patients suffering from diarrhea would cause cholera bacteria to multiply and the disease to worsen. "Yet for thousands of years, this was the normal treatment used in Ayurvedic medicine," says Khan. "By giving carbohydrate and sugar in the solution with salt, uptake was quicker, and patients rehydrated faster."[1]

The success of the treatment was covered in the British medical journal *Lancet* and made its way to a doctor at the University of Florida. The doctor saw a common problem in the need for rapid rehydration. If such a treatment worked well for cholera patients, it would surely work for healthy football players.

The Gatorade story was unusual for its era. It ran counter to the dominant innovation pattern. Innovations typically originated in rich countries and later flowed downhill to the developing world. Gatorade, by contrast, swam against the tide. It was a reverse innovation. Quite simply, a reverse innovation is any innovation that is adopted first in the developing world. Surprisingly often, these innovations defy gravity and flow uphill.

Historically, reverse innovations have been rare. Indeed, the reason most innovations flow downhill, not uphill, is intuitive. Rich customers in rich countries can afford—and indeed they demand—the latest and the greatest. Demand pushes technology forward. In due course, its benefits trickle down across the globe. You can do the innovation math: the United States and Germany have well over three hundred Nobel Prize winners in science and technology. Meanwhile, India and China, with six times the combined population, have fewer than ten. Consequently, people—especially in the West—expect the future to be invented in Silicon Valley or Houston or Munich, but not in Bangladesh.

Thus, it is natural to suppose that developing nations are engaged in a slow and evolutionary process of catching up with the rich world, both economically and technologically. They do not need innovation. They will simply import what they desire from the rich world, just as soon as they can afford it.

Under that set of assumptions, a strategy known as *glocalization* makes perfect sense. As practiced by multinational businesses, glocalization posits that the work of innovation has already occurred. Firms can tap emerging markets simply by exporting lightly modified versions of global products developed for rich-world customers—mainly lower-end models with fewer features.

But the assumptions are misguided. What works in the rich world won't automatically achieve wide acceptance in emerging markets, where customer needs are starkly different. As a result, reverse innovation is rapidly gathering steam—and it will only continue to do so.

On the surface, reverse innovation seems to be a counterintuitive phenomenon. It is easy, after all, to understand why a poor man would want a rich man's product. But why would a rich man ever want a poor man's product? The answer is that under certain circumstances, it offers new, unexpected, or long-overlooked value. Consider two modern examples.

When the giant big-box retailer Wal-Mart entered emerging markets in Central and South America, it discovered that it couldn't simply export its existing retail formula. It needed to innovate. Specifically, its big box had to be radically scaled down. The company created a version of the Wal-Mart store similar to the more "cozy" retail outlets common in Mexico, Brazil, and Argentina.

Smaller stores thrive in those places because shoppers typically lack the liquidity to buy in bulk and to maintain a home inventory. Moreover, consumers often ride bicycles, mopeds, or buses—or else walk—to do their shopping. There are limits to what they can carry home. Small Wal-Mart stores matched the needs of the local culture.

By 2011, Wal-Mart was doing something that would have been hard to imagine just a few years earlier. It was bringing the "small-mart" concept back to the United States. For one thing, its big-box market was saturated. Many U.S. consumers were suffering from big-box fatigue. Furthermore, dense urban environments, with constrained space and ultrahigh rents, could more easily—and profitably—support numerous small stores distributed around town instead of one or two that are the size of a full city block. A variant of the same logic applied in very sparsely populated rural areas, where a big box simply couldn't thrive. Wal-Mart could become a powerful rival to small-box competitors in that it still enjoys vast economies of scale in purchasing and supply-chain management even with a small store footprint. Soon enough, it seems, some Americans will be able to buy their South Asia–inspired Gatorade at a New York City Wal-Mart scaled to the dimensions of a village bodega.

Next, consider U.S. efforts to improve the cost effectiveness of—and access to—health care. Reformers would do well to look to India for new thinking.

Narayana Hrudayalaya (NH) hospital has transformed health care in India by performing open-heart surgery for just $2,000, compared to upward of $20,000 in the United States. Despite the ultra-low price, NH hospital's net profit margin is slightly *higher* than the U.S. average. Furthermore, its quality is world class. The mortality rate within thirty days of bypass surgery is 1.4 percent at NH hospital compared to the U.S. average of 1.9 percent.

NH hospital's success can only partially be explained by India's lower costs of labor. The real magic is in process innovation. NH took the radical step of adapting a number of well-understood industrial concepts that have been around since Ford's Model T: standardization, specialization of labor, economies of scale, and assembly line production.

These techniques enable NH hospital to utilize its resources much more fully, slashing the cost per procedure. For example, expensive equipment, purchased from world-renowned multinationals, is used five times more heavily than in the United States. And, surgeons perform two to three times more procedures. Furthermore, because of the hospital's high volume, an individual doctor can specialize in a specific type of cardiac surgery. This accelerates learning, improves skills, and increases quality.

These ideas may sound simple, but they run counter to the dominant logic of rich-world health systems. Doctors focus on the most challenging patients, trying to push the envelope on medical science and technology. Cost is not the first consideration, but the last. As a result, Western medicine is organized based on the expensive, and debatable, assumption that every patient is unique. Innovations in India show that, in many instances, there is another way. In fact, NH hospital is bringing its innovative business model to the rich world. It is building a large, two-thousand-bed hospital in the Cayman Islands (an hour's flight from Miami) to treat uninsured Americans at 50 percent below U.S. prices.[2]

These are just two of many examples that we will highlight in this book. The dynamics of global innovation are changing.

In his January 2011 State of the Union address, President Obama said that the United States must "out-innovate, out-educate, and out-build the rest of the world." That's a fine ambition, but it won't happen if American innovators focus strictly on American problems.

The new reality is that the future is far from home. If rich nations and established multinationals are to continue to thrive, the next generation of leaders and innovators must be just as curious about needs and opportunities in the developing world as they are about those in their own backyard. Whether you are a CEO, financier, strategist, marketer, scientist, engineer, national policymaker, or even a student forming a career aspiration, reverse innovation is a phenomenon you need to understand. Reverse innovation has the potential to redistribute power and wealth to countries and companies that understand it—and to diminish those that do not. Conceivably, it could accelerate the rise of poor countries and the decline of rich ones.[3] But it doesn't have to turn out that way. Indeed, reverse innovation is an opportunity that is open to anyone, anywhere, with the ambition to go after it.

The stakes are high. As we will explain, ignoring reverse innovation can cost many companies, especially today's world-class multinationals, much more than a missed opportunity abroad. It can open the door for the so-called *emerging giants*, the rising generation of multinationals headquartered in the developing world, to inflict pain or even severe damage in well-established home markets. There are dozens of such companies now, with names like Tata, Mahindra, Reliance, Lenovo, and Haier. They are here to stay. (See "Invasive Species: Mahindra & Mahindra in the U.S. Heartland.")

Jeffrey Immelt, chairman and CEO of General Electric, puts it this way: "If we don't come up with innovations in poor countries and take them global, new competitors from the developing world—like Mindray, Suzlon, and Goldwind—will. That's a bracing prospect. GE has long had tremendous respect for traditional rivals like Siemens, Philips, and Rolls-Royce. But we know how to compete with them. They will never destroy GE. The emerging giants, on the other hand, very well could."[4]

Reverse innovation is not optional. It is oxygen.

Why Emerging Markets Need a Clean-Slate Approach

As leaders of multinationals are well aware, the developing economies are large and are growing at fantastic rates. A few simple numbers paint the picture.

The International Monetary Fund (IMF) regularly ranks nations by various economic metrics.[5] In population, for example, China is number one, and India is number two. A whopping 85 percent of the world's citizens, 5.8 billion people, live in poor countries.[6] In measures of total gross domestic product (GDP), China is number two, India number four, and the total GDP of poor countries is roughly $35 trillion, nearly half of world GDP.[7]

Furthermore, projected GDP growth rates for China and India are at least double those of rich countries. Indeed, growth in poor countries has already outpaced growth in rich ones for several years running. The sharp recession triggered by the 2008 financial crisis made the growth gap look more like a chasm, and the uncertainty created by the U.S. and European debt crises in 2011 has widened the chasm even further. Poor countries are likely to account for *at least two-thirds* of world GDP growth for decades to come.

It is an enormous opportunity, but one that will not be easy for companies with rich-world legacies to capture. Winning in emerging markets requires far more than simple geographic expansion. As a mere starting point, it requires intense curiosity about how the needs of the developing world are different from those at home.

You can get a preliminary sense of these deep differences simply by considering just one more basic statistic: GDP per capita, the annual income of each nation's average citizens. This ranking looks little like the population or the GDP lists. The United States still ranks high, sixth in the world, first among countries with a population greater than 10 million citizens (a handful of small but very rich countries top the list). But how about China and India? Scroll down . . . Keep going. Keep going. There! According to the IMF in 2010, China is number 94 (between Bosnia-Herzegovina and El Salvador); India is number 128 (between the Cape Verde Islands and Vietnam).

The point is simple. Developing economies are different. They are not just a little bit different; they are night-and-day different. In the rich world, there are a few people who each spend a lot; in the developing world, there are a lot of people who each spend a little. Either way, total spending is vast. China and India are megamarkets with microconsumers.

This implies a starkly different business challenge. One person with ten dollars to spend has a completely different set of wants and needs than ten people each with one dollar to spend. That's why it's unrealistic to expect rich-world products and services to have much of an impact in poor countries. Doing more business in high-growth hot spots—aka poor nations—requires much more than ramping up sales, distribution, and production.

It requires innovation. Reverse innovation.

The Purpose of This Book

In this book, we will focus on what you—and we assume that most readers are leaders of, and leaders within, multinational corporations headquartered in the rich world—must do to stay strong and shape the future. Leaders within the upstart challengers, the emerging giants, will also value this book for its inside view into exactly what the established multinationals have to overcome to compete effectively in the developing world. Emerging giants can use the book's ideas to drive reverse innovation strategies of their own in their global expansion.

The purposes of this book are twofold: first, to help you grasp the theory and precepts underlying reverse innovation, including the significant strategic value achievable through its application, and, second, to provide you with highly practical guidance on how to execute successful reverse innovation initiatives. In other words, you will learn both to set strategy and to act: to identify right opportunities, build and support local teams, find creative inspiration in constrained circumstances, surmount internal and external obstacles, and avoid potentially lethal traps.

In addition to the overview presented in this chapter, part 1 of the book contains our recommendations in three categories—at the strategic level, at the organizational level, and at the project level. Strategy is our focus in chapter 2. We will explain why you must rethink global strategy, creating room, specifically, for a reverse innovation strategy. Such a strategy must be rooted in a deep understanding of the profound differences between emerging-market needs and rich-country needs, and the dynamics that can make emerging-market innovations flow uphill. In chapter 3, we will explain how you must reshape your global organization by shifting people, power, and resources to emerging markets, creating distinct business units with distinct scorecards in emerging markets and creating a reverse innovation mind-set throughout the company. Finally, in chapter 4 we will show how to pursue specific reverse innovation projects. You must assess needs, design solutions, and design teams from scratch, while still making

Invasive Species: Mahindra & Mahindra in the U.S. Heartland

In 1994, when Mahindra & Mahindra (M&M) arrived on American shores, it was already a powerhouse in its native India. The company, founded as a steelmaker in 1945, had entered the agriculture market nearly twenty years later, partnering with International Harvester to manufacture a line of sturdy thirty-five-horsepower tractors under the Mahindra name.

These tractors became very popular in India. They were affordably priced and fuel efficient, two qualities highly valued by thrifty Indian farmers, and the machines were sized appropriately for small Indian farms. Over the years, M&M continued to innovate to perfect its offerings, and its tractors proliferated throughout India's vast agricultural regions. The Mahindra brand became well established and respected. By the mid-1990s, the company was one of India's top tractor manufacturers—and it was ready for new challenges. The lucrative U.S. market beckoned.

When Mahindra USA (MUSA) opened for business, Deere & Company was the dominant brand. Deere's bread and butter was enormous machines ranging as high as six hundred horsepower for industrial-scale agribusiness. Rather than trying to develop a product that could compete head-on with Deere, M&M aimed for a smaller agricultural niche, one in which it could grow and make the most of its strengths.

Mahindra figured its little red tractor would be perfect for hobby farmers, landscapers, and building contractors. The machine was sturdy, extremely reliable, and priced to sell. With a few modifications for the U.S. market—such as supersized seats and larger brake pedals to comfortably accommodate larger American bodies—Mahindra was good to go.

But the company was far from home and hardly a household name. The few Americans who had heard of the brand thought of it variously as "red," "foreign," or "cheap." Even domestic competitors were barely aware of the newcomer. Deere gave more of its attention to Case and New Holland than to Mahindra. Flying below the radar, MUSA decided to make its mark through personalized service.

It built close relationships with small dealerships, particularly family-run operations. Rather than saddle dealers with expensive inventory, MUSA allowed them to run on a just-in-time basis, offering to deliver a tractor within twenty-four to forty-eight hours of receiving the order. MUSA also facilitated financing. In return, Mahindra benefited from the trust the dealers enjoyed in their communities.

MUSA also built close relationships with customers. Some 10 to 15 percent of M&M tractor buyers got phone calls from the company's president, who asked whether they were pleased with the buying experience and their new tractors. The company also offered special incentives—horticultural scholarships, for example—to neglected market segments such as female hobby farmers.

This high-touch strategy paid off handsomely. MUSA's U.S. sales growth averaged 40 percent per year, from 1999 to 2006. This prompted David C. Everitt, president of Deere's agricultural division, to remark that Mahindra "could someday pass Deere in global unit sales."[8]

Deere responded with short-lived—and seemingly desperate—cash incentives to induce Mahindra buyers to trade for a Deere. This had the unintended effect of promoting M&M's brand ("And we didn't even pay for it," says Anjou Choudhari, CEO of M&M's farm equipment sector from 2005 to 2010). Mahindra fired back with an ad featuring the headline "Deere John, I have found someone new."

As Mahindra enjoyed growing success in America, Deere struggled to gain a foothold in India. Unlike Mahindra, which had innovated both its product and its processes for the U.S. market, Deere tried to tempt Indian farmers with the same product that had underwritten its success at home. The strategy didn't work, and Deere was forced to reengineer its thinking as well as its product (see chapter 8).

"We gave a wake-up call to John Deere," notes Choudhari. "Our global threat [was] one of the motivations for Deere to design a low-horsepower tractor—in India, and for India."[9]

In the meantime, M&M has become the number-one tractor maker worldwide, as measured by units sold.

it possible for these teams to leverage global resources. And these teams must run disciplined experiments.

We summarize these recommendations in "The Reverse Innovation Playbook," which you'll find right after chapter 4.

Part 2 of the book, chapters 5 through 12, consists of eight in-depth case studies that, taken together, showcase the entire Reverse Innovation Playbook. Based on interviews with key principals, all of the stories include many of the challenges and frustrations that teams and their leaders faced along the way.

Frustrations are, of course, inevitable. The tapestry of geographies and cultures in which you will pursue reverse innovation efforts is likely to demand considerable adaptation, sometimes even improvisation. The case examples in part 2 show that you can be both disciplined and flexible in the pursuit of reverse innovation's rewards.

After a brief call for action in the conclusion, we offer two appendixes. The first is a tool kit that you can use to shape conversations about reverse innovation in your own company. The second, directed at academics, explains how this book builds on past work and suggests important new directions for future research.

CHAPTER TWO

The Five Paths of Reverse Innovation

To set strategy, you must understand the five most common reverse innovation paths.

I N CHAPTER 1, we described countries like India and China as mega-markets with microconsumers. We warned that one person with ten dollars to spend has a vastly different set of wants and needs than ten people each with one dollar to spend. This is a good beginning, but reaping the full benefit of reverse innovation requires a much deeper understanding of the differences between rich-country and poor-country needs.

It also requires the avoidance of a natural and instinctive assumption about paths of economic development. To see the pitfall, compare the economic advance of India with the earlier economic rise of the United States.

In 2010, the annual per-capita income in the United States was about $47,000. In India, it was about $3,000. Even under the most optimistic economic growth assumptions, it will take a long and slow march of at least two generations for India to catch up to the United States on this metric. As the income of Indian citizens rises, they will want to address pressing needs. They will demand, for example, more and better farm machinery, more and better transportation, more and better refrigeration, and more and better home entertainment.

So far, the thinking is on target. But for executives perched in rich countries, a dangerous follow-on thought trap can be hard to avoid: "These challenges were tackled in the rich world long ago. Why should innovation for emerging markets ever be necessary? Why can't we just export the products and services that we already have?"

Unfortunately, this thinking is far too simplistic. India will not follow the same path of economic development followed by the rich nations that preceded it. In particular, India has the potent advantage of being able to tackle old problems with new technology. Also, even where the fundamental needs are similar, they must be addressed under distinct conditions—different infrastructures, geographies, cultures, languages, governments, and so forth.

Because of these vast differences, business leaders who have grown up in, worked in, and are steeped in the traditions of rich countries face a tremendous challenge. Reverse innovation begins not with inventing, but with forgetting. You must let go of what you've learned, what you've seen, and what has brought you your greatest successes. You must let go of the dominant logic that has served you well in rich countries. If you want to use today's science and technology to address unmet needs in the developing world, then you must start with humility and curiosity.

In fact, it's best to assume that you've just landed on Mars.

In this chapter, we will take a major leap beyond the simple and obvious identification of the differences in income-per-capita by illustrating five enormous needs gaps that separate emerging markets from rich countries. And we will show the pathways by which solutions that address emerging market needs can flow uphill.

How Reverse Innovation Begins: Creating Far from Home

You can think of the five needs gaps as the starting points for reverse innovation opportunities. The five gaps are the performance gap, the infrastructure gap, the sustainability gap, the regulatory gap, and the preferences gap. Let's take a close look at each.

The Performance Gap

With little money in their pockets, buyers in the developing world cannot demand the sky-high levels of performance that we are accustomed to in rich countries. Indeed, in many cases, they cannot afford even what those in the rich world would consider to be low-end products. However, that doesn't mean they don't need innovation.

Consider a typical "good-better-best" product lineup. The good product offers 80 percent performance at an 80 percent price, the better product offers 90 percent performance at a 90 percent price, and the best product gives 100 percent performance at a 100 percent price.

The easy thing to do, when trying to address needs in emerging economies, is to customize the good product a bit, perhaps by watering it down to a fair product that offers 70 percent performance at a 70 percent price. Typically, however, such an offering captures only a small slice of the market.

Instead, developing nations are most eager for breakthrough new technologies that deliver decent performance at an ultralow cost—that is, a 50 percent solution for as little as a 15 percent price. It is impossible to design to that radical ratio if you begin with the existing offering. The only way to get to an entirely new price-performance curve is by starting from scratch.

For example, Nokia managed to capture an enormous market share of 60 percent in India by creating an ultra-low-cost handset that some users have bought for as little as the equivalent in rupees of $5 (discounted from a published price of $20 to $30, which is still a mere fraction of the retail price of high-end rich-world phones).

How did Nokia do it? By reimagining the cell phone. The company slashed costs by producing only a few basic models at a time when its global competitors offered dozens or more. Nokia made some customization, such as adding Hindi-language text messaging, but it did so with software, not hardware—a far less costly approach. It also added functionalities to the handset such as powerful flashlights that rural customers with irregular electricity valued. Nokia clearly understood the differences in needs—the performance gap, in particular. It created an offering that met real needs at a realistic price.[1]

The Infrastructure Gap

The rich world has extensive infrastructure in place; the poor world does not. Rich countries have highly developed physical infrastructure such as roads, telecommunications networks, power plants, and airports; social infrastructure such as schools, universities, and hospitals; and institutional infrastructure such as banks, courts, and stock markets. In poor nations, these foundations for economic development are under construction.

One naturally thinks of the rich world's well-developed infrastructure as a powerful asset. New products can be developed in the rich world under the assumption that a solid and reliable infrastructure is in place. However, a lack of infrastructure can actually be an advantage in the innovation game. Difficult constraints, such as unreliable electric power, inspire creative workarounds that sometimes lead in unexpected directions. For example, a lack of health-care infrastructure in India inspired GE Healthcare to develop a breakthrough in technology for portable electrocardiogram machines—a development that has since had an impact in the rich world as well (we will say much more about this story in chapter 10).

There are also major differences between rich and poor countries in infrastructure markets themselves. In fact, reverse innovation opportunities are particularly robust in this area. For starters, as developing countries build out their infrastructures for the first time, demand for construction services is very strong. Not so in rich countries, where investments in new infrastructure are delayed until existing infrastructure shows its age. Developing countries are robust construction markets; rich countries are tepid replacement markets.

Furthermore, when rich countries adopt innovative infrastructure technologies, they must make the new systems compatible with those that already exist. Rich countries are thus constrained by choices they made decades ago. Developing countries, unencumbered by legacy systems, have the flexibility to leapfrog to breakthrough technologies.

As a result, we have a seemingly odd state of affairs. Infrastructure is often painfully absent in the developing world, but where it exists, it is frequently cutting-edge.

There are already several examples of third-world nations with first-world infrastructure. Indeed, one sometimes wonders which are the developed and which are the developing countries. Take a flight from New York's JFK Airport to Beijing, compare the airports, and you'll see the difference. Or make a cell phone call in rural Vermont and then in rural Morocco. (One reason Nokia captured its high market share in India was that it built advanced wireless infrastructure in rural areas of the country.)

The developing world's rapid investments in wireless telecommunications has affected more than phone calls. Poor countries have leapfrogged brick-and-mortar banking to mobile banking for the masses, and they are also the early adopters of telemedicine technologies.

The Sustainability Gap

As the world economy grows, the clashes between economic activity and environmental concerns will only become more severe. Nevertheless, the intensity will not rise uniformly around the globe. On a scale from one to ten, the intensity of a certain dimension of the sustainability problem, such as air quality, might be nine in one part of the world and three in another. In some cases, intensity is highest in the developing world.

Take the case of China's extreme air-pollution problems. As a point of comparison, on an air quality scale of 1 to 500 (where 1 is cleanest and 500 dirtiest), Beijing often hits the 500 mark; a score of 100 would be unacceptable in the United States. Small wonder that China is charged up about electric cars.

The electric-car concept is a century old, but it has remained impractical for want of a cost-effective battery. Local companies are rising to the challenge. A little-known Shenzhen-based firm called BYD has announced a plug-in electric car with a lithium-ion ferrous-phosphate battery—a noncatchy name for what investors hope will be a catchy battery. One indication of the company's promise: Warren Buffet took a 10 percent ($230 million) stake in the company.

If the 5.8 billion of the world's poor consume and produce goods in ways that are environmentally unsound, the results will be catastrophic for poor countries—and for the planet. The only way poor countries can sustain economic growth is through "green" solutions. As a result, emerging markets are likely to leapfrog to several next-generation environmentally friendly technologies.

The Regulatory Gap

Regulation is a double-edged sword. New regulation almost always arises in the wake of misfortune or "bad" behavior in some market that, in retrospect, is judged to have been too free. The rich world, because of its older economies and its cultural and legal traditions, has advanced regulatory systems that, when applied effectively, keep markets fair and consumers and workplaces safe. But regulatory systems can also be needless barriers to innovation when they become labyrinthine, technologically obsolete, or captured by vested interests that seek to sustain the status quo. Under such conditions, innovation in the developing world may enjoy the advantages of lower friction and faster progress. (In making this observation, we do not mean to suggest that low levels of regulation in an emerging market are either a good thing or a bad thing; it simply is what it is, and it may sometimes provide an advantageous medium for certain innovations.)

For example, Diagnostics For All is a Boston-area start-up that has developed paper-based diagnostic tests the size of a postage stamp. When chemicals embedded in the paper react with blood, urine, saliva, or sweat, the paper changes colors. It is a quick, simple, and inexpensive alternative to diagnostic machines that cost tens of thousands of dollars and produce results requiring expert interpretation. Despite the attractiveness of such a product in rich-world markets, Diagnostics For All chose to commercialize its technology first in the developing world, where the company could circumvent the slow and painstaking U.S. Food and Drug Administration approval process and sidestep resistance to change (and even hostile lobbying efforts) from established players who rely on high reimbursements tied to expensive equipment.

The Preferences Gap

One of the more enjoyable aspects of traveling the globe is discovering, from country to country, a rich diversity of tastes, habits, and rituals. Often this diversity is revealed in seemingly mundane consumer products, such as snack foods. Many of the nutritional staples that anchor diets in developing countries are rarely consumed in the rich world. In India, for example, PepsiCo is developing new snack foods based not on corn (ubiquitous in the rich world), but on lentils—hardly a food most Americans grow up eating (see chapter 11).

As these five substantial gaps suggest, developing-world customers have problems that have *not* already been solved in the rich world (see table 2-1).

TABLE 2-1

Why reverse innovation must be clean-slate innovation

The five needs gaps between emerging economies and the rich world are so substantial that emerging-economy needs can only rarely be addressed simply by making adaptations to rich-world products.

Gap	Description	Implication	Example
Performance	Because of their low incomes, customers in poor countries are prepared to make significant sacrifices in performance—at the right price.	Design to deliver a 50 percent solution at a 15 percent price.	Nokia cell phones
Infrastructure	Rich-world infrastructures are fully built; emerging-economy infrastructures are under construction.	First, customers in poor countries need solutions that do not depend on reliable infrastructure. Second, infrastructure builders in poor countries can immediately adopt cutting-edge solutions.	Portable, battery-powered electrocardiogram machines for use where electric power is unreliable Indian telecoms leapfrogging to wireless technology in the absence of land-line phones
Sustainability	Poor countries face many of the most daunting sustainability challenges on the planet.	Poor countries are often more eager than rich ones for next-generation environmental solutions.	Electric cars in China
Regulatory	Regulatory systems in emerging economies are less developed and present fewer delays when a company is bringing innovative solutions to market.	New products may pass through regulatory hurdles in poor countries first.	Diagnostics For All
Preferences	Each country has distinct tastes and preferences.	Innovation efforts must take these differences into account.	The prevalence of lentil-based foods in India

Furthermore, poor countries have the relative luxury of addressing their challenges with modern technologies that simply weren't available when rich countries addressed similar needs decades ago.

Therefore, capturing opportunities in the poor world means starting from scratch. Reverse innovation is what we call *clean-slate* innovation.

Completing the Reverse Innovation Cycle: Winning Everywhere

So far, our message has been simple:

1. There are huge opportunities in the developing world.

2. Developing nations are different—not just a little, but *very* different.

3. Innovators win, exporters lose.

That's a good start, but it is not the full message, because it overlooks the full consequences of inaction. To fail at reverse innovation is not just to lose out on an opportunity abroad. The stakes can be much more menacing than that. A loss abroad can lead to an even bigger loss at home.

Why? Because, although reverse innovations are adopted *first* in the developing world, that isn't the end of the story. The global economy is richly interconnected. Reverse innovations can have global impact. Ultimately, they have the potential to migrate from poor countries to rich ones.

This migration is, at first glance, counterintuitive. After all, the dramatic needs gaps are what create the opportunity for innovations in emerging markets in the first place. Given those gaps, how could such innovations possibly flow uphill?

We believe there are two distinct mechanisms. Reverse innovations become attractive to the rich world through either a *marginalized market today* or a *mainstream market tomorrow.*

Marginalized Markets Today

In the rich world, marginalized markets are underserved or ignored not because they don't need innovation, but because they're too small to justify a costly innovation investment. But what if, for every marginalized potential customer in the rich world, there are fifty similar customers in the developing world? When an otherwise marginal market is multiplied by fifty, it suddenly looks much more interesting.

The very low end of the automotive market in the rich world has long been marginalized. Companies like Ford and Audi have targeted their innovation efforts at rich or middle-class customers. Poor buyers get whatever is left over after the features they can't afford have been stripped out. This may seem like a sensible approach, but it really only makes sense to an executive with rich-world blinders on. The low end of the market is a gold mine, not a ghost town, if your vantage point is Delhi instead of Detroit.

On March 23, 2009, the automotive division of legendary Indian business conglomerate Tata launched the Nano. At just over $2,000, Nano is by far the world's most affordable car. Tata practiced *frugal engineering*: it challenged every standard industry assumption to achieve its ultra-low-cost position by using clever designs, new materials, and supplier partnerships. The launch suddenly and dramatically changed the size and composition of the automotive market in India. By some estimates, the Nano will make car ownership possible for 65 percent more Indians of the middle class, all of them eager for a safer alternative to motorbikes.

It is a huge opportunity. Nonetheless, it was overlooked not just by one or two rich-world automakers, but by all of them. These automakers have not just lost an opportunity; they have put themselves at risk close to home. Tata Motors plans to scale up the Nano platform and launch it in Europe and the United States. It is likely that Tata will become a formidable new competitor at the low end of the market, challenging industry behemoths like Honda and Ford.

The banking industry has similarly ignored the low end of the market. Muhammad Yunus capitalized on the opportunity by founding Bangladesh's Grameen Bank, unleashing the microfinance revolution (and, in 2006, taking home the Nobel Peace Prize). To enable the poor to start small businesses, Grameen makes tiny loans, ones that are too small to be profitable for large banks.

At every turn, Yunus challenged the conventional wisdom of large commercial banks. Banks lend to the rich; Grameen lends to the poor. Banks lend to men; Grameen lends to women. Banks operate in urban areas; Grameen operates in rural areas. Banks ask for collateral; Grameen extends trust. Banks have legal contracts; Grameen relies on peer pressure. (If one member of a borrowing group defaults, no more loans will be made to the entire group.) Since its inception in 1983, Grameen has lent over $9 billion, with a 98 percent recovery rate. The bank has made profits every year except 1983, 1991, and 1992.

From its beginnings in Bangladesh, the microcredit banking model has spread to over one hundred countries. Today, it has even gained a foothold in a marginalized banking market in the United States—poor neighbor-hoods in New York City.

Mainstream Markets Tomorrow

When a reverse innovation hits the mainstream, it becomes a powerful force—one that holds tremendous opportunities for those with their eyes open and terrifying risks for incumbents with their eyes shut. Established players stand to lose something much more dear than opportunities. They stand to lose long-held market positions.

Reverse innovations don't always flow uphill into mainstream markets, but conditions are ripe whenever there is a trend that slowly closes the needs gap. Thanks to the gap, the poor-world innovation will be unattractive in mainstream rich world markets *on the day that it is introduced*. Because of the trend, it eventually becomes attractive. (See "GE's Ultrasound Flows Uphill.")

GE's Ultrasound Flows Uphill

How an Innovation Made in China, for China, Found Its Way into Rich-World Markets

The next time you visit your physician for a routine checkup, don't be sur-prised if he or she sets aside the stethoscope. This age-old device has long helped skilled diagnosticians recognize any number of medical conditions. Nonetheless, it may soon go the way of the typewriter. The ability to hear inside the body is powerful, but the ability to *see* is transformative. Medical imaging technology has now advanced to the point that every doctor can carry an ultrasound device in a coat pocket.

In 2010, GE Healthcare introduced the Vscan, a cell-phone-sized imag-ing device based on ultrasound technology. The battery-powered, easy-to-use handheld gadget could create a revolution in medicine. It could extend the benefits of sophisticated imaging—at a dramatically low cost—to many millions more patients worldwide.

Despite this potential, what is most interesting about the Vscan is not the magic of its pint-sized technology but its genealogy: GE planted the seeds for the device in 2002, when it developed its first compact ultrasound device in China. It is one of the premier examples of how a transformative reverse innovation can complete the migratory journey from filling emerging-market needs to finding a place in the rich world—both in marginalized markets today and in mainstream markets tomorrow.

GE Healthcare has been a leading supplier of big, powerful, premium-priced ultrasound scanners since the 1980s. Looking to stimulate growth, the company sought additional markets overseas. China, with its population of more than one billion, offered huge potential. So, the company did what seemed natural. It created a sales and distribution center in China, with the goal of distributing global products locally.

This was a classic glocalization move. After ten years in the market, GE Healthcare was unable to unlock China's potential. Sales were a mere $5 million—negligible in GE terms—and growth was slow. The company remained a marginal player.

All this changed during the first decade of the twenty-first century. In 2002, GE introduced its first portable ultrasound scanner in China. By 2008, the product was offered for just $15,000, a mere 15 percent of the cost of the low-end traditional ultrasound unit. Performance was not as good, of course, but it was certainly much better than a 15 percent solution, and performance has since improved.

How did GE Healthcare get there? By letting go of the glocalization model and recognizing that reverse innovation was the only way to address unique market needs:

- **Ultra-low cost.** More than 90 percent of the Chinese population is served by poorly funded, low-tech hospitals or basic clinics in rural villages. For these patients, the cost of receiving care is the first consideration.

- **Portability.** Clinics in rural areas lack sophisticated imaging technology, and transportation to urban hospitals is difficult, especially for the sick. Many patients in China can't travel to the ultrasound machine, so the machine must be able to travel to them.

- **Ease of use.** Rural Chinese doctors are not specialists in narrow fields, as is customary in the rich world. Instead, they must be jacks-of-all-trades. They need ultrasound devices that are very easy to use.

GE entrusted development of the Chinese ultrasound machine to Omar Ishrak, a leader with global experience. (Today, Ishrak is CEO of Medtronic.) Ishrak had sufficient clout both to ensure the autonomy of a local engineering team that had its own P&L and to facilitate the team's access to necessary global resources. The team was able to build on a conceptual breakthrough from a GE product-development group in Israel that had discovered radical cost savings by transferring the operational muscle of ultrasound technology from expensive custom hardware to far less expensive software.

Today, the portable machine is the growth engine for GE's ultrasound business in China. Between 2002 and 2008, worldwide sales from portable ultrasound products skyrocketed from $4 million to around $278 million, an average annual compounded growth rate of 50 to 60 percent. And for the team members who did the engineering work, there is the satisfaction of knowing they improved lives. In many poor countries, where infant and maternal deaths are still commonplace, women who once had to travel twenty-four to thirty-six hours by bus to reach a hospital are now receiving ultrasound exams in their own villages.

These results were rewarding, but not the whole story. A pleasant surprise for Ishrak and his colleagues was the immediate ease with which they were able to find opportunities for the new device in the rich world. Those opportunities were in marginalized markets (rich-world markets that, by themselves, are too small to justify a major innovation effort):

- **Paramedics.** Today, thanks to the development of compact ultrasound devices, paramedics are able to use ultrasound imaging in their ambulances and at remote accident sites.

- **Emergency rooms.** Because compact ultrasound devices are portable and easy to use, physicians can make quick diagnoses (for example, by locating internal bleeding and blood clots) before deciding whether the patient should undertake more-expensive tests.

- **Operating rooms.** Anesthesiologists use compact ultrasound devices to guide the placement of the needles and catheters for the administration of anesthetics prior to surgery.

Reverse innovations can also, after a delay, have an impact on mainstream markets—whenever there is a trend that closes the needs gap. In this case, steady technological improvements did exactly that. Between

2002 and 2011, GE improved the image quality of compact ultrasound devices to the point where mainstream consumers became increasingly intrigued. Higher-priced PC-based premium portable models can now perform cardiology, radiology, and obstetrics functions that once required a much more expensive machine.

Given the powerful societal goal of controlling health-care costs, the United States and other developed markets will have ample incentive to embrace lower-cost technology that delivers performance nearly equal to that of expensive premium models. GE's decade-long investment in portable ultrasound was surely begun in anticipation of the day when overall market expansion would offset the threat of cannibalization.

The delay between a new product's introduction in a poor country and the development of robust demand in the rich world is exactly what makes reverse innovation so dangerous to incumbents. By the time they realize that they've missed a giant shift in their industry—one that originated in the developing world—they are years behind in skill, experience, and industrial capacity. (See table 2-2.)

TABLE 2-2

Reverse innovations flow uphill in two ways

Destination	Time frame	Driving force	Consequence of inaction	Example
Marginalized market	Immediate	Niche markets in the rich world with needs similar to the mass market in poor countries	Lost opportunity	Microfinance in poor neighbor-hoods in New York City
Mainstream market	Delayed	A trend that closes the needs gap	Erosion, possibly severe, of existing market position in the rich world	Portable ultra-sound devices that improve in performance to the point that they can compete with traditional devices

Trends That Close the Needs Gaps

The trends that close the gaps are not hard to see, if you know what to look for. Let's revisit the five gaps.

How the Performance Gap Closes

A 50 percent solution at a 15 percent price may not hold much appeal in the rich world, where nothing less than an 80 percent solution will do. But new technologies always improve—often rapidly and relentlessly. Trajectories of technological improvement are the trends that most often close performance gaps. Fifty percent solutions can become 90 percent solutions within just a few years. And voilà! Rich-world customers are suddenly very, very interested.[2]

Consider netbooks. These small, light, ultraportable, and inexpensive laptops are a craze in the United States and other rich countries. Though they arrived with way less fanfare than Apple's iPad, netbooks are an enormous global opportunity, a fast-growing segment within the otherwise stagnant PC industry. Netbooks combine the best features of laptops and smartphones, offering a wide range of Web applications, a comfortably sized screen, a real keyboard, and easy portability.

You would expect the earliest adopters of netbooks to be in the rich world, but that's not what happened. The seeds for the netbook revolution were sown in the developing world. First came the One Laptop Per Child (OLPC) initiative in 2006, which aimed to make an ultra-low-cost laptop available to schoolchildren in poor countries. The laptop was designed by the MIT Media Lab and manufactured by Quanta Computer. It hit the amazingly low price point of $175.

Inspired in part by OLPC, Taiwanese multinational Asus, the world's largest manufacturer of PC motherboards, also designed its netbook for developing countries. The Eee PC (the three E's are for *Easy* to learn, work, and play) was priced starting at $200. From there, it was only a matter of time before technology improved, quality rose, and netbook sales took off in rich countries.

Ever-tightening budgets in the rich world can also help close performance gaps by making "good enough" performance more acceptable in certain contexts. In health care, for example, where the rate of spending growth has become untenable, solutions like GE's portable ultrasound technology or Narayana Hrudayalaya's ultra-low-cost cardiac surgeries either already have gained, or inevitably will gain, mainstream traction.

How the Infrastructure Gap Closes

Take the case of the energy industry. Poor countries have the opportunity to jump ahead to the twenty-first-century infrastructure simply because they have little energy infrastructure to begin with. They are building nearly from scratch, and thus they can invest in the latest technology right now.

By comparison, America has made mammoth investments in twentieth-century energy infrastructure—massive central power stations, fossil-fuel extraction and refining, and an extensive transmission and distribution network. This infrastructure was built when renewables were expensive and impractical, fossil fuels were cheap, and concerns about climate change were nonexistent. Many of these systems have decades of useful life remaining, and their owners will not want such assets rendered obsolete. U.S. energy companies will invest in renewables, but will demand designs that enhance, not replace, existing infrastructure.

The trend that closes the gap is the gradual aging of rich-world infrastructure. Eventually, the rich world adopts the innovation—when it is time to replace its existing assets.

The development of India's energy infrastructure illustrates just how far emerging markets might jump ahead. Most of India's population—nearly 750 million people—still lacks access to the electric grid. As India builds its infrastructure, the country will not simply follow the rich-country blueprint. It is much more likely that India will leapfrog to the next generation.

For example, renewable energy sources will be a central, not peripheral, part of India's energy solution. By the 2020s and 2030s, the proportion of India's energy that is derived from solar and wind power will be as much as five times greater than the proportion in the United States. And where wind and solar are inadequate, India will use natural-gas-powered or biogas-powered turbines that are less than one-hundredth the size of those used in the rich world. Instead of massive central power stations, India is likely to favor thousands of small units, all connected by a next-generation "smart grid" that can handle complex fluctuations in supply and demand.

We are already witnessing similar trends in China. In 2003, the country had no presence in solar energy. Today, it is the world leader. Since 2006, China has doubled its wind-power capacity every year.

If multinationals do not take the lead in shaping the energy industry in places like China and India, they will become mere spectators as local competitors (such as wind energy companies Goldwind and Suzlon, respectively) flourish not only in emerging markets, but, eventually, everywhere in the world.

We see the same dynamic in play at the level of "personal infrastructure," such as cars. The market for electric cars is likely to grow more rapidly in China than it will in rich countries, for the simple reason that most Chinese consumers do not yet own a car. For many, their first vehicle will be electric. Most rich-world buyers, by contrast, own internal-combustion vehicles that they will be reluctant to replace prematurely. To be sure, electric vehicles may face other challenges—especially in America—based on perceptions that such vehicles lack the power and performance of gas-powered cars. When such embedded attitudes change, electric cars will gain wide acceptance.

If GM and Toyota want to preempt BYD in a crucial future market, they need reverse innovation today. Indeed, in May 2010, BYD entered into a joint venture with the German automaker Daimler to develop an electric car for the Chinese market. Daimler's engineering and design expertise could give BYD the potential to compete widely—including in the developed world. Daimler, for its part, will gain expertise in battery technology and insight into a burgeoning market.

How the Sustainability Gap Closes

Poor countries, because they face some of the most intense environmental challenges in the world, are likely to become today's incubators for the new green industries of tomorrow in fields as diverse as waste management, sustainable agriculture, and water purification. The trend that will close the gap is the inevitability that sustainability pressures will rise in the rich world.

Consider the water crisis that many experts anticipate in the not-too-distant future in America's desert southwest. Residents of Phoenix and Las Vegas may be relieved to learn that GE is already working on the problem—not for Phoenix or Las Vegas, but for the city of Algiers, where the company has completed its largest desalination plant. With the entire Mediterranean now serving as a reservoir, residents of this dry city are, for the first time, living without water rationing.

How the Regulatory Gap Closes

Poor countries jump ahead when they can offer quick government approvals and minimal resistance from vested interests. Eventually, regulations in the rich world evolve, allowing innovations to make it through the regulatory thicket, at which time the gap is closed. Once the start-up Diagnostics For All clears U.S. regulations, it will enter the market having perfected its product, gained experience, and built scale.

How the Preferences Gap Closes

When a social trend closes a gap in preferences, innovations originally developed for poor countries come to the rich world. To wit: chicken tikka masala is now the number-one fast food in the United Kingdom! More broadly, rich nations are increasingly interested in natural foods and healthy ingredients. As it turns out, many of the staple foods in the developing world are exactly that, natural and healthy.

Procter & Gamble introduced a new over-the-counter cough medicine for low-income consumers in Mexico in 2003. VickMiel is a cough syrup with natural honey rather than artificial flavors. It targeted consumers who preferred homeopathic solutions for coughs and colds. The product was initially launched in Mexico and then rolled out to other Latin American countries. Starting in 2005, P&G brought this product into developed countries, including the United States, Britain, France, Germany, Italy, and Switzerland—and at a price point lower than P&G's core Vicks product, Vicks Formula 44. The new product met with considerable success as it attracted rich-country customers who either were price conscious or preferred natural ingredients. (See table 2-3.)

The dynamics of reverse innovation, characterized by five needs gaps and the trends that can close them, must become a part of the strategic dialogue in every multinational. In the next chapter, we'll look at the specific steps that global corporations must take to create a reverse innovation mind-set.

TABLE 2-3

Trends that close the five needs gaps

Gap	Description	Trend
Performance	Because of their low incomes, customers in poor countries are prepared to make significant sacrifices in performance—at the right price.	First, technological improvements raise performance to the point that rich-world customers are interested. Second, tighter budgets in rich countries force consideration of ultra-low price options.
Infrastructure	Rich-world infrastructures are fully built; emerging-economy infrastructures are under construction.	Aging infrastructure in the rich world will need to be replaced.
Sustainability	Poor countries face many of the most daunting sustainability challenges on the planet.	Sustainability pressures rise in the rich world.
Regulatory	Regulatory systems in emerging economies are less developed and present fewer delays when a company is getting innovative solutions to market.	Governments in the rich world eventually approve new technologies or revise regulatory requirements.
Preference	Each country has distinct tastes and preferences.	Customers in the rich world are influenced by poor-country preferences.

Summary of the Key Ideas

1. It is impossible to fully capture the growth opportunities in the developing world without developing new solutions from scratch. Reverse innovation is *clean-slate innovation.*

2. Five wide gaps distinguish emerging-market needs from familiar rich-world needs: the performance gap, the infrastructure gap, the sustainability gap, the regulatory gap, and the preferences gap.

3. Reverse innovations can flow uphill by penetrating *marginalized markets* in the rich world or, more consequentially, by reaching *mainstream markets* after a delay during which a trend closes the gap between rich-world and poor-world needs.

CHAPTER THREE

Changing the Mind-Set

The very organizational best practices that have made global corporations so successful to date actually get in the way of innovating in emerging markets.

I N THE 1970S AND 1980S, most global corporations divided the world into three segments: the United States and Canada, Western Europe, and Japan. If there was a fourth segment, it was "the rest of the world"—and it was regarded as inconsequential.

The rest of the world is no longer inconsequential. Yet, developed-world multinationals—especially the most successful ones—consistently struggle in emerging markets. Why? The simple answer is that global corporations are imprisoned by the past. It colors the way they think. And if they can't overcome history, it will color their futures a dull shade of disappointment.

In this chapter, we will look at how multinational businesses see the world. Unfortunately, they tend to see it through the refracting lens of dominant logic—mind-sets built from what they have experienced in the past, both in their home markets and elsewhere in the developed world.

We define dominant logic as the assorted orthodoxies that govern the thinking of key enterprise decision makers. Dominant logic is deeply held, widely shared, and rooted in past behavior and experience.

Executives are naturally motivated to repeat actions that they believe have produced success. If success continues, at some point the organization as a whole crosses a line: instead of consciously repeating those actions, it unconsciously accepts them as indisputably correct. This certitude becomes embedded not only in managers' minds, but also in the relationships, planning processes, performance evaluation systems, organizational structures, human-resources policies, and communication patterns that make the organization tick.

Orthodoxies are a double-edged sword. On the one hand, the dominant logic that supports "glocalization" is a powerful strength that has continued relevance. However, dominant logic, if left unchallenged, becomes a self-imposed barrier that limits multinationals' success in pursuing emerging-market opportunities.

It may be human nature to anticipate a future that closely resembles the past. However, we believe that the prison of the past is the single greatest obstacle to mastering the discipline of reverse innovation. The philosopher George Santayana famously wrote, "Those who do not remember the past are condemned to repeat it." With all due respect, we would modify his quote as follows: "Multinational businesses that cannot *selectively forget* the past are condemned to repeat it even as the world around them changes."

The first half of this chapter explains why dominant logic makes success so elusive; the second half offers field-tested strategies for escaping from the prison and changing the mind-set.

How Dated Thinking Inhibits Reverse Innovation

The shift in emphasis from *exporting to emerging markets* to *innovating for emerging markets* is a significant culture change. If you are going to embrace reverse innovation, and if you are going to incorporate the five needs gaps and the trends that close them into the strategic dialog, you first have to remove the embedded assumptions, traps, and fears that get in the way.

To do so, step one is simply to recognize these toxic assumptions, traps, and fears. You have to be completely aware of the current dominant logic.

We find that the best way to assess your own company's dominant logic is to consider a series of increasingly sophisticated models of the emerging markets and their role in the global economy. What you want is for everyone in your organization to reach the highest level of sophistication—level five thinking. But where is your team today? Where do its members fall on the following ladder of denial?

Level one thinking. Only the rich world matters. Poor countries are too poor to be worth worrying about.

Level two thinking. In poor countries, there is an opportunity to sell our offerings at the top of the economic pyramid. This market will slowly expand, as poor nations get richer.

Level three thinking. Emerging-market customers have different needs. We'll have to customize our existing products and services.

Level four thinking. Emerging market customers have *vastly* different needs. To capture the opportunity, we'll have to design new products and services from scratch.

Level five thinking. The stakes are global, not local.

Let's take a closer look at these five levels, one at a time.

Level One Thinking: Poor Countries Are Irrelevant

Fortunately, few global corporations remain stuck at level one. Raw facts and figures are more than enough to overcome this mind-set. Global corporations that want to grow have to go where the growth is—emerging markets.

Level Two Thinking: Just Sit Tight

Level two thinking, on the other hand, is still prevalent. It is rooted in the assumption that we touched upon in chapter 2: that emerging economies are engaged in a process of *gradually catching up* with the rich world, following the same path of development.

It is a comforting belief, as it relieves the anxieties of rich-world business leaders. They need only to sit tight and wait while customers in the developing country get richer. Then there will be greater demand for the products their companies already make and sell. "We are doing what we need to do," an executive might say. "Conditions will improve in due course. Developing nations will look more and more like home, and many more customers will want what we offer."

This is lazy thinking, even delusional. Consider a comparison between the United States and India. On the basis of GDP per capita alone, India stands today where the United States stood in the nineteenth century. The gradually-catching-up model implies that the economic history of the United States should serve as a useful guide to the economic future of India.

But can it? Visualize a crowded street in New York City in the late nineteenth century. In all likelihood, part of what you are visualizing are horses and buggies. Now, visualize a crowded street in modern-day Mumbai. The highways are clogged not with horses and buggies but with motorbikes! Indeed, at no point in the economic development of the United States were motorbikes the most common mode of transportation. Developing nations do not follow the same path as the rich nations that preceded them. Emerging economies are not engaged in a simple game of catch-up. Not even close.

The reality is that compared with the United States of the nineteenth century, India and other developing nations are actually in an enviable position. They will address their challenges with twenty-first-century—rather than nineteenth-century—science and technology. These modern solutions are unique and unprecedented.

So, if you think that the problem is that customers in emerging markets are not yet ready for your products, you've got it backward. Your products are a poor fit for emerging markets. The historical best practices of multinationals will not work in poor countries. You need *next* practices. And you need to innovate.

Level Three Thinking: Customization Is Sufficient

Because it acknowledges *some* need for innovation, level three thinking, at first glance, seems to embrace the realities of emerging markets. In truth, however, this is nothing more than level two thinking in a nicer suit.

Level three thinking is not only commonplace, but also deeply embedded in the mind-set of many senior executives in global corporations. Back in the 1970s and 1980s, global corporations established a simple model for innovation: develop great products at home. Then, distribute them around the world, with some modifications—typically minor ones—for the local market. Glocalization, in a nutshell.

As the name implies, glocalization is a compromise between global scale and local responsiveness. Corporations calculate an optimal trade-off between global scale, so crucial to minimizing costs, and whatever local customization is required to maximize market share.

Since the 1980s, the global economy has changed enormously. Global strategy has not. Glocalization is still the dominant play, not just within the walls of global corporations, but also atop the high-minded towers of academia.[1]

Glocalization is so prevalent because it has proven to be powerful as a strategy for market expansion to other rich-world countries. It delivers vast efficiencies and still manages to bridge certain kinds of cross-border differences. And it has transformed many multinationals, regardless of their pedigrees. Whether companies have globalized by expanding domestic businesses abroad (as GE did) or by creating a loose federation of acquired businesses (as Unilever did), glocalization has served them well.

The glocalization mind-set emerged when rich countries accounted for the vast majority of the market. Emerging economies had not yet begun to take off; indeed, the middle and low-end customer segments in poor countries scarcely existed. Now that emerging markets have a growing economic vitality, global strategy needs to catch up with new global realities.

Too few corporations have recognized glocalization's critical flaw. *It treats rich and poor countries equivalently.* For example, it assumes that a British company expanding into India faces basically the same set of challenges the company faced earlier when it entered Germany. For both countries, the formula would be the same: take an innovation that worked at home and sell it abroad; make adaptations to suit local tastes if needed, but do not reinvent the wheel. Table 3-1 compares the dominant logic of glocalization with the practice of reverse innovation.

While glocalization is capable of addressing minor cross-border differences, it is not up to bridging the gaps between rich and poor countries. In most cases, you can't just take a product designed for the rich world, make minor adaptations, remove a few features to reduce costs, and suddenly have a blockbuster product in China or India. Something more transformative is needed if your goal is to address the fundamental differences between a market of one person with ten dollars to spend and a market of ten people each with one dollar to spend.

TABLE 3-1

Dominant logic of glocalization versus reverse innovation strategies

Glocalization	Reverse innovation
• Optimize products for the developed-world customer	• Best solution for the emerging-market customer
• Cutting-edge, technologically sophisticated, performance-rich products with many features, new and fancy applications	• Frugal, functional, good-enough quality products
• Take the simplest possible approach to designing offerings for emerging markets: remove features to reduce cost	• Reinvent the product from the ground up; clean-slate innovation
• Premium-price, high-margin orientation	• Low-price, high-volume orientation
• Technology push; product-out approach	• Customer-centric; market-back approach
• Look for customers to sell products to	• Identify customer pain points, and develop products to solve customer problems
• Sell products to current consumers of the product	• Create new consumption among noncustomers
• Gain market share	• Create the market
• Leverage current core competencies	• Build new core competencies
• Exploitation mind-set for emerging economies	• Exploration mind-set for emerging economies
• Use developed world products to transform emerging markets	• Build new global growth platforms based in emerging markets

The humble refrigerator illustrates the difference. Refrigerators were miracles of technology when they reached mainstream adoption in the rich world nearly a century ago. By enabling longer-term food storage, they saved time and labor, and reduced food spoilage. A level three thinker would naturally assume that mainstream consumers in poor countries would demand refrigerators much like those in the rich world—though perhaps customized a bit—just as soon as their incomes rose enough to put such a purchase within reach.

The reality is more complex. The context in which the problem of food storage must be solved is very different in poor countries. First, consumers in poor countries can't rely on electricity, especially in rural areas. Therefore, a refrigerator lacking very high-quality insulation is of little use.

Second, because money is scarce, consumers are willing to accept lower performance in exchange for an ultralow price.

A new technology now coming to market meets this combination of desires. The ChotuKool refrigerator, developed by Godrej & Boyce and manufactured in Mumbai, is priced at just $69. It is stoutly insulated and can be powered temporarily by a battery. Even better, it is lightweight and rugged, with only a few parts.

Instead of traditional compressors, the ChotuKool uses a special semiconductor chip of the type used to cool computers. Such chips were, of course, not available in the 1920s, when modern refrigerators began making their way into Western kitchens. Such chips—plentiful and relatively cheap today—amount to a breakthrough technology. True, this novel refrigerator underperforms on temperature; the best it can do is 36 degrees Fahrenheit below the ambient temperature (e.g., 55 degrees on a 91-degree day). In India, however, that is a more-than-acceptable trade-off, given the other features that the ChotuKool offers.[2]

A level three thinker misses this opportunity altogether. Someone with this mind-set does not see that the combination of a very old problem (the need for refrigeration), local conditions (unreliable electricity), and a recent technology (cooling chips) can yield an innovative solution.

Could a Western multinational, such as Whirlpool, develop a similar offering and outcompete Godrej & Boyce? Absolutely. But the American company will never do so by customizing one of its existing refrigerators.

Note that we are not saying that glocalization has become irrelevant. Hardly. In fact, Nokia has ceded big opportunities in the smartphone market to Apple and Google because the Finish company put *too much* emphasis on innovation for the emerging economies.[3] Innovation in rich countries is still critical.

Indeed, glocalization accounts for the vast preponderance of global revenues today, and we expect that it will remain important for decades to come. Glocalization effectively spans rich-country-to-rich-country differences. Furthermore, some customers in poor countries do live much like customers in the rich world, and glocalization serves their needs. The problem is that there are few such well-heeled customers. The real growth opportunity in emerging markets is in the mass market. And that is where glocalization hits the wall.

Our argument, therefore, is that glocalization cannot be the totality of global strategy. Global corporations must learn to execute reverse innovation and glocalization *simultaneously*.

Level Four: Winning Requires Innovation

Level four thinkers understand that to span the chasm between rich- and poor-country needs, corporations must not only innovate, but also practice clean-slate innovation. That means, quite literally, starting from a blank page and addressing anew these most fundamental questions:

- Who are my target *customers*?

- What *value* do I want to deliver to them?

- What is the *value chain architecture* I will use to deliver that value?

The transition from glocalization to reverse innovation is a discontinuous leap. That makes it difficult, but also exciting.

Glocalization is a *product-out* mind-set. How do I take the products I have and reach as great a market as possible? Reverse innovation requires a *market-back* approach. You start with the distinctive needs of customers in the developing world, and work back to the necessary solution.

Market-back thinking begins with studying the market, but most multinationals have invested little energy in acquiring knowledge of emerging markets. Everyone involved in strategy-making must learn about local requirements and conditions. Without intense curiosity about the pressing needs of poor countries, foresight is forgone—and the future is forfeit.

Even though level four thinkers understand that a discontinuous leap is necessary, they can still fall prey to three thinking traps that cause designs to fall short.

Trap 1: Because customers in poor countries have low per-capita incomes, their needs are best met with cheap products based on old technologies. It is a serious error to view markets in poor countries as dumping grounds for sunset technologies. Capturing emerging-market opportunities is not a simple issue of lowering prices. It is about shifting to a new price-performance paradigm. Developing a solution that bridges the performance gap—that is, a 50 percent solution at a 15 percent price—usually requires an entirely new technology.

Sony sold older products and technology in China and lost ground to Samsung as a result. Poor people in rural India are not eagerly waiting in line to buy cheap black-and-white TVs. Nor are they snapping up out-of-print textbooks. Instead, they are taking advantage of the fact that the e-learning industry is advancing most rapidly in the developing economies. For example, McGraw-Hill and Indian IT firm Wipro have partnered on a product called mConnect. This low-cost education service for residents of rural India is delivered over mobile devices. For millions of India's youth, who are rabid cell-phone users (more than five hours per day, on average), this high-tech approach to skills training, English language instruction, and prep work for university entrance exams hits the mark. In a similar vein, low-cost cell phones in Africa allow customers to play the latest video games and surf the Net.

Trap 2: Reverse innovations always involve targeting the lowest possible price point. While spanning the performance gap involves dramatic price reductions, the other gaps—infrastructure, sustainability, regulatory, and preferences—do not necessarily require radically lower pricing. China's investments in alternative energy, for example, are not being driven by low price, but simply because most of China's energy infrastructure has yet to be built, and environmental constraints are already pressing.

Trap 3: Reverse innovation is product innovation. This is too narrow a view. The possibilities for reverse innovation are much broader. It's not just a matter of tinkering with product design. Many reverse innovations are business-model innovations. They may require new processes, new partnerships, and even a reinvented value chain. Furthermore, commercial innovations—that is, innovations in go-to-market strategy—can also pay off handsomely. And the most powerful reverse innovations are often platform innovations—that is, innovations that can be scaled up or scaled down to meet multiple price points.

As an example of a business-model innovation, consider Bharti Airtel Limited, the largest telecommunications service provider in India. Bharti looks nothing like its cousins around the world. The management team recognized that its core skills were branding and accurately diagnosing customer needs. Unlike most of its telecom rivals, Bharti knew little about technology. So, it took a step that a rich-world telecommunications service provider would never dream of: it outsourced network installation, maintenance, and service to Ericsson, Nokia, and Siemens and chose IBM to build and manage its IT systems.

Bharti's innovative business model dramatically lowered costs by converting the fixed costs of capital expenditure into variable costs based on capacity usage. As a result, the company can offer mobile telecom service at $0.01 to $0.005 per minute, perhaps the lowest rates in the world. Bharti has enjoyed compounded annual growth in sales revenues of 120 percent and growth in net profits of 282 percent per year between 2003 and 2010. Its market cap has steadily grown over the same period and stood at around US$30 billion as of October 2011.[4]

Even level four thinkers who can overcome these traps may not embrace a promising idea for a reverse innovation. They worry about failure. "It's too hard to make money. It's too risky. It's too different from what we are already good at."

There's no denying that reverse innovation involves the possibility of failure. However, three specific fears that frequently get in the way are dramatically overstated.

Fear 1: Margins will inevitably be too low for us to make money. This concern doesn't square with experience. Consider famous examples of rich-world companies that have made fortunes by achieving an ultralow price point. You certainly can't say that Microsoft and Apple, which ushered in the PC revolution rather than build more mainframes, or Canon, which brought us the desktop copier alternative to Xerox's mammoth freestanding machines, failed to earn healthy profits.

Executives in global corporations anticipate lower margins in emerging economies only because these business leaders are accustomed to glocalization. Reverse innovation is different. It implies redesign, of both the offering and its cost structure. It is entirely possible to earn the same or even better margins on a radically redesigned, ultra-low-cost product. Furthermore, margins are just one component of financial performance. Even if the gross margin percentage is lower, fixed costs in poor countries are relatively low and volumes are potentially *much* higher. So, operating margins and return on investment may be comparable or better.

Take the case of India's Aravind Eye Hospital, which has helped prevent blindness in more than three million Indian citizens by offering high-quality and ultra-low-cost eye surgeries—especially cataract removal ($30 per eye, compared with as much as $1,000 in the rich world). Its method is simple in concept: Aravind has industrialized the surgical process, running it as efficiently and effectively as the world's best manufacturer. To dramatically improve the productivity of its employees and equipment, the hospital tightly schedules key resources (operating rooms, surgeons' and nurses' time); it subdivides surgical procedures into phases and actions, standardizing process and technique and driving for repeatability; and it measures results, always striving to improve.

Despite offering surgeries at a staggeringly low price, Aravind performs more than 60 percent of procedures free of charge for the needy. Still, it manages to achieve gross margins of greater than 35 percent. Aravind takes no donations or charity, and yet it makes enough profit to fund a new hospital every three years.[5]

Fear 2: We'd put our premium brand at risk, or cannibalize sales of our premium offerings, if we compete in a low-cost market. These are real risks, but they can be managed. Many companies with strong brands (Honda, GE, P&G, PepsiCo, Tata, Toyota, and others) operate at multiple price points, often by creating distinct subbrands. Indeed, in an industry shaped by reverse innovation, competing at multiple price points is a prerequisite to being competitive in global markets. And the risk of cannibalization always seems much smaller when weighed against the risk of inaction—and the possibility of simply watching as an emerging giant does the cannibalizing for you.

Fear 3: Our company excels at technological leadership. That's just incompatible with ultralow cost. Wrong. Microsoft, Apple, and Canon ushered in a new ultra-low-cost era in their industries and still remained technologically preeminent.

For GE Healthcare, technology leadership and cost leadership go hand in hand. In 2010, the company introduced the Vscan, the handheld, lightweight, ultra-low-cost ultrasound device we described in chapter 2. During the development process, the product team hit a wall. Its goal of miniaturizing ultrasound devices appeared to be out of reach. The technical complexity of beam forming—the sending and receiving of sound waves—seemed to make it infeasible for a pocket-sized device to produce high-quality ultrasound images.

Help came from an unexpected source: a team working on one of GE's most expensive new ultrasound products for cardiologists. That team was trying to improve 4-D functionality (4-D shows the three spatial dimensions plus motion). The goal was to create clear images showing blood flow through the human heart—perhaps the single most challenging ultrasound application. The team had developed a breakthrough beam-forming approach that, in turn, became the lynchpin of the tiny, relatively inexpensive Vscan. Amazingly, technology developed for one of GE's most expensive machines proved crucial in its least expensive.

Level Five: The Stakes Are Global, Not Local

Level four thinkers accept that rich-world multinationals must practice clean-slate innovation to capture the tremendous growth potential of emerging economies. Level five thinkers take it one step further by acknowledging the high costs of *inaction*. They recognize that breakthroughs in India today can create explosive new markets in the United States tomorrow—new markets that disrupt incumbents.

As we explained in chapter 2, this can happen any time there is a trend that closes a needs gap. Recall that a needs gap creates the opportunity for an innovation that is adopted first in the developing world. The trend, by closing the gap, eventually creates conditions for the same innovation to be adopted in rich countries. Because of this dynamic, poor countries can jump ahead of the rich world. Therefore, multinationals that have waited around for poor countries to catch up with them may face a counterintuitive fate: having to scurry to catch up with poor countries.

When rich-world multinationals ignore reverse innovation, they empower and enable the growth of the emerging giants—the new generation of global corporations with roots in the developing world. These new kids on the block would like nothing better than to slay an old beast in its own back yard. Rich-world multinationals must confront an inconvenient truth: failure abroad can lead to failure at home.

The emerging giants can make life miserable for Western multinationals. In the IT services industry, for instance, the Indian firms Infosys, Tata Consulting Services, and Wipro have pioneered a model in which they serve clients in the developed world from distant India, where talented software engineers earn substantially lower wages. This challenges IBM and Accenture to rethink their business models. The advances in jet design by Brazil's Embraer is giving Canada's Bombardier a run for its money in regional jets. Mexico's Cemex has innovated in the cement industry to humble Holcium of Switzerland and Lafarge of France. China's Huawei is challenging global telecommunications companies like Siemens, Ericsson, Alcatel, and Cisco. India's Mahindra & Mahindra is challenging U.S. agricultural equipment icon Deere & Company in the low-horsepower tractor segment on Deere's home turf. This is just the beginning.

Nonetheless, many rich-world multinationals continue to see their rich-world peers as the *only* rivals that matter. They frame competition as a battle for market share. That's a shame. The battle for the emerging markets is not about market share. It's about creating the market. And the primary competitor is not the horse you've been racing against for years; it's the horse you may never have heard of before.

Thus do old mind-sets foment new problems.

In the next few decades, market leadership in poor countries will be a prerequisite to continued vitality in rich ones. If you stand by and watch while others solve problems in poor countries, you will discover not just that you have new rivals, but that you have fallen far behind, perhaps too far behind to ever recover.

Changing Minds and Mind-Sets

Recognizing the dominant logic, and its embedded assumptions, traps, and fears, is a good beginning. Next, CEOs can take actions to weaken the suffocating grip of orthodoxies that have arisen from historical success.[6]

With orthodoxies, however, the challenge is to weaken their grip while still maximizing their benefits. The goal is not to destroy the glocalization mind-set; rather, the goal is to enhance it with reverse innovation. Each has its place, its benefits, and its limitations.

The capacity to practice glocalization is already established in multinationals. Reverse innovation has yet to be learned. To create a reverse innovation mind-set, CEOs must take three steps: First, they must shift the center of gravity of their organization to emerging markets. Second, they must bulk up on emerging market knowledge and expertise. Third, they must change the tone by taking highly visible and symbolic personal actions.

Shifting the Center of Gravity to Emerging Markets

Try this exercise in your organization. On a map of the world, put big stickers in countries where you believe there are big growth opportunities and smaller stickers in countries where you believe the growth opportunities are less compelling. Now, put different stickers on the map to indicate where your top fifty most powerful executives are physically located.

Are the people and the opportunities in the same place? For most companies, the answer is not even close. The opportunities are in emerging markets; the people are near headquarters.

Shifting the center of gravity means shifting people, power, money, and attention to where the growth is. Here are some examples of how it is done:

- *Station critical decision makers in poor countries.* Cisco has appointed Wim Elfrink its chief globalization officer, who reports directly to CEO John Chambers. The CGO's primary home and office base is Bangalore, India—the epicenter of the world's IT services. Elfrink's central mission is to increase the focus of Cisco and its top executive team on Asia and India. Since the early 2000s, Cisco has moved 20 percent of its corporate officers to Bangalore.

- *Create new senior executive roles with oversight of emerging markets, and measure their performance with separate P&Ls.* In December 2009, General Electric sought to speed progress in India by creating a separate P&L that included all GE businesses in the country. The new unit, headed by Senior Vice President John Flannery, was given considerable power to tap GE's global R&D resources. Starting in 2011, Flannery reported to Vice Chairman John G. Rice, who relocated to Hong Kong from GE's headquarters in Connecticut. Rice oversees GE's non-U.S. operations, with a special focus on high-growth markets. This is a radical organizational change in a company where product has always come first and country second.

- *Increase R&D spending in emerging markets, and focus it on local needs.* Several companies have done so already. Nestlé, P&G, PepsiCo, Whirlpool, Cadbury, and The Coca-Cola Company have all escalated their R&D activities in India, with a specific focus on cost-conscious consumers. Similarly, in March 2010, Xerox established in Chennai, India, the firm's first innovation hub outside of the developed world. Meera Sampath, the head of the new unit, elaborated on its charter: "Our goal is to focus first and foremost on products and services tailored for emerging markets. If we can successfully figure out how to roll-out solutions for these highly challenged, low-cost environments, that gives us a tremendous platform to then roll them out globally as well."[7]

- *Encourage emerging-market P&Ls to conduct low-cost experiments.* In March 2010, Best Buy, the consumer electronics retailer, reorganized and created three divisions—the Americas, Europe, and Asia—putting three senior executives in charge, with each reporting to CEO Brian Dunn. To quote Kal Patel, executive vice president of Asia: "We are given considerable latitude to set our own strategies and business models. In Asia, this means adopting an experimental approach so that ideas can be tested and, if successful, scaled up quickly. We operate a bit like a Silicon Valley startup."[8]

- *Champion the notion that emerging markets can be incubation centers for global growth and innovation.* Highlight growth metrics that indicate how successful the company is at capturing the full potential of emerging markets.

Bulking Up on Emerging Markets Knowledge and Expertise

Even leaders located in the rich world need to break free of the glocalization mind-set that has made them successful throughout their careers. They must increase their knowledge and awareness of emerging markets—and pay attention to the potential opportunities afforded by these markets. Consider taking the following steps:

- *Change the composition of the board of directors and the top management team to include leaders with deep experience in emerging markets.* Leaders with rich-world résumés will be influenced by the people around them, so surround them with people who understand the emerging economies. In 2011, the board of directors of IBM included Lorenzo Zambrano, chairman and CEO of Mexico-headquartered Cemex. Bank of America, the largest U.S. bank by assets, named its first non-American board member, Mukesh Ambani, in March 2011. Ambani, an Indian national, is the CEO of Reliance Industries, one of the fastest-growing Indian companies, with $45 billion in sales. In announcing the appointment, the bank's management team—after focusing for years on domestic banking—stressed its ambition to become a significant player in emerging markets. Similarly, the appointments of Dinesh C. Paliwal as the CEO of Harman International and Indra K. Nooyi as the CEO of PepsiCo had a major impact on the cultures and mind-sets of these companies, as we describe in chapters 9 and 11.

- *Assign individuals to multiyear expatriate assignments in the developing world.* Expat experience is, by far, the most powerful accelerant for individual learning about the possibilities that exist in other markets. Unilever, the Dutch-British multinational, rotated high-potential executives among countries dramatically different from one another in terms of language, culture, and economy. These high potentials also rotated across different tasks in a single function (such as advertising, selling, and brand management within the marketing function) and across quite diverse business categories (such as ice cream, detergents, and tea). These highly varied assignments accomplish several things:

  - They create a deep understanding of customer problems in poor countries.
  - They transfer knowledge and capabilities to poor countries.
  - They build strong social networks that can help emerging-market innovations trickle up to rich countries.
  - Finally, such assignments are crucibles in which rising executives can develop and demonstrate steadiness, creativity, versatility, resiliency, and resourcefulness—all valuable leadership qualities.

- *Give rich-country executives short-duration immersion experiences in poor countries.* Standard Chartered, a London-based global bank, sent trainees recruited in London on two- to three-month assignments in various Asian locations.

- *Increase the strength of social ties between rich-world and developing-world executives.* Microsoft's Speech Technologies Group, an advanced research unit, had teams both in Redmond, Washington, and in Beijing. Scientists at each location served as affiliate members of the other team. And the teams met often with one another, both virtually and in person.

- *Hold board meetings, senior management meetings, and executive education programs in developing countries.* EMC Corporation (see chapter 7) holds a company-wide innovation conference and competition in a different market every year.

Changing the Tone Through Highly Visible and Symbolic Personal Actions

People don't believe in what they can't see or hear from their leaders. To make reverse innovation real to an enterprise, the CEO has to set the tone—with consistency—about the criticality of winning in emerging markets.

At GE, chairman and CEO Jeff Immelt has made reverse innovation a strategic priority. The top six hundred executives at GE meet annually at the company's Global Leadership Meeting in Boca Raton, Florida, to discuss strategic priorities. In early 2008, Immelt devoted an entire day to one theme: reconceptualizing GE as an emerging-market tiger. There were no fewer than eighteen presentations on the topic.

Immelt is clear in his priorities. He made a vivid impression on one manager in particular—the head of a major business that was doing well in China and India. Talking to Immelt, the manager seemed preoccupied with problems beyond his control in the United States. Immelt responded: "I don't even want to talk to you about your growth plans for the U.S. You've got to triple the size of your Indian business in the next three years. You've got to put more resources, more people, and more products in there, so that you're deep in that market and not just skimming the very top. Let's figure out how to do it."[9]

In all, the steps we have outlined above will go a long way toward opening enterprise eyes to a new way of seeing the world. Of course, viewing the world through a new lens is not enough. In chapter 4, we'll detail specific approaches for executing reverse innovation projects—and doing so in ways that allows for sustained excellence in an existing glocalization strategy.

Summary of the Key Ideas

1. Surface and challenge assumptions that support glocalization but that inhibit reverse innovation. Push leaders to recognize that success in emerging economies requires clean-slate innovation and that the stakes are global, not local.

2. Move people, power, and money to where the growth is—the developing world.

3. Create a reverse innovation mind-set throughout the corporation. Put the spotlight on emerging markets through the use of expatriate assignments, immersion experiences, corporate events that are held in emerging markets, creative board appointments, and highly visible CEO actions.

4. Create separate business scorecards for developing nations with full income statements and an emphasis on growth metrics.

CHAPTER FOUR

Changing the Management Model

To create clean-slate innovation in emerging markets, multinationals must embrace a new management model, local growth teams.

CHAPTER 3 looked at reverse innovation thinking. To be sure, fighting the dominant logic by creating a reverse innovation mind-set is a critical step. However, getting everyone in the company to level five thinking is not enough. In this chapter, we turn our attention to reverse innovation action.

Our main objective in this chapter is to deliver a set of recommendations for how to manage specific projects. An early warning: Our recommendations will be controversial. They will be uncomfortable for many. They will seem even more aggressive than the recommendations we have made so far.

Creating a reverse innovation mindset, the subject of the last chapter, requires *CEO-level* actions that *gradually* create *accommodating* change *throughout* the company. The goal is to *complement* the dominant logic. Executing a specific reverse innovation initiative, by contrast, requires *project-level* actions that *immediately* create *dramatic* change for a *small subset* of the company, the project team. The goal is to *overturn* the dominant logic.

Because the recommendations are dramatic, it's worthwhile to first show exactly why it is so improbable that a reverse innovation initiative could ever thrive—or even get off the ground—inside a multinational obsessively focused on glocalization. As we noted in the preface, our work with GE inspired us to write this book, and we will use GE as our primary illustration in this chapter, especially the story of its innovations in compact ultrasound devices, which we introduced in chapter 2.

Why Bad Things Happen to Good Ideas

Since organization follows strategy, it's hardly surprising that glocalization has molded the way the multinationals are structured and run. GE is a case in point. For thirty years, its organization evolved toward maximum effectiveness in glocalization. Power was concentrated in global business units that were headquartered in the rich world. The major business functions, including R&D, manufacturing, and marketing, were centralized at headquarters. Business leaders in developing countries were responsible for selling and distributing global products. (They also provided insights into local needs—insights that helped GE make minor adaptations to global products.) While many of the company's R&D centers and manufacturing operations were relocated to the developing world, the objectives in doing so were to tap overseas talent and to reduce costs. Such units reported to global headquarters and remained focused on rich-world offerings.

This approach has enormous advantages. It is very efficient. Unfortunately, an organization with a single-minded glocalization focus will present formidable barriers for reverse innovation.

Take the case of V. Raja, head of GE Healthcare's business in India in 2004. His primary task was to grow the market for GE Healthcare's global products. And yet, as Raja surveyed GE's customers in India, he saw a mismatch between their needs and the products he was able to offer them.

Consider, for example, a staple piece of X-ray imaging equipment, found in many basic surgical suites. It's called a surgical C-arm, and it isn't an especially complicated item: a rolling, C-shaped assembly, with an imaging unit at the top, which can be positioned wherever needed above a patient on an operating table. The technology dates back to before 1960.

At the turn of the new millennium, GE Healthcare offered to the Indian market a high-quality, high-priced surgical C-arm designed for the rich world. It was priced significantly higher than the local competition's alternative. Not surprisingly, that made GE's offering a tough sell for Indian hospitals and clinics. They would have been happier with a compromise product at a far lower price.

Raja saw a solution to the problem and made a proposal. He wanted the company to develop, manufacture, and sell a simpler, easier-to-use, and substantially cheaper product in India.

His proposal made good business sense, and yet it had little chance of approval. Here, in summary, is what Raja would have needed to do to overcome the dominant logic and to push his proposal forward:

- *Take initiative far beyond the call of duty.* Raja may have been the most senior executive in India, but his formal responsibilities included neither general management nor product development. His role was primarily to sell and distribute GE's global products in India. He was expected to grow revenues 15 to 20 percent per year while simultaneously boosting margins by holding expense growth down. This was a more-than-full-time job, for which he was accountable to deliver on plan. Simply finding time to pitch an India-specific product was a challenge in itself. But that is nothing compared with the challenge of the next step: selling the proposal internally.

- *Generate senior-level interest.* To do so, he would have to get the attention of the general manager at headquarters in the United States—not his immediate boss, but someone still higher in the global organization. India represented 1 percent of GE's global revenues at the time, so Raja could expect to command roughly 1 percent of the bandwidth of such a manager with global responsibility.

- *Make his case quickly.* Should Raja be lucky enough to get a meeting, he would have limited time to present his idea. The law of elevator pitches applies: go for emotion and enthusiasm. Unfortunately, he would be making the pitch to someone more familiar with world-renowned American teaching hospitals than with rural clinics outside Bangalore. At that time, global leaders in the United States did not typically visit emerging markets to deepen their insight into local conditions. How could anyone be expected to understand health-care needs in rural India while sitting in headquarters in Milwaukee?

- *Overcome bias against "small" opportunities.* Raja envisioned a modest effort at first. He anticipated that only two full-time engineers would be needed to design the product and that manufacturing could be outsourced. He estimated a $5 million to $6 million business in a market sized at $30 million to $35 million. Those are small numbers for GE, but Raja believed that the Indian market would grow significantly in the future—particularly if offered the right kinds of products. Nonetheless, global managers are accustomed to placing big bets on projected billion-dollar businesses. In the glocalization context, a new surgical C-arm for the Indian market appeared to be an unjustifiable drain of management attention and R&D ingenuity, and all for a mosquito-sized payoff.

- *Build broader support.* If Raja proved persuasive enough, he would be invited to share his proposal with functional leaders. Such conversations would be challenging. To the head of global manufacturing, simple, streamlined global products are more efficient than custom offerings. The head of marketing would fear a lower-priced product might weaken the GE brand and cannibalize existing global offerings. The head of finance would argue that lower-priced products would drag down overall margins. And the head of global R&D would want to know why engineers should be diverted from projects for GE's most sophisticated customers—buyers who know exactly what they want and can pay top dollar.

- *Deal with the capital budgeting system.* Were Raja able somehow to gain the support of these executives, the formal capital budgeting system would require him to submit a proposal with cash-flow projections supported by market research and to show that the project could meet the company's cost of capital and yield a positive net present value. Needless to say, it is nearly impossible to do market research or gather hard data when you are trying to create the market for a product that doesn't yet exist—never mind calculate an accurate return on investment.

- *Keep fighting the good fight even after the proposal is approved.* A simple initial approval would hardly have been enough. Raja's project would still have an uncertain payoff, and year after year, it would have to compete for additional capital with other, more profitable, shorter-term bets. Not only that, but Raja would still have had to sustain excellence in the operations he already supervised, while somehow executing a low-cost C-arm product within an organizational structure built for glocalization. So good luck with all of that!

Is it possible that innovation in poor countries could be so monumentally difficult inside a strong global company? Absolutely. The predicament that Raja faced is commonplace, and not just within GE but within all legacy global corporations. Each counterargument to a proposal like Raja's makes perfect sense, at least as seen from the perspective of those running the global business. After receiving an early cool reception to his idea for a new surgical C-arm tailored to the needs of the Indian market, Raja turned his attention back to the pressures and practical realities of his day job. (But as we will see in this and subsequent chapters, GE has made several changes to its organizational structure to catalyze reverse innovation, and the surgical C-arm project has since moved forward.)

The moral of Raja's real-life story? A strict and disciplined focus on glocalization creates insurmountable barriers for reverse innovation. Furthermore, the biggest hurdles to reverse innovation are not scientific, technical, or budgetary. They are managerial and organizational.

The Antidote

The solution, at least at a high level, just couldn't be any simpler or more obvious. It is to create special organizational units that are not built for glocalization, but instead for reverse innovation.

We will call these special units local growth teams (LGTs). An LGT is a small, cross-functional entrepreneurial unit physically located in the emerging market. It has a full set of business capabilities and broad authority to set strategy and develop products and services.

LGTs must follow three essential principles:

- LGTs must practice clean-slate organizational design. Building an LGT is similar to building a new company from scratch—a company with its own dominant logic.

- LGTs must be connected to the global organization and be able to leverage its resources.

- LGTs must practice disciplined experimentation.

Whether these recommendations seem controversial depends on your perspective. If you are the leader asked to tackle the reverse innovation project, you are likely quite pleased, if not exhilarated: "Life is good! My company is empowering me to build exactly the team I need. It is promising to support me with global resources and capabilities. And it is expecting me to learn quickly by running disciplined experiments."

Less excited, however, will be those charged with continuing to run the established business: "My company has taken responsibility for a critical emerging-market growth initiative away from me. It has diverted capital and talented people away from the operations I manage. Not only that, but I'm now expected to make it a priority to support this small and distant initiative. It will inevitably be a distraction, and it may or may not bear fruit. Of course, I'm still expected to be on plan and on budget—every day, every week, and every month. Meanwhile, this LGT leader is getting off easy! That manager has the privilege of running experiments!"

Despite the potential for explosive growth, the launch of an LGT-led project will encounter this dynamic—whether overt or covert—in most organizations. In fact, these initial reactions are only the beginning. Ongoing and routine conflict between the LGT and the global organization is normal. It is to be expected.

Nonetheless, there is simply no way to succeed at reverse innovation without building LGTs. Don't try to avoid the conflict. Doing so would only undermine the reverse innovation effort. Instead, the conflict must be accepted as normal, and then proactively managed and mitigated.

A strong first step is to clearly signal that reverse innovation does not replace glocalization. Glocalization will continue to be the dominant strategy. As such, rule number one when you are building LGTs is to do no harm to existing capabilities. Indeed, it is crucial that LGT leaders remember that the leaders of the existing glocalization system are not the enemy.

This is counterintuitive. Generally speaking, leaders of LGTs feel like they must "fight the system." On the contrary, they should recognize that glocalization works well for what it was designed to do: Efficiently grow rich-world markets. It remains the foundation of global competitiveness for most multinationals. If the model were to crumble, LGTs would fall too. After all, glocalization delivers the profits that pay for reverse innovation.

Thus, LGTs appear to be a more radical organizational solution than they actually are. To accept the need for LGTs is not to take a wrecking ball to the existing organization. LGTs are meant to be a supplement to, not an alternative to, the existing organization. Both glocalization and reverse innovation must thrive. LGTs depart so heavily from the norms only because they have a special mission that lies outside the organization's current capabilities. Rich-world innovation remains important.

It is entirely possible for a single company to apply both models at the same time. In fact, glocalization and reverse innovation need to do more than coexist. They need to cooperate. As discussed in chapter 3, for example, GE Healthcare's development team for the low-cost, handheld Vscan unit borrowed new beam-forming technology from a group working on a rich-world product.

Building LGTs from the Ground Up

Fundamentally, all innovation, including reverse innovation, is about assessing needs and developing solutions. The not-so-small complication is that legacy global corporations are accustomed to innovating for the rich world, and needs and solutions in the emerging economies are dramatically different. As a result, reverse innovation must begin with clean-slate thinking.

But clean-slate thinking is not a matter of simply waking up one day, flipping a mental switch, and deciding to start from scratch. The only way to achieve it is through clean-slate organizational design. In particular, LGTs must unite people who understand emerging-market needs and people who can provide emerging-market solutions. They must combine market insight with technical capabilities. They must integrate sales and marketing with R&D.

This may sound simple and obvious, but these interactions are infrequent in a glocalization-obsessed organization. Functional leaders located in emerging markets do not report to general managers in emerging markets; they report to functional leaders at global headquarters. Indeed, the people who understand the market's needs may have never even met the people who can develop solutions. Thus, these interactions must be purposefully created in LGTs.

The process of building an LGT begins with selecting team members. The wrong way to do this is to focus on who is most readily available (typically your existing colleagues). LGTs will probably require new competencies. Often these will be skill sets your company has never before needed. Thus, the key to choosing LGT members is first to identify the skills you need and then to hire the best talent you can get—whether from inside or outside the company (or perhaps through a small local acquisition).

When initiatives begin to show signs of success, the LGT will need to expand, a process that could require building new recruiting pipelines into the company. This is not always easy. Even in countries like China and India, with their large, educated populations, there is a war for talent. Multinationals compete fiercely with local firms for the same pool of talented scientists, engineers, and general managers. Individuals who offer both deep insight into local markets and experience working in Western multinationals are particularly sought-after.

Many businesses favor inside hiring, but outside hires do even more for a clean-slate initiative than just bring new skills. They help reset LGTs to a true zero point. They bring fresh perspectives that help LGTs overcome the tendency to fall back on dominant logic. Orthodoxies can be pernicious because their influence is so often unconscious and unfelt. Further, in every established organization, there are established expectations, roles, and responsibilities for people with certain titles or technical backgrounds. Even more critically, there may be an assumed hierarchy. In some companies, account managers have strong roles and engineers relatively weak roles; in others, just the opposite. Dominant logic must be acknowledged and actively questioned as an LGT comes together.

In part, this can be accomplished by creating new titles, writing new job descriptions, and having team members formally rethink their relationships with, and expectations of, each other. However, nothing is more powerful than getting new blood from outside. Outsiders are not captives of dominant logic. They are thus natural catalysts in the process of breaking down work relationships and rebuilding them from scratch.

Critically, LGTs must include their own product development teams, rather than relying solely on global R&D groups. Global groups have been staffed and organized to solve rich-world innovation challenges. They have numerous and powerful experts in the cutting-edge technologies that lie at the heart of rich-country products. However, they will have very few experts in the technologies that are the likeliest to lead to breakthroughs in poor countries. Compare the relative number and status of battery experts inside an established automaker with their counterparts in an electric car start-up. In the latter, the battery is the core technology, not a commodity component.

The evolution of GE's ultrasound business aptly illustrates the foundational principles for building the LGT. In the late 1990s, GE's ultrasound business operated in three segments: radiology, cardiology, and obstetrics. The three GE units, headquartered in the rich world, each had P&L responsibility and reported to Omar Ishrak, leader of global ultrasound business. These business units all focused on premium ultrasound products for rich-world customers. They pursued cutting-edge technologies and emphasized performance, speed, and image quality. They created unique features and functions (today, 3-D, and even motion-capturing 4-D, ultrasound images are routine).

As Ishrak set out to design a compact ultrasound device for China, he saw that the new business would have little in common with the three existing units. Therefore, he chose not to assign the development of the compact ultrasound to one of these units. Instead, he set up an LGT with P&L responsibility, headquartered in Wuxi, China. The China LGT was distinct and separate; it was empowered and expected to behave like a local player. The LGT was constructed as a full business unit with a complete value chain, including product development, supply chain, manufacturing, marketing, sales, and service.

Ishrak selected Diana Tang to lead the LGT. She had years of marketing experience in GE's ultrasound business in Asia. Through her interactions with customers, she understood quite clearly why GE's premium products were generating such a tepid response. She was also aware that the Chinese government was initiating a vigorous effort to improve health in rural areas.

The LGT's location in Wuxi was also important. Tang and her colleagues not only could keep a close eye on local competitors, but could also visit local clinics and get an even finer understanding of their needs, their work flow, and the most important ultrasound applications. Imagine how much tougher it would be for a management team located thousands of miles away to gain such insights.

Tang recruited locally, seeking experts in miniaturization and low power consumption, disciplines that were relatively unimportant in GE's premium business but crucial to the Wuxi LGT. In building the commercialization team, Tang sought deep knowledge of local market conditions. Hoping to avoid biases and preconceived notions learned while selling high-end machines, she minimized internal transfers. In addition, she deliberately chose not to hire salespeople from Philips or Siemens, GE Healthcare's global competitors. Instead she attracted people from local rivals, including Mindray, the company's most formidable Chinese adversary.

In addition to hiring outsiders with nontraditional backgrounds, the LGT departed from other organizational norms. For instance, instead of relying on GE Healthcare's global customer-support and replacement-parts organization, the LGT built in-country teams that could provide quicker, less expensive service.

Creating Links to Global Resources

So far, we have emphasized the necessity of building an LGT as though you are creating a new company from scratch. In reality, however, an LGT should be much more powerful than a start-up. That is because an LGT will—if properly chartered—have the potential to leverage the full resources and capabilities of its global parent.

If a company makes little effort to connect the LGT to the larger enterprise, the team's chances of success against local rivals—the so-called emerging giants—will diminish. Consider the overwhelming comparative advantages of local rivals:

- They have a strong sense of urgency. If they fail, they are dead. Unlike multinationals, they do not have the luxury of hedging their bets across markets and countries.

- They have an instinctive understanding of local customer needs.

- They are more nimble than the local subsidiaries of Western multinationals, which are often burdened by requirements for approvals from distant headquarters.

- They are young. They have no legacies to protect, no entrenched mind-sets, and no orthodoxies to overcome.

- All resources are local and readily accessible.

- Most of the emerging giants (such as Tata, Reliance, and Mahindra & Mahindra) are managed by first- and second-generation entrepreneurs. They are patient investors who pursue long-term bets.

- They have favorable images as local companies.

- They are well connected to important local actors, including financial institutions and governments.

- They have high aspirations. They have a passion that extends beyond business success to contributing to the economic development of their countries.

Multinationals can offset these considerable advantages only by enabling LGTs to tap into the parent company's mammoth enterprise resource base: technology, a global brand, a global footprint, existing customer relationships, distribution channels, supply networks, and manufacturing capacity. Such resources are assets that emerging-market competitors can only dream of. LGTs should be distinct and empowered, but they should not work in isolation. The most powerful LGTs engage in healthy partnerships with the parent company.

With Ishrak's facilitation, Diana Tang's ultrasound team was able to tap into GE's extensive global resource base. The engineering team "appropriated" three stellar talents from GE's R&D centers in Israel, Japan, and South Korea. They were among the company's best and most respected engineers. For example, Israeli Nahi Halmann, a software expert with a doctorate in biomedical engineering, had been a driving force behind GE's work to move from expensive custom hardware to a software-centric architecture. As such, his work was essential to the compact ultrasound's goal of radically reducing the cost of an ultrasound device.

All three of the guest engineers provided hands-on, face-to-face coaching for the Chinese team, especially as the project was getting off the ground. They also brought to the project a rich network of relationships with GE's R&D centers around the world. Each engineer was able to identify opportunities to use existing knowledge elsewhere in the company. And because of the trio's talent and status, other R&D centers were responsive to their queries. Their very presence on the LGT signaled the importance of its mission.

Nonetheless, developing healthy partnerships between the LGT and the rest of the corporation is challenging. Reverse innovation and glocalization are an awkward combination. Think oil and water. Where the two come into contact, there will be conflict. Leaders in the global business unit are likely to have several reactions to LGTs:

- Question the wisdom of allocating resources—capital, time, and energy—to a distant project with an uncertain long-term payoff

- Fear any new offerings that might eventually cannibalize existing ones

- Try to protect crucial assets, such as global brands or customer relationships, from the potential damage of risky projects

- Demand quantitative measurement of performance and progress against plans as a means to justify continued investment in the LGT

Only an inexperienced executive would expect that LGT leaders and their counterparts in the global business will be able to work out the inevitable—and sometimes quite heated—conflicts on their own. LGT heads and leaders of global business units are hardly peers. The latter typically command far greater resources, have longer tenure, and enjoy more-extensive political connections within the organization. Not only that, global leaders can justify their requests for resources with short-term needs—often to satisfy an existing customer. By contrast, an LGT leader has a smaller budget, less experience, lower clout, and fewer connections. He or she can promise, at best, a long-term hope. Supposing these parties can resolve their differences on their own is like expecting the nail to work out its differences with the hammer. It is a quick route to failure.

Conflicts can only be resolved in favor of the LGT when a more powerful countervailing force is in the mix. That is why an LGT should report to a very senior executive. Even when it was tiny, the LGT in China reported directly to Ishrak.

Executives who supervise LGTs must be able to perform the following tasks:

Identify and solidify valuable connections between the LGT and the global organization. These connections could take many forms, including occasional visits and phone calls, temporary "loans" of experts, and significant resource commitments. Such arrangements don't come about just because an LGT politely asks for volunteer help; a senior executive must facilitate the connections. Ishrak helped the China LGT to tap into GE's extensive global resource base.

Protect the LGT's resources. LGTs are multiyear bets. Unless overseen by executives with influence over long-term capital budgets, LGTs could fall prey to competing short-term priorities. And it's more than a question of budgets. Executive sponsors must also be powerful enough to prioritize the efforts of key employees. As in the ultrasound example, engineers in the global R&D organization might need to pitch in to support an LGT, even if that means shifting time and energy from the next quarter's product launch. Ishrak was powerful enough to establish the LGT as a priority not to be interfered with. Moreover, had Ishrak not shielded the LGT, its engineers in China might have been diverted to other projects—default priorities, given GE's extremely ambitious agenda for rich-country product development.

Add resources to enable the global organization to do two jobs. Before an LGT is formed, the people in the global organization have one job: ongoing operations. Afterward, they have two: ongoing operations plus supporting the LGT. Conflicts often arise when people are asked to do more with inadequate resources. To do two jobs instead of one, people need help. It may be necessary to add staff. Too often, LGTs are left begging for volunteer help, but this approach is only realistic when reverse innovation initiatives are nascent and LGTs small. Again, your project must find its Ishrak.

Modify individual performance reviews. Make it very clear that answers to the question "How well did you support our company's LGTs in emerging economies?" will weigh heavily in annual performance reviews.

Make LGTs pay for the help they get from the global organization. This can be accomplished through an internal accounting transfer. The exact amount of the transfer is less important than what it signals: when LGTs pay for what they get, they are treated more like customers than distractions.

Help recruit good "connectors." Whereas outside hires give important reinforcement to the clean-slate ethos of an LGT, insiders are invaluable in building a good relationship between the LGT and the global organization. Ishrak assigned executives from Israel, Japan, and South Korea to the China LGT. Over the long term, such global experts gain knowledge of the economic, social, cultural, and street-level realities of emerging markets. As a result, these experts become increasingly valuable contributors to

TABLE 4-1

How to manage the tensions between local growth teams (LGTs) and the global organization

Conflicts between LGTs and the global organization are inevitable and can crush reverse innovation efforts. Nonetheless, you can—and must—create a healthy partnership between the two, by taking the following actions:

- Emphasize that reverse innovation *does not replace* glocalization.

- Help LGTs leverage global resources by identifying and solidifying valuable connections between the LGT and the global organization.

- Protect LGT resources.

- Where LGTs rely on help from the global organization, add resources so that the global organization can do two jobs: excel at ongoing operations and support the LGT.

- Modify individual performance reviews so that leaders in the global organization understand that supporting LGTs is a critical responsibility.

- Through an internal accounting transfer, make LGTs pay for the help they get from the global organization.

- Help the LGT recruit good internal connectors—people who understand both the needs of the emerging market and the pressures of the global business.

future reverse innovation efforts and powerful educators of the rest of the company's leadership team. Through such symbiotic mechanisms, the legacy business culture gains comfort, confidence, and excitement regarding the value of reverse innovation in general and LGTs in particular.

Table 4-1 summarizes our recommendations for creating solid and healthy links to the global organization.

Managing Disciplined Experiments

All innovation endeavors are inherently uncertain. As a result, in the early stages of a reverse innovation effort, it is less important to deliver on plan than it is to state hypotheses about the future, test them, convert uncertainties into knowledge, and apply the lessons learned to develop a workable business model. In the battle to capture new markets, the winner is not necessarily the company that starts with the best strategy. It is often the one that learns and adapts the smartest and fastest.

The following practices will help the LGT maximize learning.

Focus on Resolving Critical Unknowns

In an established business, plans tend to be loaded with data. Leaders of LGTs should also strive to gather as much data as possible—but they should also recognize that no matter how extensive their initial research, the unknowns are likely to outweigh the knowns. As a result, the initial business plan should be seen for what it is: a best guess. Therefore, conversations during business reviews should focus on resolving unknowns, especially the following:

- How large is the market?

- What price points will unlock the market?

- Will customers be willing to take a risk on a revolutionary new product?

- Which other competitors will enter the marketplace? How quickly? How aggressively?

- Can we design the right product?

- Can we manufacture the product at the right cost?

To accelerate learning, it pays to rank the most critical unknowns: assumptions that, if wrong, could prove fatal to the strategy. Then, test these as quickly and inexpensively as possible.

Ishrak did this with the China LGT. Developing and commercializing portable ultrasounds in rural China was a process fraught with uncertainties. Appropriately, the team adopted an experiment-and-learn approach. Wherever possible, it conducted low-cost experiments to test critical assumptions about how its approach would unlock the market's full potential. Ishrak's exhortation was, "Keep the learning cycle rapid and low cost. Learn first, then invest and scale. Don't invest big and hope to learn."

For instance, the LGT knew that doctors in rural China were less familiar with ultrasounds than doctors in cities. But there was a critical unknown regarding what features—at what level of technical complexity—would meet rural doctors' needs. So the team invited doctors to use and critique prototype machines. The team members learned that ease of use, especially in primary-care screening, was far more crucial than they had anticipated.

As a result, they added emphasis to training, offered online guides, designed simpler keyboards, created built-in presets for certain tasks, and tracked after-sale customer satisfaction to gauge success.

Later on, to reduce the risks associated with building a distribution network that would reach all corners of China, the LGT pursued a phased rollout strategy. Sales teams were built first in regions where GE's local competitor, Mindray, was weakest. This both increased GE's odds of success and optimized the learning curve. The LGT was able to glean more customer insight before escalating its investment. The team observed customers' buying behavior and saw how they used the product. And the LGT learned how best to hire, train, and deploy its sales force—all before taking on Mindray in the competitor's strongholds.

Create a Custom Scorecard

Metrics commonly used within a corporation can become nearly instinctive reference points for evaluating performance. However, they may be of little use to a reverse innovation effort. Therefore, the scorecard for an LGT's progress should be customized to the project. It should especially highlight leading indicators—measures that will give the earliest indications that the strategy is working or failing.

Ishrak was careful to devise locally relevant criteria for evaluating team performance. For example, because the government approval process for new product releases is less burdensome in China than in the developed world, he set much shorter product-development cycles. And since salaries are lower and service more demanding in China, he also allowed for a bigger service staff relative to the number of installed machines—a deviation from GE Healthcare's global standards, but one that made sense in context.

Revise Plans Frequently

In most corporations, plans are fixed for one year at a time. That's fine when the past can serve as a reliable guide to the future, but that's not the case with innovation. To learn quickly, LGT leaders must revise their plans frequently. Annual iteration is inadequate.

At the beginning of the compact ultrasound project, Ishrak met often with the China LGT—monthly at least, and sometimes even weekly—to review its progress. He believed that frequent reviews would accelerate team learning.

Hold LGT Leaders Accountable for Learning, not for Results Against Plan

The profuse uncertainties of reverse innovation efforts make it neither fair nor realistic to hold reverse innovation leaders accountable for delivering on plan or to evaluate them on short-term financial metrics. But that doesn't mean they get a free pass. LGT leaders can and should face tough reviews and demanding expectations. The questions that matter most include these: Did the leader run a disciplined experiment? Did the team learn as quickly and inexpensively as possible? Did it make sensible decisions based on clearly identified lessons learned? And finally, how well is the team resolving or refining critical assumptions en route to building a workable strategy? Asking and answering these questions keeps the focus where it should be—on quick and disciplined learning.

Fully Exploiting Global Opportunities

An LGT that successfully meets the needs of local customers has something to celebrate. But that's not the end of the journey. The next step is to spread the innovation to other markets around the world.

This is where legacy multinationals have their biggest advantage over local rivals. They already have global presence. They already have global brands. They can move quickly into corners of the world that the emerging giants have yet to visit. To make the most of this advantage, senior executives must initiate discussions that include an explicit focus on identifying opportunities.

For example, during the late 1990s, Ishrak created a panel called the GE Healthcare Global Ultrasound Product Council. It consisted of the company's leading experts in the industry, its markets, and its current and future technologies. When the time came to grow compact ultrasound into additional markets, Ishrak used the council to help evaluate worldwide opportunities.

Possible moves into other developing countries are likely to be relatively straightforward. Needs from one poor country to another probably won't differ by much. Fundamental needs such as ultralow cost, portability, ease of use, and utility under conditions of minimal infrastructure are widespread among emerging markets. Consequently, it isn't necessary to commission a clean-slate innovation effort for each poor country. Instead, relatively straightforward customizations of the original reverse innovation will suffice.

It's also unnecessary to set up LGTs in every emerging market—a good thing, since there are over 150 of them. Instead, multinationals can think in terms of one or a handful of global centers of excellence for reverse innovation. These could focus on the ten biggest emerging markets that account for more than 60 percent of the population and more than 60 percent of the GDP in the developing world: Brazil, China, India, Indonesia, Mexico, Nigeria, Russia, South Africa, Turkey, and Vietnam.

Moves into the rich world might proceed into either marginalized or mainstream markets. The process of identifying marginalized markets is straightforward. A marginalized market is, by definition, one that is geographically part of the rich world but similar in key respects to poor-world markets. Even in the rich world there are poor people, or people with needs similar to those in the poor world.

Spotting the emergence of mainstream markets for reverse innovations is a bit trickier. The key is to ask questions that focus on needs gaps and on trends that can close the gaps, as we described in chapter 2. With these gaps and trends in mind, be sure your strategic discussions include these topics:

1. How long will it be before the technology underlying our reverse innovation improves to the point that our mainstream rich-world customers will be intrigued? Also, will our mainstream rich-world customers face budget crunches so significant that our ultra-low-cost reverse innovation will become more attractive?

2. Our infrastructure innovations are succeeding in numerous emerging markets. At some point, they could interest rich-world customers. How soon will rich-world infrastructure reach replacement age?

3. How soon will our rich-world customers face sustainability pressures that are as extreme as the ones that our developing world customers face?

4. How long will it be before rich-world regulatory systems catch up with innovations that are already proving themselves in poor countries?

5. Are our rich-world customers experimenting with or adopting tastes and preferences that are prevalent in the developing world?

Making the transition from innovating to propagating can be tricky. It puts new and unfamiliar demands on the LGT. During the innovation phase, LGTs grow accustomed to an extraordinary degree of independence. Their work is supported by others from around the world. However, once they succeed in the local market, that orientation shifts. They must go from being supported to becoming supportive, as their innovation spreads around the world. They must accept—and learn to play—this supporting role. LGTs only know their local markets. The effort to expand an innovation globally must be driven by leaders elsewhere, and LGTs must be responsive to their needs. This transition requires close attention from senior executives.

Individuals who can be good connectors are again extremely valuable in helping LGTs play this new role. Good connectors understand both local and global markets, cultures, and business models. They can serve as guides to the unfamiliar—for all stakeholders.

In due time, and with proper support, successful LGTs become much more than just local businesses. They become global centers of excellence in their domains. GE's ultrasound LGT in China has become the global hub for developing compact ultrasound units.

Mitigating Fears of Cannibalization

In many cases, bringing reverse innovations home will stoke fears about cannibalization. Why replace sales of premium products with sales of low-priced products?

It is certainly reasonable to be concerned about cannibalization, but it is dangerous to be frozen by its specter. After all, if you don't cannibalize yourself, someone else will do it for you. On the other hand, if you are first to get the product to market, you can control the rate of cannibalization—at least until a rival arrives with a similar offering.

GE's original entry into the ultrasound market under Jack Welch was itself a cannibalization hedge. It seemed possible that ultrasound would advance in performance to the point that it would threaten GE's higher-priced diagnostic machines such as CAT scanners and MRI machines. Even in the 1980s, GE was anticipating the need to cannibalize itself.

Furthermore, products that have the potential to cannibalize will very often also have an offsetting impact: they stimulate new consumption. Ultralow prices stimulate demand among those who would never have bought the premium model. (In the case of compact ultrasound, the new customers were small clinics and individual physicians, as opposed to large hospitals.) Also, reverse innovations have the potential to target entire marginalized markets that consist of hitherto unserved customers. (For example, compact ultrasounds can now be found in ambulances. The devices can be used by EMTs at remote accident sites).

Finally, complete cannibalization is highly unlikely, as reverse innovations usually can't fully duplicate the performance and functionality of existing products. There is generally room for both old and new to coexist. Although great improvements have been made in the full range of portable ultrasound devices, they've hardly replaced traditional premium devices, which still offer better image quality and more features than even the best portable systems.

Adding New Strength

The recommendations that we've laid out in this chapter are challenging. (See table 4-2 for a summary of the key steps for building an LGT.) However, they are not out of proportion with reverse innovation's inherently high degree of difficulty. Reverse innovation is night-and-day different from glocalization. It is not about improving an existing business model; it is about creating new business models. It is not about winning market share, but is about creating robust new markets.

To succeed at this new and starkly different challenge, global corporations must substantially depart from long-standing organizational norms. Discontinuous change in strategy demands discontinuous change in organization. Indeed, reverse innovation demands supreme institutional dexterity. It may be the most vexing organizational and managerial maneuver that global corporations have ever before attempted.

TABLE 4-2

How the logic of local growth teams (LGTs) differs from that of legacy global organizations

Organizational architecture for glocalization	LGTs
• Have functional leaders located in emerging markets report to global headquarters.	• Have functional heads collaborate closely on a small entrepreneurial team. In particular, those with market insight work closely with those with technical capability.
• Empower insiders with deep insight built over lengthy careers.	• Empower outsiders with new skills and expertise that can help meet unique emerging-market needs.
• Respect traditional and long-established organizational norms, such as how roles and responsibilities are defined and hierarchies are formed.	• Ignore long-established organizational norms. Custom-built LGTs for the task at hand, as though they are new companies being built from the ground up.
• Focus on delivering results: on-time, on-budget, and on-spec.	• Focus on resolving unknowns, learning quickly, and zeroing in on a successful business model.
• Focus on well-understood, long-standing metrics of performance.	• Create a custom scorecard that highlights metrics that will help resolve unknowns.
• Follow an annual planning cycle.	• Allow frequent revisions to plan, as often as there are new data that may resolve unknowns.
• Hold leaders accountable first and foremost for delivering results.	• Hold leaders accountable first and foremost for learning by running disciplined experiments.

As we asserted before, however, reverse innovations require targeted—not wholesale—departures from past practice. The intention is not to dismantle the glocalization capability. It is to enhance what exists with a new strength: reverse innovation.

Although the organizational challenges are steep, they are solvable. And when they are solved, it will be a win-win proposition—for both multinationals and poor countries. The vast strength of global enterprises will be put to work on the most important economic development challenges of our era. Over time, both multinationals and poor countries will be transformed. Corporations will hone new, more relevant emerging-market capabilities, and the customers they serve will gain access to goods and services with superior value and that truly reflect the way people live.

Part 2 will show how eight very different organizations are strengthening their reverse innovation muscles. Their journeys are filled with pitfalls, but also, as you will see, exhilarating rewards.

Summary of the Key Ideas

1. Commission local growth teams (LGTs) with full business capabilities for each reverse-innovation opportunity. LGTs should act like brand-new companies:
   - They must conduct clean-slate needs assessments.
   - They must develop clean-slate solutions.
   - They must practice clean-slate organizational design.

2. Enable LGTs to leverage your company's global resource base through carefully managed partnerships.

3. Manage reverse innovation initiatives as disciplined experiments, with a focus on resolving critical unknowns quickly and inexpensively.

The Reverse Innovation Playbook

HERE, we summarize the most crucial recommendations from part 1 of the book. In part 2, we'll look at eight case studies that show this playbook in action.

Strategy

1. To capture growth in emerging markets, you must innovate, not simply export.

2. Leverage opportunities to move emerging-market innovations to other parts of the world: to other poor countries, to marginalized markets in rich countries, and, eventually, to mainstream markets in rich countries.

3. Keep so-called emerging giants on your radar screen. These small but rapidly growing companies, headquartered in the developing world, have global aspirations that could one day threaten your own.

Global Organization

4. Move people, power, and money to where the growth is—the developing world.

5. Create a reverse innovation mind-set throughout the corporation. Put the spotlight on emerging markets through the use of expatriate assignments, immersion experiences, corporate events that are held in emerging markets, creative board appointments, and highly visible CEO actions.

6. Create separate business scorecards for developing nations with full P&L responsibility and an emphasis on growth metrics.

Project Organization

7. Commission local growth teams (LGTs) with full business capabilities for each reverse innovation opportunity. LGTs should act like brand-new companies:
   - They must conduct clean-slate needs assessments.
   - They must develop clean-slate solutions.
   - They must practice clean-slate organizational design.

8. Enable LGTs to leverage your company's global resource base through carefully managed partnerships.

9. Manage reverse innovation initiatives as disciplined experiments, with a focus on resolving critical unknowns quickly and inexpensively.

PART 2

Reverse Innovation in Action

CHAPTER FIVE

Logitech, and the Mouse That Roared

*If you ignore upstart rivals, you will pay
a steep price.*

HOW MANY STEALTH COMPETITORS does it take to upend a strategy? It takes only one—even one no bigger than a mouse.

This is the cautionary tale of how Logitech, the pioneering maker of computer peripherals, including input devices such as keyboards and mice, used principles of reverse innovation to avert potential disaster. It also reinforces just how crucial it is for every multinational to pay close attention to local competitors in emerging markets. If they aren't on your radar screen, they should be.

Logitech, a thirty-plus-year-old California-based multinational, had done business in China ever since its first manufacturing joint venture in Shanghai in 1993. The company believed it had a winning strategy in China. The strategy, classic glocalization, assumed that innovations flow downhill—that the same products made for Western consumers would eventually succeed in emerging markets, with small modifications at best.

Indeed, in Logitech's worldview, technology users were becoming the same the world over, as the information ubiquitous on the Internet whetted consumer appetites everywhere for the newest devices. Chinese computer users, in their behavior and preferences, would eventually become like those in the United States. It was only a question of time and patience.

In China, Logitech had been pushing wireless mice priced at about $50 and up. Logitech believed it could command a premium price for premium features. Its top model, priced at $149, required no hard surface. It could operate in thin air! Though Logitech's results in China lacked sparkle, the company was content to wait for the Chinese market to catch up with the rich world. What Logitech had not realized, however, was that, as we observed in chapter 3, you can actually be passed while you're waiting.

Strategic patience—the temperamental opposite of fast-twitch strategic restlessness—is often an admirable business asset. But a product strategy that treats poor markets as though they are evolving into markets just like today's rich ones can lead to missed opportunities. It can even be dangerous in home markets.

In late 2008, a Chinese company called Rapoo introduced a wireless mouse for $15—an ultralow price that Chinese consumers craved. Further, on the features that mattered most in China, Rapoo's offering had capabilities equivalent to those of Logitech's $50 models.

Rapoo? Who the blazes were they? At the moment, Rapoo was David to Logitech's Goliath. Rapoo's mouse was like a rock slung straight to the center of Logitech's strategy.

In fact, Rapoo had been around for ten years or so. As part of a parent company called MLK, it had been providing private-label and house-brand mice and keyboards to computer makers and big-box electronics retailers. It wasn't until 2008 that it started competing under the Rapoo name.

According to Rory Dooley, who heads up Logitech's mouse and keyboard business, the launch of the Rapoo mouse initially triggered "a little bit of denial."[1] Companies with long track records and a history of success are used to small upstarts that come and go quickly. So when Rapoo popped up with what looked like a game-changing product, Dooley says there was the requisite naysaying. Call it whistling past the graveyard: "We've seen this before, and these people always disappear." But independent market data showed that Chinese consumers were snapping up Rapoo's new mouse. According to Dooley, Rapoo had found a way to deliver just the right features at just the right price. The upstart was gaining share at Logitech's expense.

Multinational companies tend to be obsessively aware of their high-profile competitors. For instance, Logitech's main rival in the mouse market is Microsoft, so Logitech is accustomed to paying close attention to

Microsoft's technology and marketing moves. It paid little heed, however, to Rapoo.

Not a second too soon, Dooley and others analyzed the market data. They saw that the threat from Rapoo was real, and it was unlikely to go away.

What Makes a Mouse Mighty?

To the average undemanding Western computer user, a mouse is a mouse is a mouse—a commodity piece of the computing experience that gets noticed only when it malfunctions. Someone who mouses sedately, while working at a computer on a desk, will happily settle for a low-end corded model. Think of it as the Honda Civic of mice—reliable but not flashy.

Corded mice, however, are a vanishing species. Furthermore, many users—gamers, designers and developers, and consumers of graphics-rich content—want the BMW wireless mouse, not the corded Civic. If you haven't wondered lately what constitutes a top-of-the-line, state-of-the-art wireless mouse, here is its personality profile:

- *Range*. It works over long distances, up to three hundred feet.

- *Speed*. It's fast, with no noticeable delays from mouse motion to motion on the screen.

- *Shielding*. It turns out that lower-end mice don't respond well to peer pressure. Their performance can be hampered by interference from neighboring mice or other wireless devices.

- *Surfaces*. It works well on almost any surface. Glass, says Dooley, is a notoriously tricky surface, but Logitech has a glass-friendly model.

- *Programmability*. It can be customized. Users can make adjustments to the mouse's characteristics, such as its sensitivity to motion, the maximum gap between clicks that still constitutes a double-click, and more.

- *Simplicity*. It is easy to use. Just plug it in.

- *Ergonomics*. It mitigates repetitive-stress effects.

Logitech's Lineup: Good, Better, Best

At the heart of a wireless mouse is its wireless chip. There were three widely used technology standards in play in 2008. In order of increasing performance, they were the 27-megahertz (MHz) chip, 2.4-gigahertz (GHz) chip, and the Bluetooth chip. The choice of the wireless technology largely determined the mouse's performance on the first three characteristics listed—range, speed, and shielding—and was also the main driver of price.

Logitech segmented its product line into three main categories: good (low-price, low-performance, 27-MHz chip); better (medium-price, medium-performance, 2.4-GHz chip), and best (high-price, high-performance, Bluetooth chip). The good, better, and best models had ranges of 1 to 5 feet, 6 to 30 feet, and 31 to 300 feet, respectively, and prices of roughly $30, $50, and as high as $150. But as Logitech customers stepped up from the good chip to the better chip to the best chip, they got more than just improved range, speed, and shielding. They also acquired improved performance on the remaining mouse characteristics, including surfaces, programmability, and ergonomics. These bundles of features and capabilities seemed to work very well in the rich world.

Why China Needed a Mightier Mouse

Logitech's approach did not work well in China, however. Why? Because Chinese customers are different.

First, population density in Chinese cities is extremely high. Interference from a mouse in the next apartment could inadvertently jam your own mouse's signal, slowing or stopping its action. Consequently, robust shielding wasn't a luxury option in urban settings; it was a necessity.

Another distinctive characteristic of the Chinese market is that consumers favor free Internet video content over cable television. Part of the reason is that satellite and cable infrastructures in China are far less well developed than in the United States. Moreover, while U.S. consumers might not think twice about paying $50 or more for a monthly cable subscription, Chinese consumers tended to balk. "A lot of motivations in China are driven by economics," says Dooley. Chinese users plug their notebook computers into their televisions to watch downloaded movies and TV shows. They need a mouse with sufficient range to make it possible to sit on the couch and use the mouse as a TV remote-control unit.

Logitech was grounded in a Western worldview. As a result, these were easy differences to overlook. Relatively few U.S. customers suffer from hellacious interference problems. Most Americans live in detached houses on large lots, with yards that separate them from their neighbors. (The population density in China is more than four times that of the United States.) Furthermore, in the United States, cable or satellite TV is nearly ubiquitous. Few Americans are compelled to treat the Internet as an alternative to cable. So they don't hook their computers to their televisions, and they don't need their mice to double as remote controls.

Where Logitech was temporarily blind, Rapoo saw the light. There was a hole in the market—a hole that Logitech had missed with its good-better-best lineup. Although Chinese consumers—eager to get the lowest possible price—might willingly compromise on certain dimensions of performance, they absolutely needed a "better" wireless chip to get sufficient range and shielding. Rapoo had offered a mouse with the superior performance of a 2.4-GHz chip, but at the lower cost of 27-MHz (figure 5-1).

FIGURE 5-1

Wireless mouse market

Rapoo's innovation: combine "better" chip-specific features with "good-enough" other features, and sniff out the market's sweet spot—the right technology at the right price.

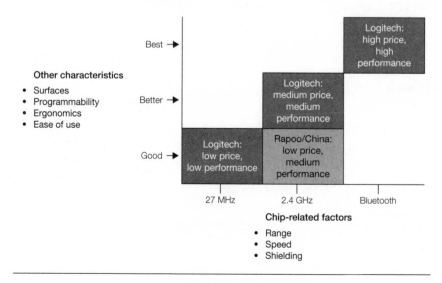

Logitech, meanwhile, had been locked in its glocalization worldview. According to Dooley, the company believed it would have to wait a few more years for the Chinese to embrace "better" wireless mice in large numbers. In actuality, Chinese consumers *were* ready. They just weren't ready to embrace it at the price Logitech had set, and they didn't care about the features that Logitech had bundled with it.

Hard Evidence

Those who practice reverse innovation must sometimes contend with potent internal opposition—frequently cloaked in devotion to the status quo. Reverse innovators who are unprepared to face such resistance are in for a rough ride.

At Logitech, denial had to be muscled aside by facts. "Data removes the emotionalism and the opinions," says Dooley. It points discussion toward evidence that helps people accept objective reality. As with any recovery process, the first step is to admit there's a problem.

Logitech had access to multiple sources of credible independent information—the perfect antidote to retrograde impulses. There were two types of data: one on product sales and market share, and the other on the extent of customers' enthusiasm about Logitech and its products. The latter research showed clear discontent with Logitech's 27-MHz mice and helped reveal a dimension of Logitech's strategic problem that otherwise might have remained hidden. The instinctive assumption among Logitech executives was that if Chinese customers were unsatisfied, the problem must be price alone. But the data showed otherwise. It was the performance of the wireless technology that created dissatisfaction.

Both sources of input confirmed the existence of a serious problem and shortened the cycle of denial. By early 2009, Logitech had settled on a new strategy, forged in a crucible of facts. The company would begin to phase out its 27-MHz technology and replace it with 2.4-GHz. But the design of Logitech's 2.4-GHz models would need to be radically changed. Otherwise, the company would never be able to compete with Rapoo's pricing.

Goliath Strikes Back

Crafting a new strategy is one thing, but making it happen is another matter. Even after the decision makers reached consensus, there was still plenty of inertia to overcome. "There was a need to accept, as a business unit, that the world had shifted," says Dooley. There came a moment of truth when the company could no longer ignore "that we had a lot of products that were no longer at the level that we would think was reasonable for the market."

Logitech now confronted an inconvenient truth. In high-tech companies, there's a tendency to fall in love with particular technologies. Within Logitech, says Dooley, there were partisans enamored of each of the technologies and features included in the three product tiers. "We had found a way of fitting them all into a view, and that view became our dominant logic and conventional wisdom."

To break free from the dominant logic, in March 2009 Logitech commissioned a small local growth team (LGT). The team drew its members from Taiwan and China and additional support from a team in Switzerland. Since much of Logitech's wireless technology is designed in Switzerland, that's where the company developed the core architecture.

The ambitious goal was to have a competitive answer to Rapoo on the market inside of six months. *No later than September!* Olivier Egloff, a Swiss national with a background in electrical engineering, was put in charge of the team. Egloff had spent three years working in Logitech's Taiwan office. Dooley describes him as a highly skilled project leader with the benefit of significant Asia experience. The LGT leader understood the urgency of the task at hand and the need to move quickly.

Before Rapoo came along, Egloff had believed that it would be impossible to manufacture a 2.4-GHz mouse at a 27-MHz price point. Now he was going to have to prove himself wrong.

One of the first places the LGT looked for savings was to exploit greater economies of scale in semiconductors—the biggest cost driver in a mouse. In 2009, Logitech had sold fourteen million 27-MHz and ten million 2.4-GHz mice worldwide. Its new strategy would upend that ratio. Nearly all production would be 2.4-GHz. Thus the company was able to tempt

Nordic Semiconductor, its main 2.4-GHz chip supplier, with a much higher volume of business. Nordic didn't make chips for 27-MHz mice. But now that Logitech was shifting to faster technology, Nordic was willing to offer an advantageous price.

The team pursued other opportunities to economize by switching to a cheaper form of system memory (which stores code that allows the mouse to behave as a mouse). Logitech's earlier architecture had incorporated erasable (reusable) memory similar to that used in digital cameras. The team instead opted for cheaper onetime-programmable memory. It also slimmed down the system program so that the software took up 16 instead of 32 kilobytes of memory.

Together, these economies in design and materials brought cost down to a point where the mouse could both perform and be priced to compete with Rapoo's. The LGT made its September deadline.

While the effort to devise a technical response to the Rapoo mouse went smoothly, there were predictable challenges elsewhere. At some point, a leap of faith was required of everyone. This wasn't always an easy adjustment to make. For example, from the start, it was important to get the China region's sales force on board. But salespeople who are used to selling mice priced at $50 per unit and higher don't warm quickly to the idea of launching a similar model priced in the teens. Because of the profit margin implications, some on the sales side deeply wished that Rapoo had simply gone away.

"If I were in sales," says Dooley, "I'd be hoping that as well. It's easier to make quota by selling a few of something at a high price than many more at a lower price."

Dooley held sometimes-heated discussions with the sales team and made a couple of trips to the region. His key message was built around the lessons of the market-share data. It was vitally important to price appropriately for the China market. It's one thing to expect a premium, but unreasonable to expect a premium twice greater than what the competition was getting. The results were in, and customers had voted for the Rapoo price point!

After considerable research, Logitech settled on a price of $19.99; it was a more modest premium over Rapoo's price but it nonetheless increased margins and placated the reluctant sales staff. The same cannibalization battle waged in China was also waged over whether to launch the new mouse worldwide. The device debuted in Europe in February 2010, and in the United States in April. In less than a year, the company had shipped more than 4.5 million units of the new mouse. Of all Logitech new-product launches, this was the first product to break $10 million in sales in China within just twelve months.

A New Strategic Alertness

What happened to Logitech was simple myopia, induced by the company's practice of glocalization. Logitech had segmented the market and developed its products in ways it believed made sense for a unified set of global technology users. Initially, the lack of an appetite among Chinese users for Logitech's higher-end offerings simply reinforced the view that the company needed to remain patient. Chinese users hadn't yet evolved to the point that they demanded premium Western goods. Patience can lead to inattention, however.

"In China, everyone is a basic user, from an economic affordability point of view," says Dooley. But that is only one piece of the picture. The reality that Rapoo demonstrated to Logitech was that the computing needs of Chinese customers didn't lag those in the rich world. They were in fact quite distinct.

In a way, Rapoo did Logitech a favor. The Chinese company forced Logitech to confront its customers' discontent. "If they hadn't come along, I might have had to invent them," Dooley jokes.

According to Dooley, the Chinese market has expanded significantly in the three-plus years since Rapoo's game-changing mouse first roared. Had Logitech not responded quickly, it would have missed out on that growth. Clearly, the value of a near-death experience in an important local market offers bracing lessons in paying attention.

"[Rapoo] was a great wake-up call," Dooley says. "I would say we were a little bit complacent . . . I think we all recognize today that the world is changing. We're looking at something like the iPad and saying, 'Maybe the iPad could replace every notebook out there. That could have a huge impact on our business.' We can't just sit there and say, 'No, no, it won't happen, because we don't *want* it to happen.'" And now, Logitech knows all too well that the Rapoos of the world can create just as much havoc as the Apples.

Beyond Rapoo, Beyond China

The Rapoo story underscores the importance of staying on top of developments in local markets. But this is not simply a defensive expedient. Local markets can be sources of strategic insight that ripples across borders and around the globe. Local threats can have global implications. Even a small new competitor in an emerging nation can grow to threaten a multinational, and even in its home markets.

When Logitech battled Rapoo, there weren't too many rich-world consumers connecting their PCs to their TVs to watch Internet video, but Logitech knew that this could change. The popularity of content aggregators like Hulu was growing rapidly. (Cable providers, watch out!) Thus, China's lack of cable and satellite television infrastructure may have actually put the nation ahead of the curve on living-room entertainment.

Logitech, freshly singed by Rapoo, is now recrafting its global strategy. The new architecture it created to respond to Rapoo now forms the basis for several products under development in mice and keyboards, as well as some new categories such as audio targeted for markets all over the world. Had Dooley and his colleagues ignored Rapoo, Logitech might have diminished itself to the status of a mere spectator watching Rapoo take the world by storm.

Logitech's Playbook Lessons

1. *Keep emerging giants on your radar* (Reverse Innovation Playbook lesson 3). Logitech was accustomed to tracking its rich-world competitors such as Microsoft, but it failed to pay attention to Rapoo, an unheralded Chinese rival. As a result, Logitech had to scramble to recover its position in the China market. To its credit, Logitech "did not waste a good crisis." The company broadly reassessed and revised its positioning strategy. And it learned to pay attention. It leveraged independent data to overcome pockets of denial and resistance.

2. *Conduct clean-slate needs assessments* (Reverse Innovation Playbook lesson 7). Don't assume emerging-market customers have the same priorities as rich-world customers. Until you ask, you'll only be

guessing at what they truly value. It turned out Logitech was charging too high a price for a product that did not meet Chinese customers' primary needs.

Questions for Reflection

1. What attributes of your company's products and services are most highly prized by your rich-world customers? Other than their sensitivity to price, how would customers in the developing economies prioritize these attributes differently?

2. How much effort does your company make to monitor the moves of small but rapidly growing rivals that are headquartered in the developing economies?

3. Can you anticipate who in your company would resist a reverse innovation initiative? Why? How can this resistance be overcome?

CHAPTER SIX

Procter & Gamble, Innovating the "Un-P&G" Way

*In emerging markets, unfamiliar customer
needs trump leading-edge technology.*

IN EMERGING MARKETS, glocalization sometimes trips over its own mistaken assumptions. One common cognitive stumble is the belief that no matter where you go, people are far more alike than different. It's the mistake that imperiled Logitech—and Logitech is hardly alone.

In the 1980s, Procter & Gamble achieved game-changing success with a feminine-hygiene product called Always. The innovative design and performance of Always were revolutionary. Among other things, the product introduced a new material that was more absorbent and less bulky, and included adhesive "wings" that secured the pad to an undergarment. The Always brand quickly became a market leader in the United States and in other developed countries. It won wide acceptance.

The global success of Always was impressive enough to reinforce the idea that menstruating women were no different in Tashkent or Tijuana than in Tallahassee. Geography might change many things, but it didn't change women's bodies or biology. As a result, Always was marketed internationally using the glocalization approach.

That seemed to work for a while, but the approach eventually stumbled. The market that first signaled trouble was Mexico. There, the brand had enjoyed some initial success, but by the late 1990s, sales were declining. The product was failing to win favor with Mexican women. Something was wrong.

Alvaro Restrepo, P&G's global vice president of R&D for feminine-care products ("fem-care," in P&G lingo), says that great successes like Always inspire "a tendency to think the whole world will like the product. But in reality, there are some markets in which you hit a wall. And then you start learning that there are consumers out there who are looking for a different experience."[1]

When Always hit a wall in Mexico, P&G leadership was eager to find out why.

Facing a New Growth Mandate and Finding a New Way to Innovate

Many of P&G's markets in the developed world have reached a saturation point. Therefore, the company increasingly seeks growth in emerging markets. That mandate began under former CEO A. G. Lafley and has been ratcheted up by his successor, CEO and chairman Robert McDonald. As McDonald told *Fortune* magazine in January 2011, "Our innovation strategy is not just diluting the top-tier product for the lower-end consumer. You have to discretely innovate for every one of those consumers on that economic curve, and if you don't do that, you'll fail."[2] McDonald had set a stretch goal of eight hundred million *new* customers by 2015, to be won by "touching and improving more lives in more parts of the world." This ambition necessitated a shift in emphasis from the West to the East.

The emerging-market opportunities are enticing. In the fem-care segment alone, demographics make the case. Nearly 90 percent of women of menstruating age live in emerging markets, according to Restrepo. These are places, he says, "where P&G typically has lower shares, and where the markets are yet to be unlocked."

The lackluster performance of Always in Mexico was the iconic coal-mine canary—an ominous early warning of large and looming trouble. Many P&G products could suffer from the same problem: offerings that are designed for global use but that overlook the specific needs of emerging economies. It was time for the company to rethink its approach to emerging markets. Indeed, it was time for P&G to rethink its approach to innovation.

Some innovation processes begin with a proprietary and patented break-through technology, for which applications are subsequently explored. Others begin with a clearly expressed customer need and then work backward to a technological solution. Inevitably, innovation is a balancing act between technology-push and market-pull thinking.

P&G has famously productive research labs. More often than not, the company's innovations have started with technology. Market-making followed after. Only when there is a clear advantage based on proprietary technology do the company's marketing stalwarts start building a strong value proposition around the technology's benefits.

For P&G, reverse innovation meant upending this characteristic process. Instead of starting with technology, Restrepo's group would start by defining an ironclad value proposition based on a clean-slate assessment of local customers' needs.

Indeed, the way Restrepo and his team responded to the Always dilemma now stands as a template for a new "un-P&G" way to innovate. Restrepo describes the dramatic shift: "We had a package design, a strong concept, and a brand name—all *before* we designed the product. The prototyping, the product development, the technology development was the *last* thing that we did. This is totally un-P&G. For us, in R&D, it was very unconventional! It was upside down from the way we typically do things."

Given the sharp budget constraints that Restrepo's team faced—typical for emerging-market innovation efforts—there really was no other option. The team had to be sure it understood the customer value proposition with absolute clarity *first*. There simply weren't enough resources to afford the luxury of technological trial and error.

Taking Nothing for Granted

In 2000, Restrepo and his team began diagnosing the problem. First, they sought to gauge the depth of consumer dissatisfaction. Maybe it would turn out to be relatively superficial. If so, simply tweaking Always might turn things around.

Initial research, however, showed that dissatisfaction was deep. Respondents were more than just a little bit unhappy with Always. Says Restrepo,

"They were negative, *totally* negative!" The response was so negative, in fact, that Restrepo's team was encouraged to design the "anti-Always brand."

P&G has a world-class reputation for successful innovation. But its great successes were, like Always, created in and for the developed world. In Mexico, P&G was discovering just how different emerging markets can be. The terrain and terms of engagement are not so easy to understand. To cultivate growth, P&G would need to identify distinct customer needs. It would need to pay close attention to local conditions. In short, it would need to become skilled at taking nothing for granted.

For Restrepo and his team, taking nothing for granted began with a simple postulate. If women's bodies and biology were indeed much the same from place to place, the context in which women lived must certainly be different.

Assessing Mexican Women's Unique Needs

The standard benchmarks for quality in a fem-care product are its ability to prevent leakage (and to keep underwear and outerwear garments from becoming stained) and its ability to absorb a sufficient volume of menstrual fluid. Restrepo and his team understood that a new product would have to achieve parity with competitors on these standard benchmarks. But they set out to identify a novel set of needs.

What the team learned from its research was that Mexican women, like women in many emerging markets, face difficult living conditions that affect their fem-care needs. In particular, women face these situations:

- They frequently endure long commutes to work via public transportation.

- They have limited access to public restrooms with hygienic toilets.

- They often live in small houses or apartments where they have little privacy of the kind consumers in developed markets enjoy. It was not unusual for several family members to sleep in the same bed.

Women often wore their pads for an unusually long duration. Wearing pads for a long time—especially in hot, humid climates—can easily lead to skin discomfort and irritation. Women therefore said they would value a hygiene product that included some emollient properties to soothe the skin. Long-duration usage can also create a noticeable odor as fluid accumulates. Women who live in close quarters with family members reported significant anxiety that others would notice the odor.

Furthermore, the research showed, Mexican women were unusually responsive to sensory stimuli. And they favored natural remedies over high-tech solutions or anything else they perceived as chemical or unnatural. It was this last insight that led to the team's branding for the product they hadn't yet developed: Naturella.

Neither P&G nor its major competitors in the Mexican market (mainly, Kimberly-Clark and SCA Group) had been responsive to these needs. The research seemed to point to a major opportunity.

Selectively Forgetting the Past

When the Naturella local growth team (LGT) began listening to Mexican customers, the team had to make tough choices about how much it heard—or, at least, how great a value to place on what it heard. Businesses often give high importance only to input that conforms to their legacy understanding of the world. Conversely, they find reasons to discount whatever challenges that legacy.

As we discussed in chapter 3, the effects of dominant logic can be very damaging to reverse innovation efforts. One of the greatest hurdles an LGT faces is to discard the distorting lens of hardwired practices and assumptions. To see emerging markets clearly will require a new lens that is open to all possibilities. It requires a rare skill: the ability to selectively forget the past. Only then can you achieve a truly open-minded needs assessment. Fortunately, Restrepo and his team possessed that skill, and Naturella was born.

For instance, as the team members sought to figure out why P&G's Always brand had failed to gain a flourishing market in Mexico, they kept hearing objections to its "plasticky," dry-woven top sheet. (The top sheet is the layer of a feminine-hygiene pad that rests next to the wearer's skin.) Success can be a ruthless captor! The dry-weave technology was the principal patented feature that had figured in the product's success to date. It must have been tempting to disregard feedback that ran counter to such a powerful history.

"In those days, talking about designing a product that had a nonwoven top sheet was the worst thing you could say around here," says Restrepo. If Naturella were to go in that direction, the product would be throwing away a competitive advantage unique to P&G. But the Naturella team understood that Mexico's cool reception of Always might derive from important differences between developed and emerging markets. The LGT was increasingly confident that P&G needed an emerging-market alternative to Always. In that context, the power of past success was less relevant.

That didn't stop others in the company from thinking it was blasphemy to turn away from the competitive advantage of the dry-woven top sheet. For that reason, there must be an institutional commitment, at the leadership level, to open inquiry. If the team hadn't won permission to create "the anti-Always brand," orthodoxy could have prevailed. And there might have been no Naturella success story. In its place, P&G would have experienced a cascading sequence of Always brand disappointments in other emerging markets.

Fighting Some Headwinds from Within

The Naturella team was eager to forge ahead, but there were some flutters of internal concern. Some people worried that it was premature to turn away from Always in Mexico. Had everything possible been done to support the brand? As paraphrased by Restrepo, the question was, "You mean we're giving up and getting into another boat?"

But Restrepo never saw Naturella as an abandonment of Always. Indeed, Always worked with some customers in Mexico—those who lived most like people in the developed world. But Always was a miss with the majority of emerging-market consumers. Naturella was an opportunity to serve new customers by addressing their distinct unmet needs: skin care, effective odor control, natural ingredients, and a pleasing sensorial experience (including an ergonomic fit). Naturella would compete in the white space, not target the core.

Ultimately, the concerns were overcome by one undeniable fact. In Mexico, the market for Always was weak and declining. While some instinctively fretted about cannibalization, in reality there was little to lose.

In addition, the project was managed with considerable discipline. It was unclear from the start of the project just how large the opportunity might be. Consequently, the team was kept small. The initiative focused strictly on Mexico at first. It received limited resources from the head of the fem-care business unit, and it flew below the radar. Up-front investments were kept manageably small. The project would have to earn its way to ever-larger commitments.

The Naturella team consisted of a small multifunctional team of marketing and R&D staff. The LGT reported directly to the head of the fem-care business. Emphasizing the contribution of the entire team to Naturella's success, Restrepo describes the work as "a total team effort."

Building by Borrowing and Scavenging

It was almost time to develop the product, but first the team had to decide how much Mexican consumers would be willing to pay for Naturella. The mass market in Mexico was typically defined by a price point 15 percent to 20 percent lower than for the premium segment. The Naturella team decided "to set that as the target price and work backwards to come up with the target cost for the different activities in the business model."

The LGT then took a clean-slate approach to designing the product. Rather than simply modify the Always design, it started from scratch.

Still, where it made sense to do so, the team borrowed raw materials from other P&G business units. For example, since the team was abandoning the dry-woven top sheet that characterized Always, it used materials available from the baby-care and diaper categories for its top sheet. The lotions and creams that would provide skin protection were found in the beauty product category. Chamomile is typically used in different skin-care products as a treatment for skin ailments such as diaper rash and facial skin and eyelid irritation. The team settled on an emollient formulation that contained chamomile oil to deliver significant protection against both irritation and malodor.

P&G possessed a diversity of additional resources from which the Naturella team could browse and leverage, including salespeople, graphic designers, and ad agency relationships. And the Naturella team was able to lay claim to a production line that was sitting idle in Canada. "We weren't asking to develop brand-new technologies," says Restrepo. "So we found a couple of old pieces of equipment that were seen as obsolete, and we got access to them."

Retiring Risks

As the saying goes, it is easy to count the seeds in an apple, but it is nearly impossible to count the apples in a seed. Creating the first market for Naturella was tantamount to sowing seeds for the future. So in a very un-P&G fashion, the team did *not* strive for up-front perfection in the product design. Instead, it tested cheaply and learned from the results. The team saw that launching Naturella was primarily a test of the strength of the value proposition. A fully perfected product and ideal manufacturing and supply-chain arrangements weren't necessary to run the test.

A gut-check arrived in 2002. The product had progressed from the prototype stage to within striking distance of what customers said they wanted. The team had done test marketing in Mexico City in April 2002 and gotten encouraging results. Now it faced a decision about whether to launch the product throughout Mexico. Within the company, says Restrepo, there were still doubters: "There was skepticism that we could win, long term, with something that was not anchored in one of our key fem-care technology building blocks." Specifically, there was concern that a product lacking such patent-protected technology could easily be copied by rivals.

The LGT didn't want to give the doubts time to multiply. Instead, in August 2002, several short months after the Mexico City test, the team won permission for a national rollout of the product in its then unperfected state. "What we finally introduced was, frankly, a fairly primitive product, by our standards. But it was good enough," says Restrepo.

The launch was a victory for the Naturella team. The target consumers responded enthusiastically. Naturella quickly gained share. "The way we saw it, there was a lot of room for improvement," says Restrepo. "But if *this* was working, imagine how great it could be when we really put the right level of resources against it!"

Strengthening the Business

With promising initial results, the LGT turned its attention to making Naturella better by both increasing product quality and lowering cost. The team's opportunistic arrangements had been necessary to get the product launched. But before Naturella could reach its full potential in Mexico—much less expand into other markets—those arrangements had to be tuned up.

For example, it was clearly not ideal to have Naturella's production capacity located in Canada, so far from the retail market. The team found comparable equipment in Mexico and moved production south. Also, the quest for quick and easy solutions had created some supply-chain issues that the team eventually needed to address. For example, the nonwoven Naturella top sheet included printed design elements. "We bought the material at one site, shipped it to another supplier that did the printing, and then had it shipped to yet another supplier to do the cutting," says Restrepo. Eventually, the LGT found a supplier that could consolidate those processes.

Simply streamlining and rationalizing the supply chain yielded low-hanging fruit, but the product design itself needed refinement. "We made modifications to the way we construct the absorbent core. This allowed us to get a better fit to the body and better utilization of materials."

The LGT also identified a better top-sheet material, improved the adhesives to ensure that the product stayed in place, developed a second-generation lotion, enhanced the aesthetics, and introduced ultrathin pads. "We were able to get R&D to focus on getting to the right construction without compromising any of the elements of the original design," says Restrepo. The result was improved product performance, better ergonomic design, and lower cost.

Increasingly, it became clear that one thing didn't need tweaking. The customer value proposition proved to be incredibly robust.

Taking the Next Steps and Learning New Tricks

Always is still marketed in Mexico, but Naturella soon surpassed the former product's market share. P&G took note. Even some of the early skeptics now started owning and celebrating the brand. People within the Latin American region were bullish about growing Naturella.

Some of the Naturella team's research reached beyond Mexico into other emerging markets, showing broadly similar needs. Once the cost-structure barriers had been addressed, Venezuela and Chile were first on the expansion list. Later came Central and Eastern Europe. Having come up with a product that was significantly lower in cost, the LGT not only had a fully baked concept and proposition, but also had a manufacturing formula and product design that were transferable from one market to another. Naturella is sold now in more than thirty countries.

Worries about competitors' ability to copy features of the product turned out to be unfounded. "As we optimized and improved the design of the product, we were also seeking to enhance our proprietary position," says Restrepo. "Today, as compared to the time of the launch, Naturella enjoys strong intellectual property. Even after we expanded coverage for the product around the world, the competition still did not respond by executing anything that even gets close to Naturella."

P&G has internalized a number of lessons in the years since the Naturella project. Chief among these is the idea that there is more than one template for successful innovation. It's unlikely that P&G will fully convert to the upside-down style of value-proposition-led projects. Technology is still—and will probably remain—the dominant driver. But Naturella offered an alternative, particularly for projects directed at emerging-markets. P&G will clearly benefit from mastering this new style of innovation as it elevates its emphasis on emerging-market growth.

The company succeeded by building a team that operated in a fundamentally different way from the rest of the business. The team took a market-back, not a technology-out, approach. This kind of shift happens only with a clean-slate organizational design. The Naturella team had a much different hierarchy than the rest of P&G. It was led by market research, not technology.

"I think the upside-down approach is applicable when you are dealing with problematic markets, where you really have to design for the toughest customers," says Restrepo. "These are the situations that require us to come up with a disruptive proposition." Breakthrough customer insights, not breakthrough technology, matter most in unlocking new markets. Indeed, in all of the stories in part 2, it is those insights that enable breakthrough products capable of bridging the needs gap between rich and poor countries.

Closing the Loop

Next, P&G must decide whether to launch Naturella in the developed world. It's still an open question, though reverse innovation has come full circle for at least some elements of the original Naturella design—including the nonwoven top sheet and the skin-care lotion, which have been added to a few other P&G fem-care products.

In the United States, the Always brand enjoys a 55 percent market share and, in the United Kingdom, a whopping 70 percent share. Says Restrepo,

"It is a lot more straightforward to introduce Naturella in markets where you have lower share, and where there is a lot of white space."

But nothing is off the table for Naturella's rich-world possibilities. One of these is in the area of what Restrepo calls "share of requirement." Research shows that women don't necessarily use one brand or type of fem-care product 100 percent of the time. During a menstrual period, a woman's requirements typically change from beginning to end. "There are occasions when they don't need the highest level of protection. In fact, they may need less protection and more comfort, or more skin-health benefits." What that means is that in a portfolio of products, perhaps P&G's optimal share of requirement could be achieved by both brands together. In that context, it is clearly to the company's advantage that each is so well differentiated from the other.

Regardless of the developed-world outcome, Restrepo believes Naturella has delivered beyond all expectations. In his view, its preeminent value to P&G was to serve as the prototype of a new way of innovating for an increasingly important set of customers: "I have to say that we were struggling at that time about how to develop an emerging-markets program . . . The success of Naturella gave us courage to get out of the box."

Procter & Gamble's Playbook Lessons

1. *Conduct clean-slate needs assessments and develop clean-slate solutions.* (Reverse Innovation Playbook lesson 7). P&G had enjoyed so much success with its Always brand feminine-hygiene product that the company was surprised when Mexican women didn't like it very much. In the effort to find out why, the LGT in Mexico questioned deeply held assumptions and ultimately developed a new product (Naturella) and a new product development approach that focused on customer value before technology. This was a dramatic departure from the norm for technology-first P&G.

2. *Enable LGTs to leverage the global resource base* (Reverse Innovation Playbook lesson 8). The Naturella team relied heavily on P&G's global assets, borrowing materials from other divisions. It even found an unused production line in Canada.

Questions for Reflection

1. How would you describe your company's innovation process? Can the same approach work in emerging markets? If not, what modifications might be needed?

2. How much energy has your company expended in trying to assess how the needs of customers in emerging markets are distinct from those of customers in the rich world?

3. Could your company create a quick and inexpensive experiment to test a distinct value proposition in emerging markets?

CHAPTER SEVEN

EMC Corporation, Planting Seeds

Start reverse innovation efforts by preparing the soil.

YOU COULD THINK of Steve Todd as a kind of high-tech scoutmaster. Todd is a Distinguished Engineer at EMC Corporation, which is a leading vendor of data-storage and information-management hardware, software, and services. In that role, he supports a global troop of up-and-coming young innovators. Members of Todd's far-flung cohort can be found in China, India, Russia, Ireland, Israel, Brazil, Egypt, and elsewhere.

This is far cry from glocalization. EMC doesn't think of these people as low-cost labor to execute an R&D agenda crafted at global headquarters and focused on rich-world needs. To the contrary, they are the starting points for innovation, and they focus on local problems. They are the leading edge of EMC's emerging reverse-innovation capability. And if Todd is the scoutmaster, his charges are beginning to pile up the merit badges.

Their activities are particularly critical in one of EMC's latest growth pushes: the consumer market. For example, two Beijing-based researchers, Jidong Chen and Hang Guo, have been in the midst of an effort to bring consumers a powerful new search technology. Its goal is to help tame an increasingly rude beast of modern life: the haphazard jungle of documents, photos, music, and videos that the average home computer disk drive has become. And it's a technology that will almost certainly be adopted first in China.

Through EMC's example, this chapter highlights moves and methods that are especially useful at the very front end of the reverse innovation process. It shows how to plant the seeds for future success.

Moving Beyond Digital File Cabinets

Headquartered in Hopkinton, Massachusetts, EMC was founded in 1979 by Richard Egan and Roger Marino. The company began life as a reseller of office furniture. Very quickly, however, it found better things to do. Instead of selling file cabinets for documents on paper, it focused on their digital analog: computer storage.

It was a wise choice. As information technology marched forward from mainframes to the modern Internet, data storage needs exploded. Massive databases grew within every company. In short order, all of the oxygen of commercial life had been digitized—customer records, scanner data, credit-card transactions, sales and supply-chain management systems. Everything.

Raw storage space on disk drives, however, was only the most basic need. EMC styles itself as an information-management company, not a mere purveyor of digital file cabinets. The company is bent on curing the diseases that too much information causes: the difficulty of finding and efficiently acquiring exactly the right information. In other words, EMC designs tools that enable its customers to locate high-value signals lost in bottomless oceans of noise.

These days, even individuals and small businesses accumulate vast troves of digital material. Home users' megabytes of need have quickly morphed into gigabytes and terabytes. Most of this growth is driven by storage-hungry music, photo, and video files. It's a tremendous opportunity for EMC.

Using Echolocation for Personal Information

As it turns out, China is a fitting laboratory for exploring the rigors of the consumer market. Chinese consumers are already storing tremendous volumes of material on their hard drives. It's the typical aggregation of documents, digital photos, and entertainment files—but there's even more of it.

In great part, this is because China lacks a widespread cable television infrastructure. Home entertainment often consists of watching movies downloaded from the Internet. Indeed, as highlighted in the Logitech story (chapter 5), China is ahead of the evolutionary curve in terms of digital content consumption. The United States, with its well-developed last-generation media infrastructure, lags behind other cultures' adoption of novel content-acquiring methods.

A second reason China's hard drives are hefty with data is that the Chinese place a high value on privacy. U.S. and other Western users are data exhibitionists by comparison. Many people in the United States casually share personal information on Facebook. They upload pictures to Flickr, and they post résumés on LinkedIn. And they use Twitter as a kind of Internet stream of consciousness, with results that range from provocative to prosaic. All of this personal information can be searched and found using public Internet search tools.

For cultural reasons, Chinese users are reluctant to share personal information in public forums. (Strict Chinese privacy laws reinforce their reticence.) Nonetheless, personal information is exploding in China. With more than 800 million mobile devices and 125 million PCs in 2011, how could it not?

The explosion is hard for individuals to manage. A typical Chinese user's hard drive is like a cluttered and disorganized office. The flummoxed user, searching for a single document, wanders amid the chaos, never knowing which intimidating pile of debris to dig into first.

Unfortunately, traditional search methods can't help. Surprisingly, it can be easier to find a needle in the enormous Internet haystack than on the humble home disk drive. That is because in a single-user environment, there's no *wise crowd* to point the way. The technology of the leading search engines leverages crowds that range in size from hundreds to hundreds of millions. Google search results, for example, rank Web pages heavily on how many other Web pages have links to them and how many visitors any given search term attracts. There is no such aggregated evidence for individual hard drives. As a result, the world's most powerful search algorithms are rendered impotent.

Jidong Chen and Hang Guo are well down the path of developing a solution—an alternative search system they call iMecho. Their design is based on associative memory. (The iMecho name is a mnemonic that stands for "my memory echo.") Here's an analogy. Suppose you met a person at a conference last month. You've forgotten his name, but you do remember who introduced you, where the person works, and much of what the two of you discussed. You probably have enough associated information to find out his name.

A search mechanism based on associative memory would be able to reconstruct the context in which you last viewed some piece of information that you now want to retrieve. If, say, you had been writing a report on echolocation in bats, the software would assemble links from that report to the various documents you used while preparing it. The associative-memory functionality would not require that you create an ongoing log of your activities; it would compile that information automatically, in the background, as you worked. The query "echolocation" would return a complete—but helpfully narrow—list of results. It would then be a simple matter to find the exact file you were looking for. And because associative memory is context-based, the results would also include other relevant documents. You might even retrieve material better suited to your current needs than the file you originally sought.

While the iMecho effort was launched with the Chinese market in mind, it is not hard to foresee the day when U.S. consumers' home storage needs will rival those of their Chinese counterparts. An article in the September 2010 *Wired* magazine amounts to a tutorial on getting rid of cable TV and building an array of digital vampires that can suck up customized mixes of programming, software, and games.[1] Further, security breaches in the United States could create a reluctance to share personal information so freely. Todd elaborates: "Over time, in the United States, I anticipate the abuse of publicly available and searchable information—and a backlash against the allure of personal information on sites like Facebook."[2]

A search technology like iMecho might easily extend beyond the home. Repositories of search-challenged information are also found in workplaces, on the hard drives of individual employees. Indeed, the iMecho researchers' ultimate goal is to build technology that solves a universal search problem. Although the predicament of Chinese users was a local source of inspiration, the solution may turn out to have widespread utility. In time, as the technology is refined and improves, it could find a welcoming home in the rich world.

Bringing Reverse Innovators to Life

EMC has made progress on iMecho not just because Jidong Chen and Hang Guo are clever technologists, but also because of the context within which they work. Indeed, EMC has taken three important steps needed to create an environment in which aspiring reverse innovators can flourish:

1. Situate innovators in emerging markets, and empower these innovators to take initiative to solve local customer problems.

2. Enable local innovators to draw on other local resources—both inside and outside the company.

3. Multiply the capabilities of local innovators by connecting them to the wealth of resources in the global enterprise.

Empower Local Innovators to Solve Local Problems

In a virtual world, conventional wisdom says it doesn't really matter where your people are located. But EMC is working to turn that wisdom on its head. Location is not a logistical detail to be overcome by technology. Instead, it's a strategic advantage. "We're finding that it matters more that employees are *not* located in the United States," says Todd. EMC is now voracious for information it might once have thought was beside the point. To gather it, the company has boots on the ground in as many locations as possible.

EMC first started to explore moving R&D activities offshore in the early 2000s. Cost savings were realized by doing development and quality assurance work in India. Ideas were pushed outward from corporate headquarters in the United States.

By the latter half of the decade, however, EMC saw that emerging markets offered much more than a way to cut costs. They were also tremendous locations for recruiting world-class engineers. Not only that, but they also offered explosive opportunities for revenue growth. Therefore, EMC broadened the charters for its units in emerging markets, morphing from development and quality assurance centers to more-comprehensive units called Centers of Excellence (COEs).

As part of that effort, the company began to encourage employees in the various COEs to propose and develop their own ideas for identifying and solving local customer pain points. According to Brian Gruttadauria, chief technology officer and director of engineering for EMC's consumer and small-business division, innovation is sometimes a matter of simply talking to the right employees—those who understand local needs. In China, one team member wanted a variety of devices, especially his BlackBerry, to be able to easily transfer material to EMC's LifeLine brand of consumer storage units. So, Bluetooth wireless was added. Now any device equipped with a Bluetooth dongle can recognize the LifeLine box and copy files and photos back and forth.

Triggering a profusion of locally relevant ideas begins with the invitation to contribute, but it only gains credibility and momentum when people see that their ideas are incorporated in real products. Adding the BitTorrent file-transfer protocol to LifeLine is a good example. The idea was based on simple research. A survey found that Chinese consumers use BitTorrent to download large media files far more frequently than do U.S. consumers. So, EMC bundled BitTorrent into its consumer storage product line and enhanced its competitive allure. Buyers were able to efficiently download movies and music and share files over their LifeLine storage networks. Downloaded material goes directly into the storage subsystem; it doesn't even tie up the user's PC.

Consumers soon asked for a further convenience. (The work of listening to the market never ceases!) The original BitTorrent functionality automatically began downloading as soon as a file was selected. But because bandwidth costs in China vary over twenty-four hours, users wanted the ability to postpone downloads until cheaper off-peak hours. A scheduling feature has since been added to LifeLine.

Connect with Local Networks

Ideas don't grow well without fertilizer. In the local market, it's important to cultivate a variety of internal and external sources of input and collaborative exchange.

Innovation can be a casualty of recession. In that context, one of EMC's shrewdest moves during the recession that began in late 2008 was to strengthen its innovation muscles by taking the low-cost step of forging deeper relationships with research universities around the globe. Indeed, the iMecho project is leveraging relationships with universities in both Beijing and Shanghai.

This outreach keeps the motor running on projects that might otherwise stall, and it also leads to ideas for future projects. Moreover, building relationships with universities strengthens the EMC brand in the local community and creates valuable opportunities to recruit promising young engineers. That, in turn, enriches the company's reservoirs of deep local insight.

Burt Kaliski, who directs the EMC Innovation Network (the company's global support infrastructure for innovation), has been a booster of active university outreach. The company hosts university partners in its local offices for in-person research lectures and sends researchers out to present briefings at the universities. Kaliski, a firm believer in face-to-face contact even in an age of all things virtual, considers it very important to be "within walking or bicycling distance of the top universities."

For best results, Kaliski says, EMC's innovators are very candid about the company's ongoing internal research projects and future needs. The idea is to stimulate ideas and contributions from academic scientists in relevant disciplines. Kaliski ensures that the material reaches the broadest possible audience and lives beyond the event. EMC engineers can join the conversations from anywhere in the world through teleconference links, and the proceedings are recorded and archived on EMC's social media platforms.

Connections within EMC can be just as important as connections to universities. Kaliski says that internally, researchers like Jidong Chen and Hang Guo are expected to market the fruits of their research to EMC's local sales and marketing teams: "Researchers wear two hats. Just like university professors, they do research *and* they teach."

Nevertheless, the dialogue is a two-way street. It is a conversation between those who best understand customer problems (sales and marketing) and those best positioned to solve them (technologists). The exchange of perspectives keeps innovations on track and grounded in practical realities. Interactions include such questions as "How is the world changing?" and "How are our customers' needs changing?" And finally, given the answers, "How should we be thinking differently about meeting those needs?"

Develop a Circulatory System for Insight and Ideas

The third and final step for bringing reverse innovators to life is to link local innovators with the broader EMC community. Indeed, when the company started down the path of turning COEs into idea hives, there was concern in some quarters that ideas generated by COEs would remain inaccessible to others. The goal, to the contrary, was to "expand knowledge locally and transfer it globally." To that end, EMC pursues strategies to introduce local innovators to their peers in other regions, and to optimize the flow of information within the company in support of the innovation process. Think of it as a circulatory system for ideas and insight.

Indeed, the ability to circulate ideas and insight is a central expectation for EMC's Distinguished Engineers—Steve Todd and his senior-level peers. The EMC Innovation Network that Kaliski directs is intended to be a hub for that circulation. Through it, the global community helps local innovators push their ideas forward. By facilitating discovery, collaboration, and sharing, the EMC Innovation Network helps combat the syndrome of "local loneliness." It engenders a stronger sense of connection to the enterprise as a whole. Those connections, in turn, more reliably convert local learning into insight-rich reverse innovation.

For an enterprise to learn—not just hear about, but deeply learn— knowledge has to travel. The objective is not just to make others in the company smarter (though that's surely a good thing). It's to keep adding value to an idea. Every project at some point needs an infusion of energy or insight from elsewhere in the company. Therefore, says Todd, it's often necessary "to collaborate with people I call 'adjacent technologists.' If somebody in China has an idea after meeting with a local customer, they may not know how to solve the problem. But with more than forty-eight thousand employees around the globe, somebody knows of a technology that can help." In a company built on engineering, the problem-solving impulse is strong. Assuming they have the time, people will generally want to help. Creating formal and informal mechanisms for kibitzing is a productive move.

Kibitzing works best when people know one another. To that end, in 2007, Jeff Nick, EMC's chief technology officer, and Mark Lewis, chief strategy officer for the Information Infrastructure Products business, launched an annual global conference on innovation. It's a gathering of the company's innovative might. The event is organized around an innovation competition, open to all EMC employees. A panel of judges, including Distinguished Engineers, evaluates the submissions. Criteria include the extent of an idea's breakthrough thinking, its potential value to customers, its relevance to EMC's strategic goals, and the ease with which it can be implemented. Kaliski says enormous esteem comes from winning the competition—or even being a finalist. Besides cash awards and recognition to their owners, the top ideas win investment, attention, and a strong development push.

Perhaps the greatest value of the conference, however, is that local innovators meet their peers. In 2009, more than nineteen hundred employees attended—hundreds in person in Bangalore and the others in satellite locations. In only a few years, the event—now typically held outside the United States—has stimulated worldwide participation among all of the COEs. The Bangalore conference drew more than fourteen hundred competing submissions from employees in nineteen countries. The geographical spread of the most prolific countries is revealing: India, the host country, led the pack, with more than 600 ideas, followed by the United States (230), China (200), Ireland (187), Israel (74), and Russia (69). Non-U.S. participation now accounts for a vast majority of internal idea generation.

Building the Capacity for Reverse Innovation

EMC believes that its future organic growth relies heavily on reverse innovation. As Todd sees it, "Unless EMC can add reverse innovation to its strategic repertoire, it will underachieve against the consumer opportunity in the rich world. The solutions that relieve pain points in developing countries will eventually be applied here at home. They'll solve problems that we don't even know we have yet. Reverse innovation is a new and important direction for us. We must master it to succeed as a corporation." High stakes indeed. Winning in poor countries today assures success in rich countries tomorrow.

While EMC has started down the path of growing a sophisticated reverse innovation capability, the harvest is as yet incomplete. Todd characterizes EMC's reverse innovation efforts as "not pervasive . . . *yet.*" The strongest roots and shoots are in idea generation—facilitated by internal networking, mentoring and coaching, and inspiring far-flung employees to both tackle local problems and participate in a global innovation process.

It remains for the company to fully develop the architecture of its local growth teams and to surround them with a full array of local business capabilities. But EMC is doing many things right. For example, LifeLine units sold everywhere—including in the United States—now have BitTorrent bundled in. The company is in an intriguing position. It could use its Life-Line consumer storage products as a flexible platform capable of adaptations for a variety of local needs and preferences. BitTorrent may be just the beginning of myriad mix-ins and mash-ups with potential appeal for local consumer segments.

EMC is endeavoring to build a truly global company, not merely a U.S.-based company with a global presence. Holding its annual innovation conference outside the United States is an important nod in that direction. Becoming truly borderless in an operational sense is a high standard.

EMC's Playbook Lessons

1. *Move people, power, and money to where the growth is* (Reverse Innovation Playbook lesson 4). EMC is smartly readying itself for reverse innovation. The company looks for—and rewards—product ideas that originate from emerging-markets employees, for emerging-market customers. It competes for young, local talent by reaching out to technical universities. And a squadron of distinguished senior experts within the company are energetically mentoring up-and-coming engineers and nurturing promising ideas.

2. *Enable LGTs to leverage the company's global resource base* (Reverse Innovation Playbook lesson 8). EMC has organized and interconnected its human knowledge base in much the same way its products strive to organize information. The company is designing a circulatory system for insight and ideas. Through online resources, live events, and facilitated peer-to-peer links, people with ideas can easily connect with each other. Though EMC develops advanced technologies, it never short-changes the value of face-to-face human interaction.

Questions for Reflection

1. Who in your company is most likely to spot the next big opportunity in the developing world?

2. To what extent are these same people empowered to take action on their ideas?

3. What global resources are your innovators in emerging markets likely to want to leverage just to move an idea forward to the proposal or prototype stage?

CHAPTER EIGHT

Deere & Company Plows Under the Past

Behaving like an underdog helped Deere
redeem its emerging-market future.

DURING THE TWENTIETH CENTURY, the inexorable trend in agriculture in the United States was toward greater consolidation. Families with small farms sold out to ever-larger players. They did so because farming was risky. Bad weather, crop diseases, and pest infestations could compromise yields. Big, up-front investments couldn't always be covered by last year's income. Market prices often profited middlemen over producers. Depending on the time of the year, farming was also backbreaking, round-the-clock work.

Understandably, farmers' children did not always choose to stay in the family business. Better educated and armed with expansive ambitions, succeeding generations of farm kids sought secure, high-paying careers in the diversifying U.S. economy.

Eventually, communities that once were home to many small, thriving farms ended up with two or three larger spreads. Farm size multiplied to a scale that enabled more industrialized operating principles and higher productivity. These big spreads either made the leap to industrialization on their own or were bought up by growing numbers of agribusiness interests.

Deere & Company, based in Moline, Illinois, was a constant witness to these changes. Dating from its founder's first steel plow, in 1837, the renowned supplier of farm equipment grew up side by side with its customers. As landholdings expanded, owners needed tractors and implements scaled to the growing acreage. Deere responded over the generations with suitable innovations. Having both seen and participated in this extraordinary transformation of American agriculture, the company learned its lessons well.

Perhaps it learned them too well. One of the hardest aspects of the reverse innovation challenge is forgetting history. As we have observed, a long track record of success can create a dominant logic, to which it is natural for a business to cling. This can be a problem even in a company's home market if the external environment changes. But when a multinational cultivates growth in emerging markets, problems often multiply. A business that enters unfamiliar markets expecting to encounter an approximation of home conditions will soon find that it has harvested trouble.

This chapter describes Deere & Company's false start in India and its impressively painstaking and disciplined effort to get itself back on track. To accomplish its recovery, Deere, notwithstanding its celebrated global brand, had to learn to behave like an underdog and upstart.

This is not easy. We can't stress too strongly that even the most successful developed-world multinationals must be humble when approaching emerging markets. Arrogance is fatal. The assumption that you know what you're doing is fatal. The only way to succeed is to do as Deere did: embrace your position as newcomer, and earn your way to success.

Deere's effort produced an assortment of positive results. These would have enduring consequences not only in India, but also in the company's approach to other emerging markets. And it began with the belated acknowledgment that in so many ways, India didn't closely resemble the markets with which the company was most familiar.

Flawed Assumptions

In terms of sheer output, India is the world's second-ranking agricultural producer. (China is in first place, with a substantial lead, and the United States closely trails India in third place.) Deere & Company has long coveted the Indian tractor market. With an industry volume of 430,000 units a year, it is the world's largest.

Nonetheless, as recently as 2005, Deere was far from becoming a force to reckon with in India. Deere's own market research that year showed that only 20 percent of those who had purchased a tractor in the previous three years recognized the John Deere brand. In the 31- to 40-horsepower tractor segment, which accounts for nearly half of all tractors sold in India, Deere's market share was a negligible 2 percent. Two local competitors—Mahindra & Mahindra and TAFE—controlled nearly 75 percent of the business.

That Deere, a venerated global brand, was a relative nonfactor in the world's biggest tractor market caused deep consternation among executives in Moline. How could this have happened? What had gone wrong?

Deere & Company makes tractors of all sizes and capabilities, with engines that range from 20 to more than 600 horsepower. The high-end tractors are monstrous, with tires taller than an NBA center, loads of high-tech gadgetry, and fully enclosed air-conditioned cabins big enough to have friends in for lunch. At the low end are so-called utility tractors. In the United States, the high end is the heart of the market, and it is Deere's bread and butter. Indeed, in the United States, a 31- to 40-horsepower tractor might easily be dismissed as a toy. It may be used for commerce—light landscaping or property maintenance, for example—but it is hardly a tool for serious agriculture. At best, it is used on small-scale hobby farms, where the primary intent is enjoyment, not earning a living.

Of course, Deere could plainly see that small tractors ruled the market in India. The company's stumble had its roots in the belief that agriculture in India would evolve in the same basic way as it had in America. By that logic, the myriad small landholdings that dotted the Indian countryside would go through a process of consolidation into ever-larger parcels. Fields would grow from postage stamps to quilts. The lower-horsepower tractors then so much in favor would prove inadequate for agriculture's growing scale. Over time, India's farmers would move up in weight class. They'd develop a need for the bigger, more expensive workhorse tractors that were Deere's main stock in trade.

The 1990s-era industry research that focused on various foreign markets pointed clearly in this direction. But perhaps even more decisive were the company's own experience-based assumptions. It is instinctive to project onto another landscape what you've already lived through. It is instinctive to presume that emerging economies will develop along the same path as the rich nations that preceded them. It is instinctive to posit that emerging economies are engaged in catching up with the rich world. It is instinctive—and often dead wrong.

To prepare to enter the Indian market in the late 1990s, Deere & Company sent a delegation from its Product Engineering Center in Waterloo, Iowa, to India to spend a few weeks studying the market. The team developed a set of requirements for the Indian market, and the company proceeded to make modifications to its existing global tractor models to meet known Indian market requirements. Meanwhile, Deere entered into a joint venture with Larsen & Toubro, a Mumbai-based conglomerate. Together, the companies put up a manufacturing facility in the city of Pune, in Western India, and prepared to build there a 50-plus-horsepower tractor—large by Indian standards.

Sales were not strong, barely denting the capacity of the factory. Apparently, if Indian farms were consolidating at all, they were doing so very slowly. It also became clear that the Mahindra & Mahindra and TAFE tractors were more successful in meeting customer needs at an attractive price point. Furthermore, both rivals had vastly more dealerships and offered a dense array of outlets for after-sale maintenance, parts, and repair services. Deere, as an unknown newcomer, inspired little confidence that it could match the incumbents' strengths.

The Road to Recovery

Deere & Company asked Jeff Benge, a senior marketer and a second-generation company veteran with more than twenty-five years' experience, to diagnose the situation. During his career, he had worked both in the home office and in emerging markets.

Benge's first priority was to deeply examine local farmers' needs—without allowing any rich-world mind-sets to contaminate the process. That required a thorough study of how tractors were actually being used and an analysis of what customers valued most highly in a tractor.

Benge understood that Deere had lost valuable time in trying to crack the largest segment of the Indian tractor market. But he did not let the perceived need for a rapid catch up trump the importance of being rigorous, thoughtful, and thorough in diagnosing customer needs. After all, it was an excess of haste—and a lack of local knowledge—that had caused Deere's earlier moves in India to go awry. Benge ultimately spent two years, in various phases of research, to develop deep market insight.

On arriving in Pune in 2005, Benge began assembling a small marketing team. Its members would be the seed corn for a project, code named Krish, to design a tractor expressly for the Indian market. It would be built in India, by Indians, and for Indians. He asked Hemant Joshi, Deere's regional sales manager in the northern Indian city of Lucknow, to join that team. Lucknow was in the heart of an agricultural region with strong sales potential, and Joshi had a keener understanding of customer needs than what visitors from Iowa could hope to achieve during a short stay in India. Ultimately, Joshi became the marketing manager for Krish, remaining with the project throughout and beyond the tractor's launch.

Benge also hired a market-research consultancy to jump-start the process of data gathering and brand building. The Francis Kanoi Group is a well-known Indian company that bills itself as "the first name in rural research in India." The local Deere marketing team bootstrapped its expertise in field techniques by going out to farming villages with Kanoi's researchers for interviews, focus groups, and direct observation. "For me, that was real learning," says Benge. "I was only aware of the techniques that we had used in other markets. This was much more personal, a much more visual kind of data collection. We lived in Indian villages and observed how farmers worked."[1] Gradually, with the consultants' support, Deere learned the methodology of getting the customer's voice and psyche into the decision-making process.

Through its various research approaches, Deere touched more than seven thousand prospective customers. They were tractor owners and nonowners alike, but all with plausible buying intentions. Deere learned that India's farmers demanded a lot from their tractors—much more than owners of similarly sized tractors in the United States. Indian consumers sought differences in the following dimensions:

1. *Price.* Indian farm communities are relatively poor. Farmers are much more sensitive to the total price of owning the tractor— including the costs of fuel and maintenance. Nevertheless, they sometimes resorted to quirky predictive indices, estimating a tractor's likely reliability and maintenance cost based on its appearance of robustness. That meant that the tractor needed to look bigger

than its horsepower would suggest. It also meant that the molded plastic hood on Deere's low-horsepower models just wouldn't do. Customers insisted on metal, despite the engineering reality that there was no appreciable gain in durability.

2. *Size.* In part because of their sensitivity to price, Indian consumers wanted a tractor that was no bigger than was necessary for the job at hand. A tractor that was too large consumed too much fuel and drove higher maintenance costs. It was also difficult to maneuver. Because fields were often quite small, turns could be tight and space restricted beyond the parcel's confines. Farmers therefore looked for tractors that had a short turning radius. Otherwise, the driver would have to stop the tractor and back up—maybe more than once—to change direction or negotiate a sharp corner. That consumed both more time and more fuel, increasing operating cost and reducing productivity.

3. *Frequency of use.* A utility tractor in the United States would not typically log more than 150 hours of use a year. It wasn't engineered for the heavy-duty dawn-to-dusk farming that would be routine in India, where owners could easily log ten times as many hours as their counterparts in the United States.

4. *Variety of uses.* Farmers in India use tractors for obvious routine farm operations, such as soil cultivation, harvesting, and field main-tenance. That, however, is only the top of a long list. Sometimes it is said of pigs that productive uses are found for every part of the animal but the oink. Indian farmers use their tractors for every conceivable purpose, giving entirely new meaning to the "utility" designation. For example, they use tractors extensively for hauling equipment, supplies, and harvested crops in two- or four-wheeled trailers. In addition, many Indian farmers were also entrepreneurs on the side, hiring themselves and their tractors out to do work for others. Moreover, in some cases, a tractor is the only vehicle a family owns, so it doubles as transportation. Towing a trailer, the tractor carries family and friends to the movies, to market, or to weddings and other social events. In other words, the tractor is a central element of village life.

5. *Reliability.* On average, India's farmers typically expect a tractor to have a fifteen-year working life, with five years of breakdown-free operation. That sounds demanding, but Deere's rich-world customers were even more demanding. It turned out that Deere's product line was actually over-engineered for the expectations of the Indian market. There was an opportunity to reduce cost—and to price more in line with the market—by tuning down certain design parameters.

Such unique market conditions mattered enormously. The modified global tractor models that Deere had launched starting in 2000 simply did not measure up, especially on the two criteria that were most important to the buyers: price and fuel efficiency. The premium price tag on Deere's machines turned buyers off. They could find satisfactory—even ostensibly superior—alternatives at a lower price. Moreover, Deere's global model only got eight kilometers per liter, whereas Indian farmers expected twelve.

The rich insight Deere gained through research prepared the company to move into the design phase. But it also sowed potent marketing seeds. The Deere team communicated with thousands of buyers of every tractor brand sold in India. In the process, it built relationships. These new friends became, in effect, adjunct marketers, strengthening the brand by spreading awareness of Deere & Company. It was a strong foundation for moving forward.

From Unique Market Needs to Clean-Slate Product Design

The job of managing the design, development, and production of a breakthrough tractor for India fell to India product program manager Robesh Maity. Maity had been involved in the market research effort from the beginning. Now, he was to translate farmers' problems and preferences into specific engineering choices.

For current markets, Deere's Product Engineering Center in Waterloo, Iowa, would typically begin each product development effort with the previous model's design. The key questions that shaped such an effort focused on adding new functionality to the predecessor design and working to improve the satisfaction of current customers. It was an approach that reduced product development costs and risks. And it was exactly the right way to serve a loyal, satisfied, and well-understood customer base.

There was, however, no significant loyal and satisfied customer base in India. Deere had approached its two-year disciplined market research effort with a mind-set of humble, agnostic, and curious inquiry. The product development effort would do likewise. The questions that shaped the endeavor focused on serving a new set of customers, about whom Deere still had much to learn. The question foremost in the product design effort was this: Of all possible tractor designs, what choices will deliver the optimum performance on the dimensions these customers most desire?

A standard practice in Deere's routine product development efforts is to put a hard limit on the number of new parts in a tractor. This reduces risk and increases reliability, but there would be no such limitation for Krish. It was a new tractor, and it would be built from the ground up, with as many new parts as were necessary.

In late 2006, Maity convened a small cross-functional team (primarily local members with support from Deere global resources). After two months of preliminary work, Maity brought a much larger group together for an intensive two-week exercise focused on generating ideas and defining specific design objectives. The group included people from Deere's U.S. and Indian organizations, including some senior-level global executives. Also invited were representatives from twenty-four of the company's India-based suppliers. In all, more than 120 people were on hand from all of the key functions: engineering, marketing, sales, finance, supply chain, and manufacturing.

Early in the two-week meeting, attendees conducted a hands-on analysis of Deere's local competition. The team had six rival tractors fully disassembled and the parts laid out on tables in an enormous room. The inquiry addressed three questions: Where were the various rival tractors adding value? Where were they saving on production cost? Where were the opportunities for Deere to stand out?

The large group broke into smaller teams, each focused on a tractor subsystem (e.g., drive train, hydraulics, electrical). The teams brainstormed exhaustively. They surfaced and documented nearly 2,000 ideas, of which roughly 500 were labeled "high confidence." Ultimately, 125 ideas were approved for further design work.

The intensive meeting also produced consensus around a variety of project goals. There were two separate, but interdependent, developmental lists: one for the tractor itself, consisting of a dozen rank-ordered customer requirements, and another for nonproduct business imperatives such as customer-financing support, branding, channel development, and service and maintenance programs. The two lists were distilled into a final agreed-upon scope and product specification. Customer requirements were further classified in three columns under the headings "Needs," "Wants," and "Delighters."

Another key meeting output was a rough estimate of the cost of the tractor and a hard goal for its retail price. While Maity saw the price constraint as an imperative, he also knew that Deere's offering had to be unique. In fact, as the Francis Kanoi team members wrapped up their part of the market research phase, they offered some parting words of caution: Deere would fail if it built a "me-too" tractor. Krish had to do more than just meet basic customer requirements.

It was from the items in the "Delighters" column that Krish's "not-me-too" credentials would be earned. Maity singled out three of these in particular: easier steering; a superior braking system; and a unique, long-lasting clutch. The new clutch in particular would be an innovative coup. Built using technology Deere had applied in more-expensive rich-world tractors, it would be the first of its kind in the Indian market. Among other advantages, it would allow for longer transmission life. Standard clutches often needed expensive repairs or outright replacement, and farmers had repeatedly mentioned them as a source of dissatisfaction.

Executing with a Clean-Slate Team

Maity now had a clear charter. The product development process kicked off in mid-2007 after winning approvals from Deere's senior leadership. Maity knew what needed to be done. Now it was a matter of making it happen.

Clean-slate projects such as Krish need dedicated teams custom-built for the task at hand. Therefore, Maity assembled a complete cross-functional LGT, from the ground up, with an eye toward local knowledge and experience.

That's not to say that Deere's vast engineering resources were left untapped. In fact, Maity was in a perfect position to leverage them. His background within the company was quite broad, and his network among the company's top engineering experts was vast. As the project encountered technical challenges, he would know who to call, and his personal relationships would help secure cooperation. To create an even more solid connection to Deere's knowledge base, Maity moved a U.S.-based engineering manager to India to facilitate information sharing on specific technical matters with the Product Engineering Center in Waterloo.

Note just how different this arrangement was from Deere's initial foray into India. For that effort, a team from the United States visited India to study the market and then returned home to develop the tractor. Here, the U.S. team was not in a lead role. It was not even in an oversight role. Instead, it was in a support role. Furthermore, Maity did not directly report back to the U.S. Product Engineering Center; he reported to a business leader in India.

Though Maity knew that connecting to Deere's deep expertise was important, he chose *not* to rely on Deere's established product development process. Doing so would certainly have been expedient— organizing the efforts of dozens of engineers is complicated. However, in Deere's established process, productivity and reliability were treated as primary constraints, often at the expense of cost and time. For Krish, however, cost had to be treated as the primary constraint, and minimizing time to market was critical. The features and capabilities to be included in Krish were exclusively those that the team's exhaustive research had shown Indian customers were willing to pay for. Consequently, Maity set priorities and structured the process to reflect the numerous characteristics.

Hard Cost Constraints

Deere's research effort had made it clear how much value customers placed on which features executed at what level of quality. With the budget and the target retail price clearly in the foreground, the team was able to make well-informed design trade-offs. At various points, the hard targets helped Maity keep conversations short whenever outbreaks of scope creep threatened to derail the team's progress. The team also paid close attention to the total weight of the tractor. Weight was strongly correlated with both price and fuel efficiency. "We monitored the weight of the Krish tractor much like somebody on an intensive diet," says Benge.

Frequent Iteration and Testing

At Deere, a traditional U.S. tractor development project typically took four to five years. But the company was playing catch-up in India. Maity didn't want Krish to take any longer than absolutely necessary. He set an aggressive target of three years for designing and marketing the new tractor. Time was thus one of the project's greatest challenges.

Inspired by his early career experience in other Indian manufacturing companies, Maity believed he could save time by organizing key design activities differently. The customary scheme was to develop components to the point of near completion before testing them. But there was a risk in that approach: it could delay the discovery of design flaws until late in the process. Serious flaws were more likely when a product was being built from scratch than in an incremental-improvement effort. To learn quickly and avoid nasty surprises, Maity favored earlier and more frequent testing, with quicker design iterations. Although frequent testing took time, Maity believed that components developed iteratively were actually completed faster and ultimately performed better. The approach also reduced suspense and gave the team confidence that it was heading in the right direction.

Parallel Development Efforts

Maity worried about the real possibility that a single setback could cause a delay of many months. He therefore resorted to a kind of parallel processing—simultaneously pursuing multiple solutions in anticipation of possible failures.

This strategy proved successful in a number of instances. For example, even though customers clearly wanted a sheet-metal hood, Maity developed a plastic alternative as a backup. (In the final analysis, the plastic option was not used, because sheet metal proved both more popular and less expensive.)

Another example: Deere attempted to design the Krish front axle in-house, but Maity knew that the team was relatively less experienced in front axle design. This was a risk that cried out for mitigation. If the in-house team's effort failed, progress would come to a halt while an alternative was sorted out. As a hedge, Maity sought bids from two competing suppliers, letting each know that Deere was pursuing its own axle design. As it turned out, the in-house design ran into trouble. Had there been no backup plan, Maity estimates it could have taken six additional months to design and develop a new axle. With an economical alternative waiting in the wings, however, the project barely skipped a beat.

Customers as Codesigners

Maity enlisted Deere's new best friends—prospective tractor buyers in India—as design partners. At significant milestones, the emerging design was shown to members of a customer research group for their reactions. As the design went from electronic form to a nonfunctional physical mock-up to a functioning prototype, the customer panel gave valuable feedback. Particularly at the functioning prototype stage, the team invited owners of competing tractors to evaluate Krish against their own tractors. Their positive reactions were heartening to the Krish team.

Sometimes, descriptions of successful innovation make it seem all too easy. It wasn't. Throughout the project, Maity struggled with thousands of variables. Nonetheless, the team proved up to the task. "Robesh was extremely competent technically," says Benge. "And I found, too, that he just had a passion for this. Krish was not an easy program. There were a lot of walls that we were constantly banging up against. Robesh was able to lead the team to the right kinds of solutions, and keep things moving forward, whenever we got into design or technology issues."

The team faced its share of tough calls. At one point, Maity grew concerned that the new clutch could be an ambush waiting to happen. It wasn't a question of failure, per se. He had confidence that his engineers would come up with a good solution, especially with help from Deere's global engineering experts, who were experienced in clutch design.

Instead, the problem was time. Maity was simply not certain the job could be completed before Krish's scheduled launch. So he initiated development of a conventional clutch design in parallel, just in case. It turned out to be needed. The decision was made to swap in a traditional clutch, so as not to jeopardize the Krish launch, but to continue developing the new clutch on its own timetable. It would be an important future enhancement.

Building the Business

Throughout the product-design process—and with growing intensity as the summer 2010 launch approached—other "nonproduct" activities were occurring in parallel. Deere's heritage notwithstanding, in India the company was the new kid on the block. And it was going to have to try harder if it wanted to build a presence in India. Indeed, it was clear to Benge and his colleagues that Deere's anemic sales were not solely caused by a mismatch between products and needs. Reverse innovation must be supported by a full array of local business functions and capabilities. Until then, however, Deere had simply parachuted into the market with a few global tractor models, hoping its brand would carry it forward. And that hadn't gone very well.

The company needed improved marketing, sales, and distribution. Benge was particularly troubled by Deere's low brand recognition. "That was a real eye-opener for me, having worked in a lot of different countries with a strong Deere brand awareness. If you looked at the challenge we had just in creating the basics about who Deere was and what it had to offer, it was a pretty startling reality. It was critical that we not only got the product right, but that we got a lot of these other elements figured out along the way, too."

Benge knew that building up customers' confidence in the local business infrastructure behind the tractor was an essential part of strengthening the brand: "We knew that we had to take some of the risk out for customers if we wanted them to consider buying this new tractor."

Potential buyers had real concerns. Would a relative "upstart" like Deere be able to provide the necessary after-sale support? When a farmer needed to replace routine parts like air and oil filters, would they be easy to find? Would there be mechanics available to deal with repairs and maintenance? Would there be a ready inventory of tractor implements and accessories?

Deere found ways to reassure customers on multiple fronts. Expanding the dealership network was the most important guarantor of credible after-sale capabilities. Adequate coverage in key agricultural regions was crucial. "In many districts, we had to seek out business owners who wanted to become John Deere dealers," says Benge. "And then we had to get them up and operating in time for the launch."

In addition, Deere bulked up its financing capabilities. The company's main competitors, Mahindra & Mahindra and TAFE, had developed relationships with Indian banks that allowed them to bundle financing on more-favorable terms than Deere could offer. Deere needed to follow suit. That meant building new relationships with well-known Indian banks, coordinating with dealers and banks to put the right processes in place, and testing to make sure the system worked smoothly. Benge and others clearly understood there was a link between sales and the availability of dealer-supported financing.

Even with more distributors and more financing options, Deere knew it would also have to offer some extra inducements, if only to get buyers' attention. It decided to offer one year of free maintenance and an unusual three-year warranty (at the time, most warranties were for only two years). The company also chose to do something particularly radical in India. It decreed that with Krish, there would be absolute price transparency. As GM's Saturn Motors division had done years ago with cars in the U.S. market, Deere would publish the price of Krish. There would be no haggling with dealers, no situations where unsuspecting customers paid more for the tractor than did others. The goal was to be open and aboveboard, to stand out from the competition, and to make sure that Krish remained firmly competitive on price versus its rivals.

Beating the Drum for Krish

Leading up to the tractor's launch, the marketing team worked aggressively with dealers to stoke their excitement. The dealers, in turn, were expected to stoke the excitement of the customer base. Nothing would be worse than if the new tractor simply appeared in the market without proper advance fanfare.

Such a possibility was unlikely. The marketing effort that had tapped customer insights in order to define Krish's specifications had really never paused. As market research made the transition to product planning and development, marketing sustained its customer engagement, even as its purpose changed. With the launch in sight, the purpose became to sell tractors, in large quantities.

During the months before launch, Deere held two-day training sessions for dealers and sales teams in thirty locations throughout India. The sessions included hands-on demos using early Krish production models. The dealers were genuinely impressed with the tractor and the groundwork that had preceded it. These events built dealers' confidence that the product was superior to those of its rivals. And the sessions engendered enthusiasm that Krish would succeed—both for consumers and for the dealers themselves.

Dealers then scheduled local customer events. The audiences included owners of competing tractors, would-be buyers and influencers, and bankers. Many dealers made buyers out of prospects. More than 670 tractors were sold in advance of the launch.

The 35-horsepower Krish tractor was launched, on schedule, in July 2010. The marketing team did its best to create a media circus through newspaper and magazine interviews and a variety of live events. There were also television commercials and newspaper ads. Splashy celebrations were held in each of thirteen Indian states. Deere executives from the United States and India joined Indian government officials to crack a metaphoric bottle of champagne over Krish's new sheet-metal hood. Because the number of tractors needed to fulfill advance orders were still being manufactured, giant toy Deere ignition keys were given out to buyers.

Beyond the glitzy galas, sales teams were out in the field during the weeks after launch. More than ten thousand farmers took test drives on Krish. In the first four months after launch, 2,505 Krish tractors were sold—surpassing a stretch sales target of 2,350 units.

The company had won solid customer acceptance. It had succeeded because it had developed a product from scratch and built in India a full range of business capabilities.

Deere could also claim a stable platform for continued growth in *all* emerging markets. Indeed, it was clear to the company that the processes that Maity used in developing Krish were a worthy reverse innovation in their own right. Several elements of the effort stood out: the exhaustive front-end customer research phase (reminiscent of P&G's development of the Naturella concept); the primacy of cost as a constraint; the accelerated and overlapping design cycles; the development of multiple solutions in parallel; and the continuing involvement of customers.

The company has since applied the Krish product-development model to other projects in India, China, and other emerging markets. Further, the company is moving product features around the world. A new utility tractor for the Chinese market has appropriated some Krish-style elements.

The Krish team was recognized with the inaugural CEO award for its alignment with the overarching company strategy to grow in emerging markets. Further, Deere designated India as the global center of excellence for utility tractor development and manufacturing.

Deere & Company's Playbook Lessons

1. *To capture growth in emerging markets, you must innovate* (Reverse Innovation Playbook lesson 1). Deere's dominant logic led it to wrongly assume that Indian agriculture would become like that of the United States. As a result, the company exported global tractor models—with limited success. To recover, Deere had to gain deep insight into customer needs and develop innovative solutions. This involved a tremendous amount of work. To Deere's credit, it rose to the occasion with the zeal of a convert.

2. *LGTs must conduct clean-slate needs assessments, develop clean-slate solutions, and practice clean-slate organizational design* (Reverse Innovation Playbook lesson 7). Applying characteristic discipline and thoroughness, Deere developed a new model for emerging-market innovation that it now applies in other markets and across its line of products. The clean-slate approach involved extensive market research; creative parallel development strategies for hedging risk; disciplined experimentation through rapid prototyping, learning, and frequent iteration; extensive customer feedback; and the formation of unique cross-functional teams.

Questions for Reflection

1. What is the source of your assumptions about emerging markets today? What kind of effort would be required to deepen your understanding?

2. If your company currently has a well-honed new product- or service-development process, is it flexible enough to deliver products or services suitable for emerging markets?

3. In your industry, how similar are customers in different emerging markets? For example, do your potential customers in Brazil have needs similar to those in India?

CHAPTER NINE

How Harman Changed Its Engineering Culture

Clean-slate solutions can kick the hornet's nest.

I N 2006, Sachin Lawande joined Harman International Industries as chief software architect in the company's automotive division. Harman was the leading tier one manufacturer of high-end infotainment systems. These factory-installed in-dash systems integrate GPS navigation, music, video, and cell-phone and Internet connectivity. They have become hot, competitive differentiators for luxury automakers, and Harman was the dominant player at the high end. The company's earliest customers were BMW, Audi, and Mercedes-Benz.

Lawande quickly found himself flying around the world to troubleshoot software problems. As he got to know the proprietary software that ran Harman's infotainment products, Lawande realized how complex its under-lying architecture was. The luxury automakers' insistence on a high degree of customization further tangled Harman's code base.

In a situation free of constraints, an evolution toward complexity is almost inevitable. Designing products for big-ticket luxury cars is a rela-tively low-constraint undertaking. It's just the sort of project that appeals to a complexity-loving engineer. In technology companies like Harman, engi-neers are the ruling class. Problem solvers par excellence, they are among the most creative people in any business. But they can sometimes fall prey to hubris, preferring to demonstrate their virtuosity rather than travel the shortest distance between two points.

The automotive division's main software engineering group was based in Germany. The team excelled at designing the complex infotainment products that the high-end automotive segment craved. The German team was justly proud of its success. But it also had a very particular way of doing its work. "People have highly structured role definitions," says Lawande. "They take pride in building the best component that was ever built by anybody."[1]

Lawande had a different mind-set. Much as he admired the elegance of the German team's engineering, he was also a practical man. He appreciated, above all else, the virtues of simplicity and flexibility. As a software engineer, Lawande had spent twenty years developing embedded devices—combinations of software and chips that perform dedicated functions within a larger, noncomputer system. At companies like Bell Laboratories, 3Com, and QNX Software, he learned the prime directive of embedded devices: do more with less. Get the greatest functionality from the fewest lines of code and bits of hardware. And do it all in ways that are unnoticeable by users.

The collision between Lawande's mind-set and Harman's dominant logic might easily have caused him extreme frustration—perhaps even a quick exit from Harman. But it didn't turn out that way. Instead, he was asked to lead a project, code-named SARAS, that perfectly fit his natural instincts. The goal was to design a completely new infotainment system, one with a vastly simpler architecture and the potential to stimulate Harman's growth where the opportunities were greatest: in the emerging markets. (SARAS is not an acronym. In Sanskrit, *saras* means "adaptable" and "flexible," two top design objectives of the new system.)

New and Improved Catnip

Ever since Henry Ford stopped insisting that cars could only be black, automakers have competed on the basis of features having little to do with the fundamentals of transportation. Motorists quickly took basic utility for granted. Only car buffs debated the finer points of carburetion, turning radii, compression ratios, and drive trains. For most customers, smart styling, amenities, safety features, and other options were the dominant reasons to buy.

In today's dealer showrooms, infotainment systems are the new catnip for car buyers. Virtually every form of digital information and amusement available in the home or office can now be bundled in a four-wheeled vehicle.

In the luxury segment, Harman had a position to envy. Its market share for infotainment systems exceeded 70 percent. The automotive group was the largest of Harman's three divisions, accounting for $2 billion of its $3 billion in revenues. In addition, there's a $400 million consumer audio business (Harman Kardon, Infinity, and JBL are three of its brands) and a $600 million professional audio division that provides public-address and other sound systems to stadiums, arenas, auditoriums, and nightclubs. Each division has its own engineering group.

The company has a long history of groundbreaking innovation. Founders Sidney Harman and Bernard Kardon were engineers and inventors. Together, in 1953, they launched Harman Kardon, which produced the world's first high-fidelity and, later, stereo receivers. They also began the practice of marketing home stereo systems as collections of components. Customers picked out the speakers, receiver, turntable, and amplifier they wanted, then took them home and wired them together (often not without some anxious trial and error). The company has won many awards, including a technical excellence Grammy Award in 2010 for its AKG microphones and headphones.

With its strong engineering bloodlines, Harman was known for staying ahead of the curve. But now it was in danger of falling behind. There was little room to improve on its market share in the high end, and little growth in that segment. Harman had to seek new growth downstream.

The infotainment phenomenon may have begun in the luxury space, but it did not stay put. Demand soon penetrated the midmarket and lower, stimulated by advertising, pop culture depictions of infotainment systems, and the growing availability of dashboard GPS and other features as add-on options in rental cars. Worldwide, the high end accounted for, at most, 10 million of the 70 million cars manufactured annually. The fastest growth, of course, was in the developing nations, as new manufacturers, like Tata and Maruti in India, achieved price points unimaginable in the rich world.

To move into these new markets in a meaningful way, Harman would need to change its culture, beginning with its approach to engineering. The company's early efforts hadn't gone very well. In a typical glocalization move, Harman engineers created a scaled-down version of its high-end system. They took what they had on the shelf and reduced its cost by subtracting top-of-the-line features and functionality. In one instance, they tried to pair their high-end software with low-end hardware and silicon. The mismatch compromised performance and made the product virtually unusable. After spending a lot of time and money on fixes, Harman shipped a system that managed to satisfy no one.

Reshaping Harman to Capture Emerging Market Growth

Dinesh C. Paliwal became Harman's CEO in 2007. He had spent twenty-two years at ABB, a $35 billion Swiss-based technology company, where he had worked in six countries on four continents and established ABB's presence in China and North Asia. Paliwal brought to Harman a rich global perspective, depth of experience, and a grasp of engineering culture—he had graduated, with highest distinction, from the renowned Indian Institute of Technology, India's MIT. He also brought a reputation for busting silos and demanding cross-cultural collaboration.

Paliwal's mandate was to raise Harman's profile in emerging markets. He began making substantial changes right away, hiring two new regional managers to run Harman's Chinese and Indian operations: David Jin had been CEO of Philips Healthcare group in China; M. Lakshminarayan was a joint managing director for Bosch India. Both men, like Paliwal, had proven successful in growing regional market share for Western multinationals.

Harman's five-year growth targets for China and India were aggressive. China was expected to grow into a billion-dollar business from current revenues of $120 million. India, starting from a mere $15 million, was slated to grow to $250 million. Paliwal understood that glocalization alone was not the way to achieve that kind of aggressive growth. Emerging markets demanded a fresh approach. He commissioned project SARAS and entrusted Lawande with leading a crucial thrust in Harman's growth strategy.

SARAS's charter was to design a new infotainment platform from scratch, with the goal of delivering functionality similar to Harman's high-end products *at half the price and one-third the cost*. But Lawande's ambition went further: he wanted to develop a more modern and scalable architecture capable of meeting a broad spectrum of Harman's future requirements. He foresaw a system adaptable enough that it would someday span a broad swath of the automotive market, from the entry level to the luxury brands.

Unbeknownst to Paliwal and Lawande, they had embarked on a reverse innovation journey. They didn't yet know there was a name for what they were doing. In the end, Lawande—with Paliwal's crucial support—would succeed by drawing upon much of the Reverse Innovation Playbook.

Challenging the Established Way

When new ideas or approaches come along, they often trigger an immune response. Unsurprisingly, SARAS ran into resistance.

"There were multiple attempts, at various points, to derail [the project]," says Lawande. One of these was a bid by the former chief technology officer (CTO) to take control of SARAS. With roots in the German engineering ranks, he disagreed with Lawande's start-from-scratch approach. The CTO hoped that by taking over, he could lead the project down a more conservative path. But Paliwal intervened and supported Lawande's leadership. (In January 2009, the CEO even made Lawande Harman's new CTO.) This is just the sort of highly visible personal action, on the part of a CEO, that can help change mind-set and culture.

Indeed, says Lawande, "Without the backbone that Paliwal displayed in pushing for SARAS—if it had not come from the very top—I would not have been successful at all."

Despite such support, in some corners of the company the idea spread through grapevine gossip that SARAS was a form of slumming. It was inferior. It was only meant for India and China. It couldn't possibly be technically sophisticated enough to be sold into more mature Western markets. Because of the project's expansive potential, says Lawande, "We wanted, from the very beginning, to kill any of that talk."

Resistance was rooted not only in the project's disruptive ambitions, but also in Lawande's organizational model. From his earliest experiences at Harman, he had seen the strengths and weaknesses of the dominant product-development approach. Given the goals of SARAS, he knew a much different roadmap was needed.

Harman's established approach was hierarchical, complex, and highly specialized. Engineers typically stayed within their narrow technical domains. A significant infotainment-system function, such as navigation, might combine several hardware and software technologies. The German approach would first segregate the technologies and then subdivide each technology into many smaller components. To each of these components a team would be assigned.

These teams were typically not called upon to extend themselves. One team might know little about an adjacent component to which its own work would eventually be joined. Indeed, it might know scarcely more than generalities about the functionality it was working on.

This fine parsing of labor was highly efficient as long as the intent was to produce incremental design improvements. Over time, it produced highly crafted, world-class individual components. Nothing at Harman was leveraged from third-party designs or open-sourced. Each element was 100 percent "invented here."

The approach worked well for the luxury segment, but it was also both rigid and expensive. For SARAS, however, the top priority was to radically reduce costs—while still delivering disproportionate customer benefits. That challenge cried out for a clean-slate solution.

To succeed, SARAS would need an organizational model as thoroughly reinvented as the product it was meant to produce. We have stressed that LGTs must be organized from scratch and exactly as the needs of the project dictate—setting aside prior organizational wisdom, even though it might have led to great historical success. Harman is one of the clearest demonstrations of this principle.

Building the Team

Work on SARAS began in earnest in late 2008. Facing a radical new engineering challenge, Lawande chose to set up his team far from the company's traditional design centers in Germany and Farmington Hills, Michigan. SARAS's center of gravity would be primarily in India and China.

The decision was controversial. The German engineering group was important and powerful. Establishing new engineering centers was a threat to its stature.

Lawande shopped within Harman to find the right people to lead the local growth teams. He handpicked two top talents from Farmington Hills: Arvin Baalu, an Indian who had spent four years with Harman, would head up a team in Bangalore, and Kelei Shen, who is Chinese, would put together a team in Suzhou, China. Baalu's team would develop the new software architecture, while Shen's focused on the hardware.

Baalu and Shen had established reputations within the company as strong leaders with high credibility. They would be able to create a bridge between the corporate and local cultures and bring a deep understanding of Harman's products and technologies to SARAS. Further, their local roots would help the project credibly reach out to the local customer base and accelerate market development. Their origins gave them one kind of credibility, and their reputation within the organization gave them another. Baalu's and Shen's association with SARAS gave the project greater leeway within Harman than it otherwise would have enjoyed.

Crucially, the teams reported to Lawande rather than to automotive division leadership. This is a key to success in reverse innovation. LGTs reporting up to senior corporate executives are insulated from the effects of unit-level decision making that could compromise their work or threaten access to vital resources. Moreover, the automotive division leader might naturally evaluate an LGT using criteria that make sense for an established business but not an emerging venture.

Lawande also chose three engineers from Germany to be on the core engineering team. It was one thing to rock the boat, but he wasn't looking to sink it. Despite their initial resistance to SARAS, Lawande saw that the German engineers were as important to the company's future as they had been to its past. Because of their formidable expertise, they could make crucial contributions to SARAS. As with his U.S. draftees, Lawande picked people with talent, credibility, and influence. Through their participation in the project, they would become change agents. Once they returned to Germany, they would help build support among their colleagues.

It's hard to overestimate the implications of such decisions. The goal was to create a *new* design capability, not to penalize, punish, or dismantle the one that already existed and performed so well. After all, Harman would not be abandoning the luxury end of the business. Lawande saw that he needed an LGT that was unique, but also one that partnered well with the global organization.

Lawande kept his team small. Low head count would drive high efficiency and opportunistic decision making. All told, there were fewer than thirty people working full-time on SARAS: fifteen in India, five in China, and three each in the United States and Germany.

Lawande asked the team members to think in terms of—and to organize themselves around—whole functions rather than components. For instance, one subteam brought together all of the competencies needed to tackle the navigation unit.

In retrospect, Lawande saw that changing the organization (dividing the work by functionality of the infotainment system, not by component, for example) was as important as the innovations in the product itself. The latter came about only because of the former. You don't get clean-slate innovation without clean-slate organizational design. Ultimately, the team's method was as engineered as the infotainment system itself.

Shaping a Radical Product Redesign

His team in place, Lawande became the straw that stirred the drink: "My role was to challenge the group and make sure they were thinking aggressively." He also helped the team remain true to five major design philosophies.

SIMPLICITY. Overarching the entire design process was an imperative to keep things as simple as possible—never more complicated than was absolutely necessary. Complexity would be the enemy of economy. If SARAS was to deliver the same functionality found in high-end infotainment systems, it was imperative to keep the feature sets for any given function (navigation, communications, multimedia) to the required minimum. One of the well-kept secrets of infotainment systems is that they offer many more features than most end customers typically use. Says Lawande, "A high-end navigation system is likely to have more than a hundred features. But what we find is that most of our customers don't go beyond the first twenty." Simplicity demanded better alignment between the new system's feature sets and real-world usage patterns.

COST. SARAS's most radical aspect lay in the ambitious mathematics of cost. Providing close-to-high-end functionality at one-third the cost was a tall order. It mandated that Harman break through the cost floor quite dramatically. At every step, Lawande exhorted the team to be creative in bending the curve. The team's incessant mantra became "half the price, one-third the cost."

Such a seemingly oppressive constraint can actually be liberating. When regarded as an opportunity, a constraint can inspire breakthrough thinking. Cultures of constraint produce people who become, by necessity, both resourceful and resilient.

For example, India is a country with a large rural population living in poverty. Many millions of people lack convenient access to decent health care. Many also suffer from eye diseases that often lead to blindness. The innovations of the Aravind Eye Care Hospital go beyond the cataract surgery we described earlier. The constraints of poverty, geography, and deficient infrastructure led Aravind to innovate around access to care. Since patients can't travel to distant hospitals, Aravind sends well-equipped mobile eye clinics out to rural villages. Doctors and nurses screen villagers. If needed, the staff uses a satellite link to connect patients with specialists in their urban hospitals. If a patient requires surgery, Aravind provides transportation to the hospital and back. These services are offered free of charge to poor patients, their care underwritten by those who can afford to pay market rates. These sorts of solutions come readily to the minds of people who viscerally understand local constraints and can tap them to drive creativity.

MODULAR DESIGN. Much of the complexity of Harman's incumbent system had been created by the heavy after-sale customization that each automaker demanded. Modularization would help Harman minimize the amount of painstaking and time-consuming custom work. The company would look across the customer base and identify common elements automakers most often demanded. Then it would create an inventory of locked-down modules from which to choose. This modular menu would preserve the design's architectural integrity and save work on the back end.

There's nothing new in pursuing a modular approach. But temptations to stray from the righteous path arise predictably. At some point during the development of a product, people forget that modular design was an important part of the spec. That happened with the existing high-end system, says Lawande. SARAS was designed using the strict discipline of modularity.

OPEN SOURCE SOLUTIONS. Lawande wanted to get away from developing expensive proprietary systems. Rather than invent everything, SARAS would leverage what it could. It would adopt open-source solutions wherever possible and remain friendly and open to third-party applications.

Lawande set restrictions on how much work would be done internally versus leveraged from third parties or the open-source movement. It required discipline to sustain that commitment. "What happens, especially in this very insular industry, is that there is almost a disdain for what's happening in the outside world," he says. "It's like, 'We are *special*. We understand automotive . . . and nobody other than us can figure out what needs to be done.' The underlying attitude among some within the company was that software programs with more general applications can't ever be quite right for us."

The team was encouraged to look for available outside technologies that would meet the performance needs of each set of features. But it made selected exceptions. For example, the open-architecture philosophy led to a particularly important breakthrough that had to be programmed in-house. Called OpenNav, the application would allow the new platform to work with almost any third-party navigation software from around the world. Developing OpenNav took a great deal of time and effort, but it was judged to be worth such an investment since it would power the product's openness to a wide array of valuable third-party mapping content.

The open-source philosophy, too, was challenged. A particular moment of truth arose around the messaging technology that enables system modules to communicate with one another. For years, developing proprietary messaging technology had been a particular competency of the German engineering group. But adopting it would have prevented SARAS engineers from drawing on a host of open-source applications and hindered third parties in developing new applications for SARAS.

There was pressure from the Germans to use the existing technology. Heading off an unproductive political debate within the ranks, Lawande, in his capacity as CTO, made a unilateral decision in favor of an open-source approach, rather than encouraging dialogue and taking the time and energy to build consensus.

STANDARD CHIPS. Harman designed its high-end systems with custom silicon chips. Because the company's orders to chip manufacturers were in small quantities (by semiconductor industry standards), this had proven expensive. The chips were a significant factor in setting the floor for total system cost.

The SARAS team looked to slipstream on another industry's greater scale. As it turned out, the chips made for smartphones were fast becoming functionally akin to those used in Harman's infotainment systems. The smartphone market was vast. It made sense to leverage chip manufacturers' investments in what they were building for the smartphone industry. Harman thus became an extension of that far larger market. The impact of this alone on system cost, says Lawande, was "a game changer."

Pushing the Team Toward Completion

Lawande managed the design process using a methodology called Scrum— a flexible, iterative approach to software development. Scrum is ideal for helping teams tackle large, cross-functional projects. The approach parses a project into "sprints," each lasting from two to four weeks. Sprints are themselves divided into tasks. Instead of facing formidable, far-off deadlines on which the entire project could rise or fall, the team is given weekly goals. Short deadlines lead to frequent feedback and rapid learning—keys to success in innovation initiatives.

The SARAS team tracked each sprint daily using so-called burn-down charts—visual representations of success in specific tasks. Adherence to the Scrum method allowed the team to spot danger before it turned lethal.

Lawande set a date in March for the first demo. He would be traveling to India for it, and he made it known that he was expecting to be wowed. That first prototype functioned well enough that Lawande scheduled a second demo, this one for the board of directors, to be held in June at Harman's Stamford, Connecticut, headquarters.

It was a bold move, but Lawande wanted to establish SARAS as a legitimate program inside the company once and for all. What better way to accomplish that than by giving the work such a prominent showcase? Not only would it rally the team, but it might also inspire some of the doubters—those still unconvinced that the project would fly—to "get on the right side."

The demo went smoothly. It was a big confidence booster for the team, and it gave the project the high internal visibility it would need to ensure that the next phase—commercialization—would go as smoothly as the demo.

Overcoming Sales and Customer Hurdles

With a product he was proud of, Lawande focused on going to market. He adopted a hybrid sales strategy. In the emerging markets of China and India, there were dedicated sales teams. Harman was a new presence in those regions and hadn't yet built up its sales relationships. In markets where Harman was already established, however, the current sales force simply added the new platform to its existing offerings.

Winning over the established sales force proved to be a high hurdle. Like the engineers, Harman's sales force was schooled in the high-end model. The sales process consisted of sitting down with each customer and defining the desired—and extensively customized—system, then going off to implement it in the traditional way.

The new system's menu of modular features greatly reduced the extent of customization. Systems could be more quickly configured and delivered. But the salespeople were accustomed to a long and painstaking development process. They interpreted the lower degree of difficulty as an indication of low quality as well. Consequently, they were initially reluctant to present the new platform to their customers as an option. They were finally persuaded when Paliwal and Lawande expressed their wishes in the form of an order.

Customers also showed early reluctance. Even though some OEMs had pressed for changes to the legacy platform, they were caught off guard by the extent of SARAS's departure from what they'd grown accustomed to. Lawande invited customers to visit the development centers in China and India. After meetings, presentations, and demos, they were reassured that the new approach was solid.

In late 2009, Toyota came aboard as the first customer. Toyota was known as a most discerning client, making painstaking evaluations of any technology before adopting it. Harman had been trying for five years or more to win a contract from the automaker. Now it had one.

It felt like a tremendous victory, and it helped to overcome the sales force's misgivings. Ultimately, says Lawande, salespeople became happy having something new to sell. It also helped that profit margins did not erode, as many salespeople feared. "What was interesting, and what really opened eyes, was that our net profit margin using this technology actually went up. It's almost double that of the high-end business," says Lawande. With a higher net profit per unit over a much larger volume base, sales force commissions stood to rise, and there was a compelling, self-interested pull toward the new architecture.

In fact, just six months after the Toyota win, orders had reached the $1.5 billion mark. The five-year target for the new architecture was $5 billion. According to Lawande, as of late spring in 2011—eighteen months after launch—SARAS has generated more than $3 billion in new business. "We are now using SARAS to ensure our success in the fast-evolving market in China."

Committing from the Top

In retrospect, it seems remarkable that this effort unfolded during one of history's most hellacious economic calamities. Typically, businesses pull in their horns, reduce risk, and ride out the rough weather. The Great Recession had knocked the octane out of the auto industry and had hit Harman's automotive division hard. Revenues had dropped by a third—from $3 billion to $2 billion. Projects within the company were far more likely to be scrapped than launched.

SARAS faced further hurdles: determined opposition from the German engineering corps, an initially lukewarm response from a sales force that didn't like the sound of a low-cost system, and the increased investment required for staffing new offices in its target markets. Had it been run under the aegis of Harman's automobile division, the project would almost certainly have been canceled. With all of the work being done across Harman to get costs under control, it took plenty of backbone on the part of Paliwal to continue investing in the new program, but he was determined to build a low-cost platform to unlock new markets.

So SARAS was on the hot seat. "I was having many sleepless nights, thinking about what would happen if I have the system ready, I have people in India and China, but no business!" says Lawande, who credits Paliwal for not succumbing to short-term pressure. The pair today presides over a firm that is poised to expand while much of its competition in the automotive space is struggling not to contract.

Building a Multidirectional Platform

The sales victories were satisfying, but Lawande was already looking ahead to the next phase. From the beginning, his goal had been not just to win in the initial target market, but to move uphill over time. From the beginning, the modular architecture of SARAS was meant to be readily scalable. Eventually, the new architecture would be able to address high-end expectations. Its return to the West was foreseen in its conception.

Whether destined for high-end or midsegment cars, infotainment systems offer similar functionality: navigation, multimedia, and connectivity to cell-phone networks and the Internet. The differences lie in the number of features in any given functionality, such as navigation. There were also differences in the level of each function's execution: the size of the navigation display; the level of detail in the maps; the gradations of color the system offers; the number and richness of the information feeds. For example, a high-end display is likely to be a ten-inch screen showing high-resolution 3-D graphics, whereas a low-end version might have a seven-inch screen with 2-D graphics.

Such differences are not functional so much as aesthetic. And the performance gap between low- and high-end components—chips, displays, and other high-tech hardware—is narrowing. In reality, what the SARAS teams had produced could be configured to closely resemble the functionality of the high-end system.

Nonetheless, bringing aspects of the new architecture into the luxury markets won't happen overnight. Automotive suppliers like Harman serve customers that operate on long lead times. When Harman sells an infotainment system in late 2011, the vehicles into which it's installed won't come to market until 2014 at the earliest.

As it turns out, Lawande is just as eager to move downhill as he is to ascend. Indeed, the SARAS team—now grown to fifty people—is also tackling a design for the Tata Nano, the world's most affordable car. Again, the goal is to dramatically lower the system's cost while sustaining most of its performance. "Doing more with a lot less" might be SARAS's motto. The Nano system's cost is to be between a quarter and a fifth that of a high-end system, while still offering three-quarters of the performance. Since most drivers use only their system's core features, the infotainment experience in a Nano and a Mercedes won't be all that different.

Lawande even has his eyes on another radical redesign—for motorbikes. The market for motorbikes in India, China, and Southeast Asia remains vast, and Harman management sees a big, unappreciated opportunity. The project, code-named NALANDA, is entirely original: new hardware and software will run on a new platform, all to be designed in India. NALANDA has an ambitious price target of just $20, which it will strive to hit through the novel approach of leveraging the processing power inside of owners' cell phones. If there are any skeptics left at Harman, this is the SARAS team's chance to prove them wrong for a second time.

But it probably won't be necessary. Even the German engineers—the ones originally most resistant to the project—have come full circle. And, since winning the Toyota contract, Harman has seen a sustained rally in its share price, which as of late 2011, had nearly increased fourfold from its 2009 low.

More importantly, the company has a platform for global growth. SARAS appears poised to move in any direction, giving Harman the opportunity to compete effectively in any corner of the world. It is a classic reverse innovation story.

Harman's Playbook Lessons

1. *Create a reverse innovation mind-set throughout the organization* (Reverse Innovation Playbook lesson 5). Most emphatically, Harman CEO Dinesh Paliwal, through highly visible, unambiguous actions, supported the goals and methods of the SARAS project (and its leader Sachin Lawande). He likewise made clear the urgent imperative of achieving more growth from emerging markets and untapped segments of the automotive industry. At important moments, Paliwal intervened to ensure that key functions (especially engineering and sales) understood that their cooperation was crucial—and nonnegotiable.

2. *Create separate business scorecards for developing nations with full income statements and an emphasis on growth metrics* (Reverse Innovation Playbook lesson 6). Paliwal created new regional manager positions for India and China, hired leaders with deep experience in

each country, and focused each leader on winning through reverse innovation.

3. *Practice clean-slate organizational design* (Reverse Innovation Playbook lesson 7). Lawande built the SARAS LGT in India and China, far from the legacy design centers in Germany and the United States. His clean-slate organizational design created subteams that focused on functions, not components. He encouraged project principles that would enforce simple, opportunistic, cost-effective design choices.

4. *Manage reverse innovation initiatives as disciplined experiments* (Reverse Innovation Playbook lesson 9). The LGT executed quick and low-cost experiments with short-term deadlines. It evaluated progress and lessons learned based on weekly goals. Overall, the process was flexible and iterative.

Questions for Reflection

1. In your company, how much power and authority are vested in people with responsibility for emerging markets? Are the people with power located where the growth is?

2. How has your company traditionally organized its innovation efforts? How do people specialize? By feature? By component? By phase in the process? By engineering specialty? Does the same organizational form make sense for your innovation efforts in emerging markets?

3. What conflicts are likely to arise between your LGT and the rest of your company? How can these conflicts be resolved? Who has sufficient power to resolve them in a way that gives the LGT a realistic shot at success?

CHAPTER TEN

GE Healthcare in the Heart of India

In several inspired ways, determined local engineers helped grow markets and broaden access to care.

WHEN VISITING THEIR LOCAL DOCTORS, members of a Bangalore-based GE Healthcare engineering team noticed something troubling. More precisely, it was what they *failed* to notice that frustrated them.

Starting in 2001, they had been developing and manufacturing GE's high-end electrocardiogram (ECG) machines in India. Naturally, whenever they were in their own doctors' offices, the engineers would look for the machines they'd worked on. Alas, the machines were nowhere to be seen. Indeed, if any machine was in evidence—and often there wasn't—it was one made by a local competitor.

Electrocardiograms are noninvasive, risk-free, relatively low-cost tests that measure electrical activity in patients' hearts. The ECG is the most widely performed cardiac test in the developed world. In cardiac units in hospitals in rich countries, GE's ECG machines have long been a fixture. In poor countries, however, GE's "global premium" ECG machines have typically been available only in hospitals in major urban centers. The price of the machines, their weight, and their power requirements have put them out of reach for rural India. As a result, heart problems that could have been detected early and treated have too often gone undiagnosed.

GE Healthcare (2010 revenues of $17 billion) is among the dominant manufacturers of medical-imaging, diagnostic, and health-information technologies. Its traditional competitors are large global technology manufacturers (such as Siemens, Philips, and Toshiba) that offer their own lines of medical diagnostic equipment. The prices for GE's ECG machines range from about $3,000 to $10,000. These high-end devices are typically heavy—certainly too cumbersome to carry—and they are usually tethered to a specialized, full-size printer and a computer display. Since the test is somewhat complicated to administer, a reasonably skilled operator is needed. Most of the technology is proprietary and expensive to repair or replace.

By 2005, as the Bangalore engineers' mastery of ECG technology grew, so did their eagerness to build something specifically for India—a product whose design would reflect the economic, infrastructural, and cultural realities the engineers understood intimately. The country had a mega unmet diagnostic burden that they believed they could shoulder. They envisioned a product that would become ubiquitous in Indian health care. Moreover, they had acquired enough confidence in their capabilities that they were ready to act.

The story of GE Healthcare's ECG project highlights common themes in reverse innovation tales. Local innovators pay their dues and develop their skills. In light of what they've observed in the marketplace (or know in their bones), they are driven by a growing passion to fill an important gap—one that hasn't yet been grasped by the larger enterprise. They flesh out their vision. They turn frustration into a plan. They lobby for the plan. In time, they are heard, and they seize the day!

But as you will suspect, it's not quite that simple. Reverse innovation is not a tool for mavericks—though such personalities may find congenial roles within its framework. Indeed, reverse innovation requires much more than individual action; it demands excellence in organization as well. LGTs must be unique and start-up-like, yet fully able to draw on the resources of the larger global enterprise.

Therefore, this is not just a story about a few local engineers aspiring to big change. It is equally the story of GE's effort to develop an emerging-market growth strategy that puts reverse innovation at its center. The only way to address the full opportunity in emerging markets is to build products that truly satisfy local needs—products that, in GE parlance, are designed *in country, for country*. This chapter looks at how the India team did this and, just as important, how GE enabled the LGT to do it.

A Crescendo for Change

The group that champed at the bit to build an India-worthy ECG worked at the John F. Welch Technology Centre in Bangalore. Built in 2000, the facility was GE's first multidisciplinary R&D lab outside the United States. At that time, it was one of GE's clearest expressions of a commitment to invest in emerging markets. By 2011, it had become one of the company's largest R&D facilities, sitting on a campus with 1.1 million square feet of lab and office space and housing four thousand scientists and engineers across all GE businesses. Of this group, thirteen hundred worked for GE Healthcare. In the early years, the health-care teams focused solely on software programming—traditional outsourcing fare. Gradually, confidence in the team's performance grew. New skill sets were added. The scope of work expanded, from subsystems and electronic components up to higher-level clinical functions. Nonetheless, the work still focused on global products and was directed from the United States.

Until 2005, GE Healthcare continued to pursue a glocalization strategy. In India, it offered a version of its high-end product for $3,000, the low end of the premium price range. The results had been underwhelming. By then, the company saw that a more sophisticated approach was required, but it hadn't yet entrusted its local talent with the challenge of designing breakthrough products for Indian consumers.

Late that year, the market provided a timely nudge. The division's Indian sales force was becoming every bit as frustrated as the engineers. It was failing to get traction with customers. As the salespeople put it, GE Healthcare "wasn't even a player" in the rural market. They didn't mince words with V. Raja, president and CEO of GE Healthcare in India (in chapter 4, Raja illustrated how hard it is, in a glocalization culture, to win support for a new business idea). Salespeople told him, "If you give us products with these features at this price point, we can create the market for value products. We can then play in the entire price range, and at multiple price points, and not be only a premium player."

Raja was sympathetic. "They could see that we had all these beautiful ECG products available," he says. "And yet, none of them met the requirements of the bulk of the Indian customers. Products developed for Western markets don't work well in situations where there is erratic power supply, low customer affordability, space constraints, and heat and dust."[1]

Local competitors, particularly BPL Healthcare, were filling the gap and "eating our lunch," Raja says. Indeed, by his estimate, BPL could claim 60 to 70 percent of the Indian low-end ECG market. GE Healthcare had less than 5 percent.

Raja worried that such competitors were more than just a local threat. There was always the chance that one of them could eventually prosper enough to challenge GE Healthcare on other fronts as well, most likely with a technology adopted first in India. "We must play in their backyard," says Raja, "otherwise we run the risk of losing global share to BPL, if they or other local players moved into premium segments."

Eager engineers, frustrated salespeople, and rising competition created a crescendo of unease that was further bolstered by the simple reality that GE Healthcare faced a saturated ECG market in the developed world. Where could future growth come from? The obvious answer was the emerging markets, and that required tapping the value segment with lower-cost products.

Increasingly, India was a focus of urgent attention and high hopes within the company. Unfortunately, GE Healthcare's value segment cupboard was bare. Looking for a way forward, the company turned to Oswin Varghese, one of the engineers who had chafed at working on products completely unsuited to the needs of rural India. He had a degree in biomedical engineering and had joined GE Healthcare in 2001, after working for a few years at other companies doing hardware, software, and systems design. Now, he was in charge of a making the case to GE headquarters for building a radically different ECG model.

Making the Pitch

As our earlier story of V. Raja revealed, new business ideas within GE had to clear many hurdles. Not the least of these was convincing the corporate office that you had the capabilities needed to see the project through to success. This was an especially tough sell for a group that had never before owned a development project. Historically, it had functioned as a provider of subsystems for units designed in GE Healthcare's Milwaukee headquarters. So, the highest hurdle was building confidence at the corporate level that the group could execute a complete system. This required some persistence.

"We probably had to give more presentations than any other group would have," says Raja. Nonetheless, the tides were shifting in Raja's favor. GE's emphasis was increasingly on capturing growth in emerging markets. It took persistence, but for its trouble, the team got a $500,000 investment for a product the engineers were calling the MAC 400.

Clean-Slate Needs Assessment

The mission of the MAC 400 would be to extend the lifesaving diagnostic power of a traditional ECG to a mainly poor population of 700 million in rural India. This was where the bulk of India's chronically underserved, undiagnosed patients were to be found. "The most frequent cause of death in India is heart attack," says Raja. "Cardiac disease is a big social issue. Mitigating its impact requires early detection. GE had to think of a solution that could be used by every one of India's seven hundred thousand general physicians."

To achieve its ambitious mission and defeat local rivals, Raja's team would have to fully understand just how distinctive the Indian health-care market was. As is so often the case, the company needed to get over its past: leaning too hard on its potent brand, its high-end legacy, and its strategy of glocalization. Instead, it would have to recognize that Indian health care operated under a number of basic constraints—mainly those of income and infrastructure—that compromised access to services. Together, these constraints established the necessary specifications for the MAC 400.

Income

Both patients and clinics had far less to spend than their Western counterparts.

- *Low cost to patients.* India has a high rate of poverty. At US$5 to US$20, the cost of an ECG test, done with a traditional machine, is not trivial. It is expensive enough to discourage a great many people from promptly seeing a doctor when they experience chest pains, even though the consequences of an undiagnosed condition can be ruinously expensive and possibly fatal. Therefore, the cost of a single MAC 400 ECG test for the patient would need to fall to the point where no one would have a reason to refuse it.

- *Low capital cost.* GE Healthcare's $3,000 ECG model was also too expensive for most physicians and clinics. Indeed, there was virtually no market for the company's product except in the best hospitals in India's largest cities. The MAC 400's price would have to come way down to be affordable by small clinics and individual physicians.

Infrastructure

With transportation, reliable power, and medical experts in short supply in India, medical equipment needs qualities and features seldom considered in the rich world.

- *Portability.* Especially in India's vast rural areas, health clinics and practitioners are relatively few and far between. The population is widely dispersed. Though routine screening makes an enormous difference in long-term patient outcomes, most patients are too far from the nearest clinic to travel for routine care. They only bother to travel when symptoms are worrisome. Therefore, the MAC 400 would have to be easily portable, so that physicians could carry it with them to the patients, rather than expecting the patients to travel.

- *Battery power.* India's electric power grid is not fully developed, and electric power is either unreliable or unavailable in rural areas. A machine that must be plugged into an outlet has limited or zero usefulness in such settings. The MAC 400 would have to be able to run on a battery when power from the grid was unavailable.

- *Ease of use.* A traditional unit requires a competent, well-trained operator, but there is a severe shortage of medical professionals in developing countries—even worse in rural areas. GE Healthcare's premium ECG models come with a fifty-page user's guide. The MAC 400, by contrast, would have to be radically simple, usable by nearly anyone.

- *Ease of maintenance and repair.* The infrastructure for maintaining and servicing medical technology is likewise not well developed outside of the largest cities. If a traditional high-end GE Healthcare ECG unit broke down in a rural area, users would have difficulty finding someone to fix it. Thus, the MAC 400 also needed to be very easy to repair.

Finally, of course, the machine had to be better than the ones offered by BPL and other local competitors.

Clean-Slate Solution

Soon after funding, two parallel creative challenges arose—building the team and designing the product. Both needed to be clean-slate efforts.

There was little chance that the project could move forward within the existing organization. Creating the MAC 400 would require rich cross-functional collaboration across engineering, marketing, sales, and service teams, but there was little history of such collaboration. All of the functions pretty much kept to their silos, each reporting back to functional heads at global headquarters.

GE needed an LGT. The company built one that was led by Varghese and that unified the functions in a dedicated unit. The team was fully empowered and was freed from the short-term performance criteria that typically preoccupied business units at GE.

The LGT set out to build a new product from the ground up, not adapt an existing one for a new market. The team was given permission to challenge the "GE way" of product development. At the same time, as was necessary, the team availed itself of GE's enormous technological and human resources. Indeed, LGTs depend on just the right mix of insulation and collaboration.

The goal of the Indian LGT was to build from scratch an ECG machine that would retail for no more than $800. This tall order kept Varghese and his team up late on many nights. They sought ways of holding costs down while still delivering on the ambitious requirements for portability, battery operability, ease of use, and ease of repair. One of the LGT team members describes the challenge this way: "Capturing the mass market in India requires a shift in mind-set from value for money to value for many. As a result, frugal innovation is the answer."

The team found many ways to cut costs. For example, GE has historically designed entire ECG machines in-house, based on proprietary technologies. High-end units had custom-made components: GE-designed chips, GE-designed printers, GE-designed keyboards, and even GE-designed cables. Since proprietary technology can quickly drive up product cost—both to manufacture and to operate—the LGT scrupulously avoided it. Instead, like Harman in chapter 9, the team looked to leverage existing technology wherever possible.

During an ECG exam, electrical signals from the patient's body are made intelligible by what's known as a digital signal processor (DSP). Because GE's proprietary DSPs for high-end machines were manufactured in relatively low volumes, costs were high. Like both Harman and Logitech (chapter 5), the India LGT chose a standard DSP chip, readily available from such manufacturers as Texas Instruments and Analog Devices, thereby gaining significant economies of scale. (Though semiconductors can be a significant driver of product cost, they are also a category of component whose performance improves rapidly and relentlessly. Each technology generation makes dramatic leaps forward. Thus any innovation built on silicon chips is a good candidate to quickly close performance gaps!)

After a series of experiments to design a cost-effective printer in-house, the team hit upon a novel idea: to consider the suitability of the kind of ticket printer used on public buses and in movie theaters. The Bangalore bus system used a printer that was of the right size, weight, and durability to be used for MAC 400 ECG printouts. Millions of these printers are sold every year. GE Healthcare could buy it off the shelf and enjoy additional irresistible economies of scale—versus commissioning a custom solution for only ten thousand units a year.

As they found the technical solutions one by one, the team's mind-set changed from counting dollars to counting cents. The team, Varghese says, "was under constant pressure" to shave away cost in every aspect of the design. "Working on global products, we never worried about cents!"[2]

The team also made progress on shrinking the form factor so that the machine would be easily portable. The goal for total weight was between 1.1 and 1.2 kilograms. This required aggressive shaving of grams as well as pennies.

Minimizing the size of the printer reduced the footprint and weight. Eliminating the monitor reduced overall technical complexity, weight, and power consumption, which in turn contributed to longer life for the rechargeable battery. The team achieved its goal of recording a minimum of one hundred ECG tests on a single charge.

The LGT also found clever ways to meet ease-of-use and ease-of-repair requirements. The MAC 400 interface consisted mainly of a green button that started the machine and a red button that stopped it. As Varghese puts it, "If the person knows how to read traffic signs, he should be able to operate a MAC 400." The LGT prepared a short, simple training manual. Furthermore, the team's design called for a small number of standard replacement modules that were easily swappable. If the device failed, users themselves could swap modules.

The LGT kept headquarters apprised of its progress, but used a distinct method to do so. The standard drill within GE was to fire off a PowerPoint slide summarizing a project's current status versus its goals. But because of corporate's initial worries about the LGT's capabilities, the team wanted to show tangible demonstrations of progress. Instead of PowerPoint slides, the team held hands-on demos of its latest prototype. "With every review, the prototype would have evolved substantially, demonstrating real progress," says Raja. The global executives were able to see "the body language, see the team's excitement. They could see the brilliance in people's eyes. They felt we were making progress, and they backed off."

In line with our recommendations in chapter 4, Raja understood that reverse innovation projects demand custom criteria for evaluating progress. "We suspended regular P&L review standards and assessed progress by other metrics, such as the rate of risk reduction. We also submitted to frequent reviews from experts elsewhere in the company. We learned a great deal from such reviews."

As the design of the MAC 400 approached completion, a final objective was to comply with all relevant certification and testing requirements. "We wanted the new product to meet international regulatory standards, such as radiation emission, so it could be sold anywhere," says Varghese.

The Launch

The MAC 400 launched in December 2007 and quickly proved itself. To be sure, it had made significant sacrifices to achieve its goals: compared with premium models, it lacked a monitor, a digital memory, a full-sized keyboard, and a large, freestanding printer. But it also offered compensating benefits. At just over 2.6 pounds, it could be carried easily in a briefcase or hooked to a shoulder strap. Moreover, under the hood of this small device, there was considerable ingenuity. For example, it used the same patented GE analysis algorithm that runs on premium ECGs.

The MAC 400 extended affordable diagnostic testing to a poor rural population whose needs had hitherto been neglected. Despite the machine's bare-bones architecture, it recorded and printed clinically accurate electrocardiograms, detected cardiac illnesses, and helped to save lives.

Patients in Bangalore, or some other urban center, would be charged 90 rupees (about $2) for an ECG. Patients in rural areas would pay forty-five rupees (about $1). Either price point compared quite favorably with the $5 to $20 cost of an ECG taken on a premium model.[3] (Figure 10-1 shows the traditional ECG machine and the MAC 400.)

FIGURE 10-1

Traditional electrocardiogram machine (left) and the MAC 400

 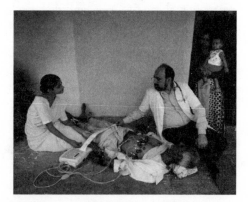

Source: Manoj V. Menon, communications leader, GE Healthcare South Asia. Used with permission.

To drive sales up quickly, GE's LGT developed a new go-to-market approach. Historically, GE Healthcare distributed high-end ECGs in India through dealers in big cities and large metropolitan areas. As those were not the target markets for the MAC 400, the company built a separate direct sales force to reach physicians located in the smallest of villages in the country. It was another illustration of clean-slate organizational design.

As we have noted throughout, however, the journey from inception to launch will, from time to time, require an LGT to get help from the larger organization. But how, in a vast enterprise like GE, do you give a ten-member LGT ownership and empowerment *plus* access to the company's much-needed deep global resources? From an organizational approach, you are, in a sense, asking King Kong and Bugs Bunny to play nicely with each other.

"The key was getting the two to work together," says Raja. "We encouraged the LGT to develop the culture and mind-set of an underdog. Oswin Varghese was the instrument behind creating the culture of a start-up. Still, his team was able to leverage GE's vast reservoir of global technology and global distribution. Ultimately, we won because we took advantage of the strengths of being both very large and very small."

Playing well together was a hallmark of the project. "This was a big team effort, not an individual effort," says Varghese. Part of the secret to effective collaboration lay in the uncompromised allegiance of the cross-functional team (consisting of engineering, supply chain, sales, and distribution) to the goal of making the MAC 400 a resounding success. The fact that GE had disrupted its usual model of having functional staff report up to global function leadership left the LGT clearly accountable only to the project.

Beyond India

Although the MAC 400 was designed for the unique circumstances and needs of India, it quickly found a market in the developed world. Much to the surprise of everyone involved, the fraction of MAC 400 sales made in Europe grew rapidly to half. The machine was a perfect solution for physicians in individual practice who could not afford the bigger systems. The quick win validated the LGT's foresight in complying with all international standards.

The MAC 400 is now sold in virtually every country (except the United States and Canada, where GE instead sells a model developed in China). "We are not just innovating for India," says Munesh Makhija, CTO for GE

Healthcare in India. "We are innovating for the world." As another example, Makhija cites GE's line of lower-cost baby warmers—units that maintain a consistent thermostatic environment for newborns: "Infant mortality is a major problem in India. We developed the Lullaby line of baby warmers in Bangalore. We launched the product in May 2009 at a price point of $3,000." (Rich-world prices for these units start at $12,000.) "This made-in-India product is now sold in over sixty countries, including rich countries in Western Europe."

The successful spread of the MAC 400 and the Lullaby baby warmers to new markets highlights a key point: innovations for the developing world sometimes move into the developed world unexpectedly, into niche opportunities in marginalized markets that previously went unnoticed or were too small to justify a product development effort.

GE Healthcare used several mechanisms to facilitate MAC 400's move from India to other countries. First, it displayed the MAC 400 in international medical equipment shows, making potential customers everywhere aware of the breakthrough product. In addition, the company's marketing effort positioned the MAC 400 for doctor's offices. That way, the global sales team saw the potential for incremental growth, not a threat that could cannibalize GE's core hospital market. Finally, senior leaders gave the MAC 400 extensive visibility internally, including a two-page spread in the 2007 GE annual report and a spot in GE's "Imagination at Work" advertising campaign. Jeffrey Immelt personally showcased the product in several high-level management meetings—always with this message: "If *we* don't launch it globally, other Chinese or Indian companies will!"

MAC India

The initial reverse innovation is sometimes just the beginning. The first salvo later becomes a platform for subsequent forays both up market and down market (table 10-1). Says Raja, "One of the things we learned from this process is that there is a segment even lower than the value segment."

GE's first product extension was a scaled-down version of the MAC 400, dubbed MAC India and launched in the first quarter of 2010. MAC India delivered an ultralow price. At just nine rupees, an ECG scan from a MAC India cost a bit less than a bottle of water. Raja notes that at forty-five rupees, "MAC 400's ECG scan is still too expensive for patients in rural areas. If somebody has a pain in the chest, he will say, 'Oh, this will cost me forty-five rupees. Maybe the pain will go away.' But it doesn't. Then, three days later, he has a heart attack. Either he dies or, if he survives, he incurs the cost of further medical care, which burdens his family with debt. But if the ECG costs only nine rupees, he will say, 'All right, let me spend nine rupees.'"

The cost to buy MAC India was also dramatically lower than MAC 400—twenty-five thousand rupees, down from forty thousand. "India is not about value," says Raja. "India is about *super value*." One of the LGT team members provides a quantification of this standard: "Generally speaking, to win in India, you need a ten percent solution in the urban market and a one percent solution in the rural market. If a product is sold for a hundred dollars in the West, you need to hit a ten-dollar price point in urban India, one dollar in rural India."

MAC India looked similar to its older sibling, but the printer—a major cost factor—was smaller (58 rather than 80 millimeters wide). That led to lower material costs, and ongoing savings in both paper and power consumption. The most radical difference was MAC India's elimination of a power supply. It runs exclusively on its rechargeable battery. Thanks to power-management efficiencies achieved with the smaller printer and improved performance of the central processing unit, the MAC India can record an impressive five hundred ECG exams on a single battery charge.

MAC India included innovations in nonproduct areas as well. GE Healthcare made financing available on relatively easy terms, at 0 percent interest. A physician who couldn't afford to buy the machine outright could choose to pay a daily fee of twenty-seven rupees—the equivalent of three ECG scans—debited electronically.

MAC 600

The next iteration aimed up market. There's no question that the MAC 400 involved difficult trade-offs. For one thing, it lacked any digital memory. It was therefore impossible to perform and store more than one ECG exam before printing out the results. If the printer were to break down in the field, the machine would be rendered unusable. Another trade-off was the lack of a monitor. If one or more of the electrodes were attached to the patient improperly, the mistake would be discovered only in the printout,

TABLE 10-1

GE's initial reverse innovation, the MAC 400, moved both up marked and down market

	High-end standard	Innovation 1: MAC 400	Innovation 2: MAC India	Innovation 3: MAC 600	Innovation 4: MAC 800
Description	Bulky—integrated, full-size monitor, keyboard, and printer	Highly portable and lightweight (less than three pounds); can be carried to patients' homes	Scaled-down MAC 400, but with same footprint, portability, and ease of use	Upscale version of MAC 400 using same basic footprint	Higher-end version of portable ECG with more advanced software and contemporary look and feel
Features	Top-notch functionality Requires a rolling trolley	Simple, two-button operation, for use by untrained personnel; small, built-in printer for ECG results; eliminates freestanding monitor, printer, and keyboard	Smaller onboard printer (58 mm versus 80 mm) reduces weight, paper cost, and power usage	Adds built-in monitor (operator can see that tests are recorded properly); cell-phone-type keyboard (patient identifiers can be entered in test file); digital memory (tests can be stored and e-mailed)	Includes more features: integrated cell-phone-type keypad (SMS text input); monitor display 7 inches (versus 4.3 inches on MAC 600); larger printer; built-in connectivity
Power requirements	Runs on house current; can run on battery for 50 ECG tests	Runs on house current or rechargeable battery (good for 100 ECG tests)	Battery operation only; eliminating power supply reduces weight, cost, and power usage; this, plus improved chip performance and other economies, drives big gains in battery life—up to 500 ECG tests per charge	Runs on house current or rechargeable battery	Runs on house current or rechargeable battery

Target	Developed countries and infrastructures; unsuited for conditions in India, which call for portability, low purchase price, low operating costs, and available battery power (in response to unreliable electric grid)	Value segment of smaller cities, larger villages	Super-value segment of small and medium-sized villages	Cities of all sizes	Tier 2 and 3 Chinese cities and rural areas
Surprise markets	None	Sold in 194 countries (sells well in Europe, especially France)	Not yet	Not yet	Sold in the United States
Trade-offs	High price	No memory card—exam results must be printed out immediately rather than stored; no keyboard means no way to enter patient name or numeric identifier (operator must write name on printout)	Same as in MAC 400, but with smaller printer and no power supply	More technical complexity, weight, and power usage than MAC 400	More technical complexity, weight, and power usage than MAC 400.
Cost to buy	$3,000 to $10,000	$800	$500	$1,200	$2,000
Price per ECG test	$5 to $20	$1 to $2	As little as $0.20	$1 to $2	$2 to $3

after the test had been done; it would then have to be redone. Finally, it lacked an alphanumeric keyboard or keypad. Operators couldn't key in the patient's name or any identifying number. A name or number would instead be written on the printout once the test was completed. This was rightly seen as a cumbersome workaround.

So the MAC 600 added a cell-phone-like keypad. It also added a memory card capable of storing up to five hundred ECG tests. If the printer failed (or if each test no longer had to be printed immediately), the stored tests could be printed later from the memory card. Tests were stored as PDF files rather than in GE's proprietary data format. That meant they could be read on any computer, printed on a standard office printer, and easily shared via e-mail or mobile phones. Seeds of telemedicine were sown.

The machine also boasted a 4.3-inch monitor. Operators could quickly verify that the leads were taking proper readings. If, say, a patient's chest hair interfered with the signal from an electrode, the operator could spot and fix the problem before the test was done. This capability both saved on paper and lessened patient discomfort. Moreover, this on-screen review feature enabled one MAC 600 to save as much as one tree per year (or fifty-nine kilograms of paper), making it an eco-friendly medical product.

These enhancements were all accommodated within the same basic form and footprint as the MAC 400 and MAC India models. The MAC 600 was launched in the first quarter of 2011 and retailed for $1,200. Whereas its less-featured siblings were intended for smaller cities and rural villages, the MAC 600 was suited to large urban clinics and physician practices.

The brilliance of the MAC series of ECG machines shows what big companies can do when they organize themselves to tap into the hunger and intensity typically associated with start-ups. On a modest $500,000 budget, the Bangalore LGT had to be mindful not only of every dollar but of every cent that went into the design of the MAC series. To reach its goals, the team had to draw both on cutting-edge proprietary in-house technologies and off-the-shelf signal processing and printing methods. And, only by harnessing the forces of iconoclasm, opportunism, and efficiency could the team create an adaptable product that could be easily upgraded or downgraded to address a variety of underserved markets, from second- and third-tier cities in the developing world to remote rural areas to doctors' offices in Western Europe.

Since their launch, the MAC series of products have sold over fifteen thousand units. The company's initial $500,000 investment was recouped many times over. Margins on MAC products compare favorably with those of high-end machines.

MAC 800

Concurrent with the Bangalore effort, GE Healthcare pursued one other ECG innovation. An LGT in Wuxi, China, developed a quasi-premium machine called the MAC 800. It can't properly be seen as a platform extension, since the China LGT took a different approach. Indeed, it's a separate platform with a separate operating system. It has a seven-inch monitor, a bigger printer, and a cell-phone-like keypad.

The Chinese team began its project later than the MAC 400 LGT did. It set out to build a more sophisticated product, more in line with China's market requirements. The Wuxi LGT had learned that Chinese customers were willing to pay extra for a level of sophistication that Indian customers weren't. CTO Munesh Makhija says that the MAC 800 interface has a contemporary look and feel, more-advanced software, and built-in connectivity.

Ideas were freely shared back and forth between the Bangalore and Wuxi teams. For instance, although the China LGT specified a bigger printer, the team sought a noncustom solution and sourced it from the same manufacturer used by the Bangalore team.

The MAC 800, which sells for $2,000, is identifiably a cousin of the Bangalore platform. It has portability, simplicity, and battery operation. In terms of features and value, it is roughly comparable to GE Healthcare's high-end models priced at $5,000. (In some respects, the MAC 600 was an effort to close the gap between the MAC 800 and the MAC 400—a smart compromise upward from India's value obsession.)

Perhaps a good place to end this story is to note that by 2011, the MAC 800 was being sold in the United States to new customer segments—rural clinics, visiting nurses, and primary-care doctors. These medical professionals either cannot afford the big-ticket diagnostic machines or else need equipment they can easily tote. Reverse innovation isn't complete until the circle closes and the product meant for an emerging market finds its way back to the developed world.

GE Healthcare's Playbook Lessons

1. *Leverage opportunities to move emerging-market innovations to other parts of the world* (Reverse Innovation Playbook lesson 2). The line of MAC portable ECG machines did not cannibalize GE's higher-end products. It has expanded the market by reaching large populations of underserved patients. The machines quickly found additional new customers around the world, in rich countries and poor countries alike. The extraordinary reach of a large multinational confers an enormous advantage over emerging giants. GE exploited this advantage well.

2. *Manage reverse innovation initiatives as disciplined experiments* (Reverse Innovation Playbook lesson 9).Rather than judging the success of the project on standard measures, GE increased the frequency of reviews, focusing on learning based on mini-experiments and reducing risks.

Questions for Reflection

1. Does your company have realistic expectations for what individual innovation leaders can accomplish *on their own*?

2. How does your company assess the progress of risky innovation efforts?

3. If your company had a successful innovation in an emerging market, could variations of it be created to serve customers with similar needs throughout the world?

CHAPTER ELEVEN

PepsiCo's Brand-New Bag

*To make a more healthful product, you need
to think globally, snack locally.*

YOU COULD SAY that the mission of Mehmood Khan is to find a higher purpose for the lowly snack. Khan, now PepsiCo's chief scientific officer, was once a Mayo Clinic physician and researcher specializing in endocrinology, metabolism, and nutrition.

It's exactly the expertise that the company's chairman and CEO, Indra K. Nooyi, must lean on in order to achieve her ambition to deliver on the company's "Performance with Purpose" mission. First and foremost, this credo means creating products that do more than just please the palate. They also should embody properties of health and wellness. In simplest terms, that has meant committing to reduce fat, sugar, and salt in all of its products. People now seek more from their snacking. Health-sustaining calories are in. The PepsiCo challenge, therefore, is to create snack foods—everywhere in the world—that are not just "Fun for You" but also "Good for You."

It's a necessary ambition, Nooyi asserts, because "all the employees of PepsiCo are first mothers, fathers, children, husbands, wives, aunts and uncles. So, how do we articulate our strategy in a way that makes everybody feel very good about the company? It can't be because of our financial performance alone—although that's necessary—but in terms of the holistic impact we have on society."[1]

The company will tackle this challenge much more readily if reverse innovation is part of its repertoire. And yet, until recently, PepsiCo took a glocalization approach. The company developed products for the United States and then sold and distributed substantially similar products throughout the world. As a result, PepsiCo's growth, particularly in emerging markets, hit a wall. The company's brands bumped up against local needs, tastes, and habits that could not be satisfied by lowest-common-denominator global products.

In case after case in part 2, we have encountered this syndrome of stalled emerging-market growth. Under the glocalization scenario, what first appears to be promising momentum hits a wall—often sooner than later. The renown of even the most potent global brands wears thin when the offered product is neither designed expressly for local markets nor priced for local means.

These days, PepsiCo is finding ways to address sharp differences across borders by designing products with local tastes and consumer needs in mind. And it is capturing a greater share of the opportunity in emerging economies.

But that's not all. PepsiCo is finding that its innovations in emerging markets have the potential to have impact—and deliver performance with purpose—all over the world. When ideas and creativity start circling the globe in multiple directions, interesting things can happen. Monologues become dialogues, and innovations spawn more innovations.

For example, PepsiCo is finding that some long-popular ingredients in emerging economies, such as lentils in India, have healthy profiles that suggest new directions for snacking across geographies. Further, cuisines travel. The popularity of Asian tastes, for example, is growing in the West.

In this chapter, we will show how PepsiCo—through its Frito-Lay snack food unit—is making reverse innovation happen. We will take a particularly close look at Aliva, a new savory cracker developed for the Indian market (and PepsiCo's first foray into cracker production). The company's approach to reverse innovation combines local product development efforts, strong support from global resources, plus efforts to ensure that the raw material of PepsiCo's innovations—ideas, flavors, ingredients, marketing expertise, packaging materials, manufacturing methods, and so on—can flow in any direction within the organization.

Bringing Health Science to Snacks

Mehmood Khan has enjoyed a multifaceted career, which has led to his developing a multifaceted mind. Before he came to PepsiCo, Khan worked in the pharmaceutical industry. He had come to the attention of big pharma as a result of research he'd worked on looking at the safety and efficacy of weight-loss drugs. He was an expert on obesity—including its various negative health consequences—before it had become a well-established medical subspecialty or a matter of urgent public-health concern.

Khan went to work for Takeda Pharmaceuticals North America, a division of Japan's largest and most venerable pharmaceutical firm. Takeda, which had been founded in 1700, was then developing an anti-obesity drug similar to those Khan had researched.

Big pharma is an industry where long horizons make special sense. Drug discovery takes a long time. There are many misses for every hit. After Khan had been with Takeda for a while, he was about to be promoted into a very senior R&D role. He had a formal interview with the CEO, who was also named Takeda and was a direct descendant of the founder. During the interview, Takeda told Khan, "You know, we had a president of our company before you had a president of your country."

"It was quite a statement," says Khan, looking back. "And it was exactly in line with the company's culture." The experience of working at Takeda, he says, made him realize "that leaders should worry about legacy. They should focus on the next decade, not just the next quarter."[2]

All of his experiences have carried Khan, step by step, from being a physician to becoming a business leader. In turn, his preoccupation as a business leader incorporates all that he learned as a physician.

Concerns about childhood and adult obesity are on the rise, especially in the United States. The problem is frequent grist for discussions of public health policy. It's not news that snack foods are not commonly associated with health and wellness. Nonetheless, Khan saw that there was enormous opportunity for impact in creating options for healthier snacking.

"Consumers interact with our products on three levels: the neurological level, the gut level, and the metabolic level," says Khan. Traditionally, food and beverage companies have focused only on the first. The neurological level is where brands, marketing, and sensory payloads operate. "I look at the problems of emerging markets, where the majority of our future customers will be. What do our products do to the person's gut? What do they do to their body chemistry? If I ignore those effects, then all I've got is indulgence without any balance."

That is not to say that indulgence takes a backseat to other goals. Achieving the right balance is crucial. As Khan bluntly asserts, "If we don't own the space of taste, we don't have a right to exist."

Building on a Past Success: Kurkure

As PepsiCo geared up for its effort to develop Aliva, Khan wondered whether there were any examples in which PepsiCo had already practiced successful reverse innovation, without realizing it or calling it by that name. In India, he found such an example.

It was a lentil-and-rice-based snack called Kurkure. Introduced more than a decade ago, Kurkure (meaning "crunchy" in Hindi) had grown to be Frito-Lay India's top-selling product as measured by the number of bags sold. Moreover, it had surpassed products from Cadbury and Britannia, two venerable competitors who have operated in the Indian market for over one hundred years. PepsiCo had learned a lot from the Kurkure experience, says Khan. "The fact that it was conceived *in* India *by* Indians was very different from PepsiCo norms."

Once, emerging nations aspired to have access to rich-world products. But these days, they want rich-world *quality* baked into products *with local origins*. Kurkure exemplified the idea that innovation shouldn't simply be handed down from on high. It starts with understanding customer problems in India.

To develop that understanding requires the right kind of research. "Conventional market research asks the consumer what they think of your product offering," says Khan. "You don't get consumer insights that way. It gives you hindsight about their past experiences with the product. It is retrospective. What you need is insights that will help you develop solutions for the future. You need consumer *foresight*. Now, put this in the developing-world arena. Customer problems in developing countries are fundamentally different. They require fundamentally different solutions."

Central to Kurkure's development was a clear understanding of fundamental shifts in the Indian market. Changes such as the following would have been largely invisible to distant observers in New York but were addressed by Kurkure:

- *Lifestyle changes in India.* Traditionally, in middle-class Indian homes, snack foods were consumed at tea time, and they were homemade. There's little time for that these days, however, as in many households, both husbands and wives have jobs. As a result, consumers increasingly put a premium on the convenience of ready-made snacks.

- *Local flavor preferences.* In form and texture, Kurkure resembles Cheetos—the twisty-shaped, crunchy, cheese-flavored Frito-Lay snack popular in the United States. But that's where the similarities end. Indians prefer savory snack foods whose seasoning is rich and complex. They also like multiple flavors and textures. By contrast, Western (and especially U.S.) consumers like their snacks to be either salty and crispy or sweet. Kurkure is now sold in a half dozen flavors that please the local palate, including green chutney and tomato with hot pepper.

- *Local ingredients.* Kurkure's batter is made with lentils and rice. Cheetos is corn-based. According to Khan, there are few basic foods richer in protein than the humble lentil. It is a staple widely cultivated in primarily vegetarian India. Besides being nearly 30 percent protein, lentils are low in fat and rich in fiber, micronutrients, and complex carbohydrates. Lentils therefore make perfect sense as a healthy snack food ingredient.

- *Messaging tailored to the Indian psyche.* According to Gautham Mukkavilli, who headed the foods business for Frito-Lay India, Kurkure's slogan, translated from Hindi, means basically, "Hey, it's imperfect but it's mine."[3] That sentiment embodies what Mukkavilli calls "the product truth and the country truth." India, he says, is now confident enough to accept its own imperfections. "We are who we are, take it or leave it." Such an insight is detectable only at the street level.

Khan also saw that while Kurkure was an innovation executed by the Indian team targeting the Indian consumer, it benefited mightily from

PepsiCo's global capabilities. For instance, producing Kurkure required solving a nettlesome problem of production technology. Lentil-based batter was much harder to extrude than the corn-based batter used in Cheetos. Solving that manufacturing problem, says Khan, "required a global team."

The Aliva Story

Kurkure showed Khan that PepsiCo had the capabilities to develop a snack specifically tailored for the Indian market. Now it was time for a reprise.

The India team members conceived Aliva as a marriage between a fried salty snack (*fun!*) and a baked cracker (*healthy!*). Their ambition was that it would be even more popular than Kurkure and that it would vanquish the stereotype that healthy snacks are dull.

Aliva would be made using wheat and lentils and would be baked rather than fried. It would contain no trans fats or cholesterol. It would be produced in an eccentric triangular shape with curved sides. The central brand message, targeted at the young-adult demographic, would be that Aliva could transport you to the cusp of the weekend, delivering an exuberant Friday feeling. Overall, Aliva was to be the embodiment of Khan's and PepsiCo's agenda to deliver affordable, accessible, and healthier snacking.

Building a Dream Team

The Aliva project was managed by Vidur Vyas and executed by a small local growth team. Vyas had formerly worked for Colgate-Palmolive and, before that, had been a consultant with Accenture. The full-time "staff" of the LGT consisted only of Vyas and one other full-time dedicated collaborator. The rest of the Aliva contributors were drawn from what Frito-Lay India marketing leader Deepika Warrier calls "a dream team" of regional and global experts. They represented the best talent available internally—or through consulting partners—across all of the relevant disciplines: marketing, sales, distribution, production, flavors, packaging, and design. "What we have in PepsiCo are informal networks that connect global and local," says Warrier.[4]

Coordinating such loosely coupled resources might appear to be a tall order. But Vyas insists that there were compelling guarantees of cooperation

in place. There was support for the project beyond the region, most con-
spicuously in the person of Khan, who helped the Aliva LGT get the help it
needed in key areas, including the following:

- *Production technology.* The challenges of achieving the desired
  cracker shape and texture, ensuring resistance to breakage, and
  establishing a new baking system were all beyond the capabilities of
  the LGT.

- *Packaging standards and technology.* The team designed an innovative
  bag for Aliva, but there were assorted difficulties that required the
  assistance of multiple experts from the global organization.

- *Flavoring support.* PepsiCo maintains a global flavoring expertise that
  worked in concert with the Aliva LGT's experts on Indian seasonings.

Trial and Error

From its inception to its 2009 launch, the Aliva project took nearly four
years. Aliva was evaluated against criteria that took full account of potential uncertainties. Such latitude was indispensable. Aliva had to make its
way through a predictably fraught gestation. There were plenty of bumps
in the road, and plenty to learn along the way.

Aliva's most vexing challenge was its packaging. Packages are hugely
important to snack food performance. If snacks had remained in the era of
the general-store cracker barrel, great branding opportunities would never
have materialized. Aliva's packaging needed to be as distinctive as the shape
of the cracker. The packaging had to communicate that Aliva was both
healthy and fun. Decisions about the package would have implications for
Aliva's texture and shape, the way the cracker was produced (through
baking), and the attractiveness of the offering at the point of sale.

The Aliva bag featured a number of innovations. Vyas claims that nothing like it had ever been tried before. It was to be made from new materials
on brand-new—and untested—machinery. The bag was designed to be flat
on the bottom. Unlike typical snack bags in the United States, it could
stand up straight on a retail shelf, tabletop, or counter. The packaging material was therefore heavier and stiffer than conventional plastic film. It
turned out that a more rugged package could actually be made using only

two laminate layers, not three. This solution was both more cost-effective and environmentally friendly.

The package specifications needed to address certain constraints of local infrastructure. It often took a long time to distribute perishable goods through a vast, predominantly rural retail network. Crackers can spoil more quickly than other types of snacks. Aliva therefore had to be protected from spoilage as well as breakage. A rugged, lightproof, hermetic package was key.

Vyas and his team endured a perfect storm of complications on the way to satisfying these needs. Because the Aliva bag was a first-of-its-kind package design, it seemed that every element of the package's structure and manufacture either had to be invented or endlessly troubleshot. To start with, the new packaging machinery was touchy. In limited test runs, things seemed fine. But once Aliva launched, in May 2009, problems cropped up during production-scale runs, particularly with the heat seal at the top of the bag. So, new material had to be designed. This required help from squadrons of global experts on polymers and lamination technologies.

There were nettlesome challenges on other fronts as well. Because Aliva would rely on a new baking system, which had only recently been used for the first time to produce cookies in PepsiCo's Mexico region, Vyas's team needed time and technical guidance to learn how to operate it reliably.

Finally, the team aspired to create a cracker in an eccentric triangular shape. The cracker's unique design was considered an important aspect of the values the brand would communicate. The triangle shape was meant to connote speed, stimulation, and taste. The triangle's curved edges were meant to connote health. At first, however, the crackers suffered unacceptable levels of breakage. Coming up with a workable version—a cracker with a low rate of breakage and a pleasing combination of textures—required innumerable trials.

But if Aliva's journey to market had an unusual share of difficulties, that is only because it was forging entirely new paths in a number of areas. To its credit, PepsiCo patiently tolerated a high degree of necessary experimentation. There were rounds of iterative experimentation with packaging, with the baking system, and with the architecture of the cracker itself.

Patience Rewarded

Indeed, the launch demanded great patience all around—from Vyas's virtual LGT, from the region, and from PepsiCo itself. Though the various birth pangs added time to the development cycle, patience paid off.

High hopes had been placed on Aliva. Says Mukkavilli, "Once the product was ready, it was a huge energizer for our entire organization—because it was potentially going to be the next big platform." Kurkure had expanded to become a broad, multiline product, and its success was the benchmark against which Aliva would be measured.

In the postlaunch period, performance was tracked by sensible new-product metrics: growth in consumer awareness, response to trial offerings, and repeat business after trial offerings. "We know that new products go through ebbs and flows, highs and lows," says Mukkavilli. "During 2010, we said that Aliva was an absolute must-win battle for everybody in the organization. We said everybody must have one goal related to Aliva. You know, 'Tell me what you're going to do to make Aliva win in the marketplace.'"

A spirit of competition fired up the Aliva LGT. Its ambition was to grow Aliva at a faster clip than Kurkure. By mid-2010, performance had been very strong on some metrics and weaker on others, according to Vyas. Having set a stretch goal to exceed Kurkure by 40 percent, Aliva was forecast to end its first year "slightly ahead of or equal to Kurkure."

Mukkavilli anticipates that Aliva will expand both within its native region and beyond. There are already several versions of the cracker, offering distinct Indian flavors that have been inspired by local spices unique to different parts of the country. And although Aliva has multiple textures and is spiced in the savory style that Indians favor, the production technology behind it is adaptable. So it's not far-fetched to think that Aliva versions flavored for Western palates will make their way to Stop & Shop supermarkets and 7-Eleven stores.

PepsiCo's Recipe for Reverse Innovation

Nooyi's ambitions extend far beyond Aliva. To fully capture the growth opportunity in emerging markets, she is focused on building a company that can make reverse innovation happen routinely.

That starts with shifting power and money to emerging markets. Nooyi has changed the organization so that emerging-market heads report directly to her, not to a head of international business, as was the practice in the past. She has also increased investments in emerging markets. Further, she has institutionalized a framework for managing innovation, with four key elements:

1. Innovate locally using global capabilities.

2. Strike the right balance between local autonomy and global authority.

3. Take local innovations across geographies.

4. Establish systems and processes to enable items 1 through 3.

Local Roots, Global Resources

Though Kurkure and Aliva were locally conceived and executed, the ability of each team to draw upon a deep and well-coordinated bench of global experts and other resources was critical. Warrier describes PepsiCo as a company with highly fluid "informal networks" that knit together local and global concerns. Vyas extols PepsiCo's highly collaborative culture.

These qualities are reinforced by PepsiCo's reward system. For instance, the entire Aliva team—the Indian LGT as well as the global packaging, baking, and seasoning gurus—collectively won PepsiCo's 2010 Marketing Innovation Award. Absent these shared rewards, it would be much harder to choreograph the challenging pas de deux between fully empowered local growth teams and well-developed global support capabilities.

So fluid was the interplay of the local and global assets brought to bear on Aliva that in a conversation about whom to recognize for Aliva's achievements, Khan is stumped. He cannot single out individuals, only the entire extended family of contributors. "I can tell you whose project Aliva was," Khan finally says. "It was PepsiCo's."

Freedom Within a Frame

Khan is very clear on the boundaries of autonomy between global and local. If a local region decides to develop a product, it has the freedom to do so—freedom within a frame: "If you need to invest in a local product, you have your own budget. You don't have to go to headquarters [to ask permission]." The only caveat is that the product must align with global brand standards. But within that framework, there is wide latitude for autonomous decision-making and action.

On the other hand, Khan centralized and consolidated a group to deal with regulatory and safety issues across PepsiCo's divisions. That group reports to him, and he reports to CEO Indra Nooyi. "There's no dual reporting line for safety to any commercial person other than through me to Indra. That gives us absolute control. I cannot decentralize that. And I can't rely on a commercial business leader, and P&L owner, to be the tiebreaker. A safety call is a safety call!"

There are also clear boundaries in the exercise of LGT autonomy versus, say, that of the support team providing guidance on a new baking technology. "We have a global baking team," says Khan. That team makes its expertise available to local product teams, as it did for the Aliva LGT. "But nobody from the global baking team tells the local teams what to make."

Lifting and Shifting

PepsiCo seeks ways to make innovations with local origins easily transferable. How much of a new snack's basic recipe, or the technology for its production, can be lifted and shifted? Why couldn't a lentil-based snack migrate beyond India, if it had the right flavorings for local tastes?

One opportunity for lifting and shifting was rice bran oil. Noting India's high rate of cardiovascular disease, PepsiCo looked for an alternative to palm oil, an ingredient widely used by snack food manufacturers but also relatively high in saturated fats. Many of Frito-Lay's international units have switched to sunflower oil, but sunflower oil is very expensive and hard to come by in India. Rice bran oil turned out to be a better choice. It was seen as a heart-healthy alternative. Moreover, rice is plentiful in India, making the oil highly affordable.

Rice bran oil has become one of Frito-Lay India's most successful—and purest—reverse innovations. It was developed locally, but it has migrated to Africa, the Middle East, and other Asian countries where sunflower oil is expensive and consumer incomes low.

The company's global support capability around flavors shows how ideas can flow bidirectionally. Dallas-based Eapen George, who runs the team, works directly with Khan on global projects, but was also available to Vyas to help with the Aliva launch. (Indeed, Vyas describes a "close collabora-tion" with the U.S.-based flavor team.) But Frito-Lay India also has its own local flavor expertise. Just as India can learn from global, global can learn from India—dialogue, not monologue! As much as Vyas profits from hav-ing strong input from George's group, the global capability is also enhanced when George is in a position to discover local taste innovations that deserve to be transported elsewhere.

Instituting Systems and Processes to Support Innovation

To ensure that PepsiCo is able to routinely leverage global assets for local innovation, find the right balance between global authority and local autonomy, and move innovations across geographies, the company has taken several additional steps.

ESTABLISHED PRINCIPLES FOR RESOURCE ALLOCATION. Many businesses are overwhelmed by the demand for near-term performance. However, reverse innovation requires reserving some bandwidth for inventing the business of tomorrow. It's a matter of balance. PepsiCo has devised a resource allocation formula that sees to both key needs—the *70/30 rule*. The company exhorts innovators and executives to devote 30 percent of all energy, attention, and investment to working on entirely new ideas. These would be the kinds of high-potential but speculative projects that can become future lines of business. The remaining 70 percent of development energy must entirely align with current global strategy and priorities. Performance is evaluated against the 70/30 metric.

CREATED SPECIAL INCENTIVES. The resource allocation process needs to be reinforced with a little extra motivation. For example, the company has created incentives for lowering salt and sugar in products and increasing whole grains and fiber. It also put in place metrics to track—and reward—local innovations that are lifted and shifted.

BUILT MECHANISMS TO SHARE KNOWLEDGE. If they are to accelerate lifting and shifting, employees must know where promising ideas are being developed and pursued. The company has initiated several mechanisms to facilitate the spread of such ideas: PepsiCo rotates scientists between developed and developing countries (also between the food and beverages units); there is a global online R&D portal; and global food and beverage summits are held regularly to share best practices.

Nooyi has put in place an efficient, well-designed system for globally supported local innovation. There is a clearly understood commitment to identify which elements of local innovation can become global in their impact. And the company has the means for making those transformations happen. It's only a matter of time before the circle is closed.

PepsiCo's Playbook Lessons

1. *Enable LGTs to leverage the global resource base through carefully managed partnerships* (Reverse Innovation Playbook lesson 8). PepsiCo has carefully balanced central authority and local autonomy and has nurtured partnerships between LGTs and global resources. When a reverse innovation succeeds, no single leader is recognized. Instead, all the contributors—LGT members and global experts—are rewarded together.

2. *Move people, power, and money to where the growth is* (Reverse Innovation Playbook lesson 4). PepsiCo CEO Indra Nooyi has clearly signaled a commitment to emerging market growth. For example, the heads of developing countries report directly to her, rather than to an international executive. Nooyi has increased the company's investments in emerging markets. And she has adopted an institutional framework for reverse innovation practice that provides for systems to support and enable it. PepsiCo now conveys a mind-set—embodied in Nooyi herself—in which both developed and developing world markets are increasingly on an equal footing.

Questions for Reflection

1. How deeply embedded in your company is the attitude that one size fits all—that any customer, anywhere in the world, has the same basic needs?

2. Is your company ready to entrust leaders in the poor world with the responsibility for high-risk business experiments? If not, what will it take to get there?

3. Where are the most powerful people in your company located? How does this distribution of power affect the flow of ideas, knowledge, and innovations around the world?

CHAPTER TWELVE

Partners In Health's Radical Model for Care

Developing world medicine can improve rich world health.

W HEN MIGUEL LEARNED that he had been infected with HIV, he did not see it as a crisis. He didn't even show up for his next doctor's appointment. Miguel had more pressing concerns. He had grown up in a one-room shack made from bits of trash collected from the streets. His father had been an abusive alcoholic. When his mother fled, Miguel had dropped out of primary school. In desperation, he had begun trading sex with men and women for money.

After his father died, Miguel had started his own family in the same shack. He worked temporary jobs, always on the economic edge. Then, he started to get sick—*very* sick. Believing that he was dying, Miguel focused exclusively on work, hoping to support his family as long as he could. His immune system became so weak that he contracted tuberculosis. When his wife finally persuaded him to seek help, he tested HIV positive.

Bernadette's story is as grim as Miguel's. She first tested HIV positive at age twenty-seven. She believed that she acquired the virus from her husband, who had since died. Bernadette had a sixth-grade education. She never had a job. She relied on government disability checks. She had been a repeat victim of domestic violence. Her current partner was abusive, and her daughter became pregnant at age fifteen.

But in the lottery of life, Bernadette had a major advantage over Miguel. Bernadette was born in the United States; Miguel was born in Peru. Bernadette lived in Boston, just a few blocks from the neighborhood that contains one of the highest concentrations of medical talent in the world. Miguel lived in a slum outside Lima. Bernadette also had insurance with full prescription coverage. She had a primary-care doctor, an HIV specialist, and two social workers attending to her care. She had access to the medicines that have changed HIV from a death sentence to something she could live with.

Nonetheless, it was Bernadette who was at death's door. Doctors analyze blood samples to count the number of CD4 cells, which are the critical immune system actors that HIV destroys. A CD4 count gives an accurate picture of the extent to which HIV has progressed in a patient. Healthy adults have CD4 counts of roughly 1,000. Bernadette's had dropped to 4. She weighed a mere eighty-four pounds. At any moment, an opportunistic infection might have invaded Bernadette's nearly nonexistent immune system and killed her.

One of the greatest medical communities in the world had failed her.

As it turned out, however, what Bernadette needed most wasn't medicine alone. She needed a different kind of intervention. Indeed, what she needed most was the same type of treatment that gave Miguel hope in distant Peru—a treatment not just of the disease, but also of the patient's whole life.

Bernadette needed an advocate—one who had learned from innovative approaches to health care created in the resource-poor developing world. And that is exactly what she received, from a doctor named Heidi Louise Behforouz. Adapting a model that Partners In Health (PIH), a Boston-based global health organization, had pioneered in Haiti and Peru, Behforouz employs community health workers to provide home-based services to the sickest and most marginalized HIV/AIDS patients in Boston. After less than a year, Bernadette's CD4 count had risen to nearly 300, and she had gained sixty pounds.[1]

A reverse innovation was saving Bernadette's life.

A Doctor's Career Choice

By her own account, Behforouz hit bottom toward the end of her second year of medical school in Boston. She had always wanted to be an advocate for the poor and saw medicine as a natural outlet for that desire. But

Behforouz found that her medical training was taking her farther from her goals, not closer to them: "I was thinking of taking a year off and going to Iran to work with nomadic tribes there."[2]

An interaction with Paul Farmer changed her direction. Farmer, an expert in infectious diseases, saw patients at Boston's Brigham and Women's Hospital, where Behforouz practiced during her training. But Farmer was also the driving force behind PIH, which began by caring for Haiti's rural poor using innovative strategies and treatment plans. Farmer was living the life Heidi Behforouz aspired to. He had spent much of his time at Zanmi Lasante (meaning "partners in health" in Haitian Creole), the clinic he had helped start in Cange, a village in Haiti's central plateau.

When Farmer said, "Come work for us," Behforouz eagerly accepted.

Farmer graduated from Harvard Medical School and had long been affiliated with Brigham and Women's. He had recruited classmates and fellow interns and residents to do stints in Haiti. And he sometimes used the Boston hospital's resources and expertise to help treat his Haitian patients. Nonetheless, PIH had no programs in the local community—or anyplace else in the United States, for that matter.

But that was soon to change. And Behforouz, a cofounder and now the director of the PACT program (for Prevention and Access to Care and Treatment), based in Boston's Dorchester section, would find herself at the center of that change. She would adapt methods PIH developed in emerging nations and apply them in major American cities. In doing so, she would complete the reverse innovation circle.

The Lessons of Haiti

"The world is full of miserable places. One way of living comfortably is not to think about them, or, when you do, to send money." So wrote Pulitzer Prize–winning author Tracy Kidder in *Mountains Beyond Mountains*, a penetrating profile of Paul Farmer's complex nature and the work of PIH.[3] Haiti, one of the world's poorest countries, ranks high on any list of miserable places.

Farmer would not be one of those who only sent money. He first came to Haiti in 1983, after graduating from Duke University with a degree in anthropology. During his years at Duke, he had studied Haitian farm workers who toiled in North Carolina's nearby tobacco fields. The more he learned about Haiti and its people, the more fascinated he became. Gradually, he formed the view that "Haitians were the underdogs of underdogs, the shafted of the shafted."

Farmer had also developed an interest in medicine. He applied to medical schools with the hope of becoming a professional hybrid of doctor and anthropologist. He chose Harvard Medical School, one of the few that would grant a combined degree. Of the fateful 1983 trip, Kidder wrote, "[Farmer] figured he'd find out if that was what he really wanted to become by trying out both disciplines in Haiti."

The country quickly got into Farmer's bloodstream and gave a sharper focus to his opposition to injustice. Indeed, Kidder paints Farmer as a man haunted to the point of sleeplessness by the idea of fellow humans forced to go without life's basics: shelter, food and water, and access to health care.

The saying "An institution is the lengthened shadow of a man" is an apt description of PIH. Its mission and philosophies were shaped by Farmer's determination to fight injustice. PIH embodied three core values:

1. The poor are entitled to equal access to quality medical care.

2. Treatment must be understood within the social context that defines all aspects of a patient's life. To get good health outcomes, one must attend to nonmedical issues such as poverty, hunger, sanitation, and racism.

3. Community-based delivery of care is not only cost-effective for chronic illness, but also likely to produce better outcomes.

When Farmer arrived in Cange, the area was in the grip of a tuberculosis epidemic. Tuberculosis can be treated with medications, but the treatment is lengthy (typically several months). If anything interrupts the treatment, not only is the disease let off the hook, but it also usually gets worse. Surviving bacteria often become resistant to standard drugs. Once that happens, there remain fewer treatment options, and they are much more expensive and more difficult to obtain. Worse, the drug-resistant strains of the bacteria can then spread to other people.

Farmer quickly saw that an adequate supply of medications was a necessary condition for successful treatment but not a sufficient one. Even if the medications are readily available, the patients still had to take them faithfully. Often, they did not.

Trying to understand why, Farmer studied the problem as much from an anthropologist's perspective as a doctor's. He saw that in order to treat a patient, you had to understand more than their disease. You had to understand their life.

Farmer examined every aspect of his patients' lives. What were the non-medical complications in their treatments? Could they pay for transportation to and from the clinic? Did they have food and clean water? Were their living conditions sanitary? What were the causes of stress in their lives? Did they have a source of income? Were they depressed? Did they believe that the medical treatments would work, or did they put their faith elsewhere? And, who else besides the patient lived in the home, and what was the state of *their* health?

Farmer dedicated PIH to improving outcomes by doing whatever was necessary to remove barriers to treatment. The typical Western approach would have been to throw more medicine at the problem. That was not an option in Haiti, where the medical infrastructure was limited and doctors were scarce—though that would not have been Farmer's first thought, anyway. His instinct was to focus on nonmedical conditions. He decided that if achieving better outcomes meant PIH needed to provide patients with food and water, education about hygiene, or transportation to and from the clinic, then that was what it would do.

But how could this pledge be made practical?

Ultimately, Farmer developed a solution as simple as the problem was complex. He experimented with assigning local community health workers (CHWs)—also called *accompagnateurs,* or accompanists—to each patient. Their responsibilities extended well beyond simply making sure that patients complied with the treatment programs. Each worker was also to become a partner in health. The *accompagnateurs* went into patient homes to understand their lives, diagnose barriers to treatment, and eliminate those barriers.

Behforouz describes the role this way: "What do we mean by accompaniment? We mean that you walk *with* the patient—not behind or in front of her—lending a shoulder, a sounding board, or a word of counsel or caution. The key is *solidarity with our patients*. You provide medical and psychological support; empowering, not enabling; together facing and managing challenges that neither you nor they can fix—poverty, racism, illiteracy, social isolation—so that you can help them swallow their pills every day and get to their appointments on time."

Critically, the *accompagnateurs* in Cange were residents of the community. PIH trained them on diseases and treatments, but their real value lay in their deep insight into local life. They often had greater influence over patients than did the doctors.

The approach worked astoundingly well—especially given that Farmer spent only $150 to $200 to treat tuberculosis, as compared to $15,000 or more in the United States, where the practice is to hospitalize tuberculosis patients.

The approach worked so well, in fact, that Farmer became a major figure in global public-health circles. He did not hesitate to challenge conventional wisdom. He believed that global health authorities were complacent and that they misunderstood the real nature of the problem they were facing. Tuberculosis, he argued, was not a disease that could be treated with medicine alone.

Farmer and one of his earliest PIH colleagues, Jim Kim, argued that the cost of medical treatments for tuberculosis would escalate as new multi-drug-resistant strains appeared. The physicians also warned that although tuberculosis was most prevalent in poor countries, the bacteria that caused the disease were indiscriminate. They could easily cross geographic and economic boundaries.

Meanwhile, under the leadership of Kim, PIH expanded its operations from Haiti to a slum in Lima. (Kim is now the president of Dartmouth College.) With some adaptations, Kim took the PIH model—community health workers' partnering to treat the patient's whole contextual life—and applied it in Lima to improve the lives of people like Miguel. The success in Peru led to substantial progress in convincing the World Health Organization and other global bodies of the effectiveness of PIH's approach.

Bringing the Partners In Health Model to the United States

The campus of Harvard Medical School is a stone's throw from the Roxbury neighborhood, home to many of Boston's poorest citizens. In 1997, the *Boston Globe* published an article calling attention to HIV/AIDS treatment disparities between rich and poor communities in the Boston area. It was a problem that Behforouz was familiar with. As a medical student, she had done research that showed alarmingly high AIDS mortality rates in Roxbury, Dorchester, and other poor enclaves of the city.

Spurred on by local health activists, PIH launched PACT in Boston in early 1998. The new organization's most urgent priority would be to improve the success rate of treatments for HIV/AIDS.

Behforouz began by endeavoring to build an organization that fully understood the CHW-centric model and was fully capable of executing it. The steps she took are instructive for any leader who is tasked to bring a reverse innovation home:

1. Behforouz traveled to Haiti and Peru to see the method in action firsthand.

2. She called frequently on Farmer, Kim, and other PIH leaders for advice and support.

3. She studied PIH's operating manuals, training syllabi, and guides for patients and physicians.

4. She hired people who were familiar, from direct experience, with the health and living conditions in poor countries.

5. She adopted PIH's core values as PACTs.

As indispensable as this transfer of knowledge was, Behforouz learned that PIH's methods couldn't be replicated verbatim in Boston. "We can take core elements from PIH, but we've also had to adapt for conditions here," she notes.

Doing so required experimentation. For example, at first, PACT did not know how frequently, or over what period, community health workers would need to visit patients. The program learned from experience, fine-tuning its methods for determining the intensity of treatment and for assessing when and whether a patient could be discharged. PACT developed a three-tiered hierarchy of daily, weekly, and monthly visits. Patients could graduate from level to level.

PACT also had to learn where it fit into the Boston medical community. Quite unlike PIH, which "builds" health care in poor countries where there is little existing infrastructure, PACT had to find ways to insert itself into Boston's dense network of health-care institutions.

In the telecommunications business, there is a concept known as *the last mile*. It refers to the final piece of enabling infrastructure that connects the backbone network to the individual customer's home. Without that last connecting element, the rest of the network has no practical value for an individual customer. In health care, for many poor patients, the last mile was missing. They did not benefit equally, or at all, from the healing powers of the nearby great institutions, gifted physicians, and proven treatments.

Behforouz saw PACT as the last mile for poor patients. But it wasn't easy to implement. Troublesome turf issues arose quickly.

One source of conflict proved serious enough that PACT had to reposition its mission. In its early days, PACT acted as a community-based provider of case-management services. But individual clients might have as many as seven case managers from various agencies and clinics. Behforouz quickly understood that in the battle against HIV, skirmishes among overlapping case-management agendas could create confusion and ill will. Worse, they could compromise patient outcomes.

PACT needed to find ways to complement, not compete with, existing programs. So, after considerable research, Behforouz shifted PACT's role from *case management* to *health promotion* for patients who were failing treatment in hospitals with Western-style methods. Hospitals were only too happy to hand over such patients to PACT, Behforouz says. "We did a lot of different iterations of the model. Our approach has always been 'experiment, learn, adapt, and change.'"

But Behforouz also faced an even deeper challenge. The PIH model treats CHWs not as social workers but as health interventionists. That was welcome in poor countries, where there was no ready alternative, but the shift was a profound challenge to institutional norms in the United States. "Community health workers had been viewed as facilitators of access to care, but not interventionists in their own right," explains Behforouz. PACT's model proposed giving CHWs a more central role in delivering care.

Health care is loaded with venerated traditions. Perhaps foremost among them is the exalted placement of physicians at the top of the pecking order. (Even organizations that have recently promoted patients to the center of the universe often have an asterisk giving physicians a dominant role in interpreting patients' best interests.) To be sure, physicians are very important. However, Behforouz—a physician herself—believes their outsized status exerts too great an influence on the way care is organized and delivered.

"We don't really support a wellness model in this country," she says. "Health care is focused instead on the end result of poor health behaviors. Incentives are built around a 'sick care' system. We have to turn the system upside down—from treating people when they are sick to preventive medicine. My argument is that community health workers should be a cornerstone of the health system." In that model, she says, physicians would "provide care at the top of their skill level only when wellness measures fail. Instead of having the CHW be an extender arm of the physician, have the physician be the extender arm of the CHW. We have to turn our current health-care system on its head."

Turning the dominant logic upside down is often necessary when reverse innovations make their way back home. Reverse innovations often bring transformation—that is, elevating the role of CHWs to interventionists and putting them on the leading edge of health-care services. Such changes are never easy, and venerated logic dies hard. Says Behforouz, "It drives me crazy that everyone wants to know the cost-effectiveness of a CHW, but we never question the cost-effectiveness of a physician."

These types of tensions are to be expected. As we have seen throughout this book, nothing is more powerful than success in helping to get past them.

Once PACT began to demonstrate strong results with clients, it won respect from providers of HIV medical services. PACT's launch was fortuitously timed, in that the HIV care community in Boston was desperate to find a solution for its toughest cases—patients who were failing treatment in the traditional medical system, primarily due to their inability to take prescribed medications. These were the patients on whom providers had simply given up. Often, these patients had histories of trauma, depression, substance abuse, and persistent social isolation. Such patients were being referred to PACT.

PACT's results were stunning—not just for the patients, but for the medical system. The CHW approach dramatically reduced the cost of patient care for Medicaid, the main insurer for PACT-referred patients. That's because the CHWs were extremely effective in helping people adhere to their prescribed treatment. Better treatment compliance significantly drove down hospitalization rates. An analysis of hospital billing records for forty PACT patients showed a 35 percent drop in inpatient hospital day use and an even bigger decline in hospitalization costs, from an average of $22,443 per patient to $12,926 per patient. This more than made up for PACT's cost of $3,600 per patient. Furthermore, patients became healthier. They had a clinically significant increase in median CD4 count from 145 to 220.[4]

Hiring, Training, and Supporting Community Health Workers

This kind of success can only be sustained if PACT is effective in recruiting, training, and retaining CHWs. Selecting the right people starts with a clear understanding of their role. Behforouz believes that the most important thing CHWs do is to eliminate the communication gap between doctors and patients. In her view, the unequal power dynamic in the doctor-patient relationship interferes with trust: "The fact that the community health worker is your neighbor, has had similar life experiences, is of the same culture, is *not* a person in a white coat, is in your territory, and can traverse both worlds—yours and that of the health-care system—is incredibly powerful. They are uniquely qualified to bring sophisticated medicine to patient homes and deliver individualized care within the conditions and belief systems that shape their patients' lives."

Because the ability to establish trust is so crucial, Behforouz seeks matches in culture and language between CHWs and the client base. Indeed, PACT's CHW corps is as multicultural as the client base. Out of twenty-five employees, ten speak Spanish. Others speak Portuguese, Haitian Creole, Ugandan, Cantonese, and Bengali. Most have experience working with disadvantaged populations in poor countries. Several were once PACT clients. "They understand poverty and marginalization," says Behforouz.

Not surprisingly, hiring is not solely résumé-based. "We have to really get to know the person. They go through a series of interviews with us. We do a lot of role-playing and case-based scenarios, and actually just listen to them talk. And that's how we select them."

Managing CHWs also brings unusual challenges. Behforouz notes that deep engagement between management and physicians isn't typically a high priority for health-care organizations. But she has seen that the PACT model simply cannot work without energetic engagement: "You have to be willing to invest in their training and supervision in an ongoing way."

PACT's community health workers are thrust into quasi-professional roles, but they may not have much formal education. And because they live in the neighborhoods they work in, they might struggle with some of the same problems that bedevil their clients: child-care issues, violence, and a lack of resources. PACT managers need to be creative, flexible, and supportive when such issues arise.

Moreover, community health work is compelling, intense, and draining. A CHW is, by definition, a prime candidate for burnout. To keep that prospect at bay, Behforouz has created an atmosphere of open communication: "We encourage people to talk frequently, with each other and with their supervisors, about their experiences. One of the things that shocks people is that our community health workers probably have four to five hours of training or supervision a week. In most other models, they're lucky if they get an hour a month."

Extending the Impact

After building a track record of success in Boston, Behforouz faces the natural question "What's next?" PACT is endeavoring to attack other chronic conditions—diabetes, for example. It partnered with a clinic across the street from its Dorchester office to adapt the HIV/AIDS health-promotion mission to care for diabetics. Behforouz notes that diabetes outcomes depend on many factors other than medication adherence, including nutrition and exercise.

PACT is also working on geographic expansion. In 2006, the New York City Health Department asked Behforouz to consider expanding PACT to help the city manage its most difficult HIV patients. Rather than create a wholesale replication of the program in New York, PACT "trains the trainers," who implement its intervention techniques within twenty-eight clinics and hospitals in the New York boroughs.

But this is a little like franchising a delicate art. Being so removed from patients and CHWs is a slightly uncomfortable stretch for a hands-on organization. "We are learning a lot about that dynamic and how to manage it," says Behforouz. "We're working towards this idea of integrating our model into existing health treatment centers, as opposed to being a separate community-based organization. To make progress, we're having to learn how to be effective consultants. It's a real struggle for us. We get a lot of calls for our help, but we're not the fly-in-and-fly-out types, saying 'This is what you need, and thank you for our check.' And the reality is that if you don't have full buy-in, if the institution isn't willing to make investments at all levels, it's very difficult to make changes as an outside force."

More and more, though, that's what PACT is being asked to do: be the outside force that transfers the model and integrates it into clinic and hospital operations. Increasingly, PACT is giving technical assistance to other health-care providers.

Implications for Health-Care Reform

It is clear—from the growing demands on PACT and from the multitude of experiments elsewhere in the health-care field—that the world is starting to catch up with Farmer's innovation. The use of community health workers has become one of many dimensions of the ongoing conversation about health-care reform in the United States. And there is now a wider understanding of the link between poverty and the risk of bad health outcomes.

For example, *New York Times* columnist David Bornstein looked at the work of Health Leads, an organization that places trained volunteers in urban hospitals to work with patients whose conditions have been caused or worsened by conditions of poverty. Doctors at these facilities, writes Bornstein, "now regularly 'prescribe' a wide range of basic resources—like food assistance, housing improvements, or heating fuel subsidies—which Health Leads' volunteers 'fill,' applying their problem solving skills (and tenacity) to identify resources anywhere they may be available."[5]

Behforouz worries, however, that such experiments, though inspiring, are still inadequate: "I'm involved with a lot of different committees that are thinking about health-care transformation. What's hard is that we're trying to fix a model that is fundamentally broken. We have accepted our current model and try to improve it. It won't work. You can put lipstick on a bulldog, but it still looks like a bulldog. We need to look to community-based models of care that are effective but often go unrecognized, perhaps because much of the care is delivered by paraprofessionals who have not been extensively schooled in the biomedical model and don't practice office-based care."

Reverse innovations are never incremental. If they were, they'd take root in rich countries, not poor ones. Only organizations that dispense with the lipstick-on-a-bulldog approach—at least for purposes of running an experiment—can be successful in bringing a reverse innovation home.

We see great promise in the CHW model. But it is likely to grow far more explosively in the developing world than in rich countries, where its spread will be hindered by the extensive infrastructure that already exists. That's the nature of reverse innovation stories that are shaped by a large infrastructure gap. The rate of adoption in rich countries is paced by the rate of replacement of the standing infrastructure.

Nonetheless, there are signs of movement. The Mayo Clinic and Kaiser Permanente have implemented programs to closely monitor patients with chronic conditions. It's an area receiving intense focus, as chronic care accounts for an ever-rising proportion of total medical spending. It is also the area in which nonmedical spending is likely to have the greatest impact. The two organizations are using both live visitation and computerized telemedicine applications to bring effective disease management into patients' homes. The result is a lower cost of care, a reduced rate of hospitalizations, and better health outcomes.

We hope that these organizations and others push their endeavors further. In fact, there are many promising areas where rich countries can adopt poor-world health-care solutions. Several organizations in poor countries, for example, have shown that taking an assembly-line approach to surgical procedures to correct certain medical conditions can dramatically reduce costs. As we mentioned in earlier chapters, India's Narayana Hrudayalaya Hospital and Aravind Eye Hospital perform surgeries for sums that are orders of magnitude less expensive (yet of equal quality) than comparable procedures in the rich world.

Health care in developed nations is entering an era of fundamental transformation. Historically, medical knowledge and medical technology have established the limit of what we can accomplish. In the new era, cost will be the primary constraint. It seems obvious that the places to look for breakthrough cost-cutting innovations are in parts of the world where resources are scarcest. As such, reverse innovation has enormous potential to help reshape health care.

Partners In Health's Playbook Lessons

1. *Leverage opportunities to move emerging-market innovations to other parts of the world* (Reverse Innovation Playbook lesson 2). This, the last step in reverse innovation, requires intense effort. PACT director, Heidi Behforouz, had to fully understand the CHW model first developed in Haiti and Peru, through studies, mentoring, travel, and hiring people who had done the work. Then, she had to be flexible, adapting the model for a rich-world environment dense with health-care infrastructure.

2. *LGTs must develop clean-slate solutions and organizational designs* (Reverse Innovation Playbook lesson 7). Only through fierce, independent thought—shown, for example, by PIH in Haiti and elsewhere and, in turn, by Behforouz in the launch and continuous refinement of PACT—can truly radical goals be achieved. Critically, this includes challenging the dominant logic of the organization or industry when establishing organizational designs for LGTs.

Questions for Reflection

1. Are the managers of rich-world operations in your company at least aware of ways in which your company has innovated in the developing world? What would it take to fully exploit those innovations worldwide?

2. What organizational sacred cows need to be challenged if your organization is to succeed at reverse innovation?

3. In your industry and in the developing world, what is the intersection between "good for your company" and "good for society?"

A Call to Action

Reverse innovation has the potential not only to transform your company, but also to transform the world.

THE CENTRAL PURPOSE of almost every business book is to galvanize readers to take action. *Reverse Innovation* is no different. Our deepest wish is that you *will* take action!

Let's not, however, minimize the difficulties that you will face when you do. If you have read this far, you should now have a healthy respect for the many varieties of jeopardy a reverse innovation effort will need to overcome. You've seen this in several of the examples in this book. Projects hung in the balance. Failure seemed all too possible.

But this is to be expected. Reverse innovation efforts inevitably test the commitment, resiliency, and passion of the innovators. Equally, they test the gumption and long-term vision of the leaders to whom the innovators report and of the organization as a whole.

Nonetheless, the reverse innovation journey is one worth embarking upon. Let's look at what one possible successful journey could look like from the perspective of a business unit general manager in a global corporation, using the Reverse Innovation Playbook as a guide.

The journey often begins, as it did for several of the case examples in this book, when your core product hits a growth wall in the developing world. It's an immediate hot-button issue, because these days, the emerging economies account for the bulk of world GDP growth. If your company is not growing in poor countries, it is not growing much at all.

The most likely diagnosis is that your product is simply a poor fit for the emerging economies. There is a tremendous needs gap between what your customers in the rich world want and what mainstream customers in the poor world crave. You can't simply *export*; you must *innovate* (Reverse Innovation Playbook lesson 1).

Your anxieties are heightened by a relatively unknown company headquartered in the developing world. This company is growing much more quickly than you are and is even starting to make noise in your home market (lesson 3). It's time to take action.

Recognizing that you can't simply visit China or India for a week and understand the market's needs, you embark on a rigorous, clean-slate needs analysis (lesson 7). You question every one of your company's deeply embedded assumptions about what customers want. You call on outside experts that can help fully research the market.

Once you are sure you have a clear understanding of what customers want, you charter a local growth team (LGT) and name a leader. The LGT also adopts a clean-slate mind-set. It develops a solution from scratch and designs its organization from scratch (lesson 7).

With the LGT leader, you identify one or more opportunities to leverage the global organization's skills and resources. You dedicate significant time and energy to ensuring that the LGT and the global organization develop a healthy partnership (lesson 8). The relationship allows the LGT to build on what already exists without reflexively or subconsciously duplicating assumptions about needs and solutions. You further commit to routine and thorough reviews of the LGT's plans, helping the team structure disciplined experiments that resolve critical assumptions quickly and at minimal cost (lesson 9).

With a lot of hard work and a little bit of luck, the product launch is a success. You immediately look for opportunities to duplicate the success in other parts of the world (lesson 2). You discover that many other emerging markets around the world have very similar needs and that even a few marginalized markets in the rich world are of interest. You anticipate trends that might close the needs gaps, and you make preparations to launch the product into mainstream rich-world markets when the time is right.

Meanwhile, around your company, interest in your project is rising.

Disappointing growth results in the developing world are not unique to your product line—they are commonplace throughout your corporation. Increasing the win rate in poor countries has become your CEO's preoccupation. Before you know it, your project has become your company's premier example of how to win.

Your CEO begins to make some powerful steps to catalyze reverse innovation. He or she starts pouring more money into LGTs. The CEO reassigns experienced executives to developing-world responsibilities and adjusts the reporting structure so that the most senior executives in the developing world have general-management responsibilities and report directly to the CEO (lesson 4). For these new general managers, the CEO even establishes distinct scorecards that focus strictly on the developing world (lesson 6). And he or she launches several initiatives to strengthen the reverse innovation mind-set throughout the company, moving several critical annual company events each year to the emerging economies and making growth in the emerging economies the top theme (lesson 5).

Meanwhile, you are in line for a promotion. The CEO calls you to the office to assess your interest in becoming the company's new head of China.

That's what the success scenario looks like. It sounds easy when condensed onto one page, but you will have all of the normal uncertainties inherent in any new business launch. On top of that, you'll have to contend with the overt and omnipresent tug of your company's shorter-term pressures, plus the more subtle tug of its dominant logic. These are daunting barriers, but you can overcome them with a bit of smarts . . . and a basket of passion.

Passion as a Motivating Force for Reverse Innovation

Indeed, all the leaders whom we have spoken with exhibit an extraordinary level of passion about their reverse innovation efforts. Much of this consuming passion is rooted in the potential to address so many unmet needs in emerging markets and, in doing so, to improve people's lives.

Consider, for example, Mehmood Khan's determination not only to please the palates of PepsiCo's customers, but also to lower their risk for certain diseases. Or contemplate the intense ambition shared by GE Healthcare's India-based ECG engineers to deliver affordable, easy-to-use, and portable diagnostic tools. Or recall the commitment of Heidi Behforouz, director of Partners In Health's PACT program, to radically reform the doctor-centric way health care is delivered.

To be sure, we have focused this book primarily on the inner workings of multinationals and the specific challenges they face in catalyzing emerging-market growth. Nonetheless, in reverse innovation, we have seen that the interests of business and the interests of people are more nearly aligned than in most other contexts. It is, in fact, nearly impossible to overlook the power of reverse innovation as an instrument for solving some of the world's most vexing social problems.

Let's step back and reflect just briefly on a bigger picture—not the needs of individual corporations, but the needs of individual citizens of planet Earth. From that vantage point, it matters less whether the legacy multinationals or the emerging giants win the great reverse innovation contest. What matters are the benefits the contest will deliver over time.

It will produce enormous change. It will accelerate innovation in the developing world, where innovation matters most in people's lives. It will lift economies. It will lead to higher standards of living—better health, wider access to quality education, and greater economic opportunity.

It took generations for the United States to advance from poverty to its present level of prosperity. If all goes well, today's developing countries can make that journey in half that time. And if multinationals aggressively bring their full capabilities to bear, it might happen faster still.

Indeed, to have a tremendous impact on the emerging economies, multinationals need not abandon their business mission or redefine their charters with a focus on charity or corporate social responsibility. Our call, quite to the contrary, is for businesses to do what they *must* do to thrive: identify unmet needs, innovate, compete, and grow. To describe business's participation in efforts to improve the lives of the poor, some executives and academics use terms like *social innovation, inclusive innovation,* and *inclusive growth.* We'd like to suggest a different term. Let's just call it *business*—business at its best.

A Reverse Innovation Opportunity: Affordable Housing

An example of a critical unmet need in the developing world is affordable housing. In 2010, Vijay Govindarajan and Christian Sarkar proposed the aspiration of a $300 house on the *Harvard Business Review* blog network (www.300house.com). The response was overwhelming—nothing less than a revelation. Thoughtful critiques poured in and inspired volunteers came forward to contribute.

A $300 house would transform the lives of hundreds of millions of the world's most desperately poor citizens. It would turn strangers into neighbors, slums into neighborhoods.

Despite the ultralow price point, a $300 house could include basic modern services such as running water and electricity. More importantly, it would create a community that shared access to computers, cell phones, televisions, water filters, solar panels, and clean-burning wood stoves. In so doing, it would enable the poor to leapfrog the limits of slums. It would make possible healthy and safe living conditions and a decent education.

The idea of regenerating slums is certainly not new. In the past, however, the focus has been on potential solutions from nongovernment organizations, nonprofits, and governments—all on the assumption that the poor can't be customers.

That assumption is mistaken. A $300 house is not charity; it's a challenge for commerce. Not only are the world's poor relevant customers, but they represent the fastest-growing customer segment. Meeting their needs requires innovative solutions that have to scale—something that multinationals know how to do. Building $300 homes and servicing their residents is a mega-opportunity, with billions of dollars of profit at stake.

When we think about this idea, we think of our children. They are incredibly smart, but not necessarily smarter than a young child now living in India's filthiest slum. Our children have what that person does not—the ability to choose among many opportunities and to determine their own path. Reverse innovation represents not only the open door to an affordable home, but the door to a world of opportunity.

We hope you share our passion. And we welcome your ideas—not only about the $300 house, but also about other social purposes to which reverse innovation might contribute.

Your Role in Advancing Reverse Innovation . . . and an Invitation

Finally, we are mindful that the discipline of reverse innovation remains a work in progress. Indeed, while researching and writing our book, we have thought of this as a next-practice topic rather than a best-practice one. Much is still to be learned!

For example, while there are growing numbers of stories about innovations developed in and for emerging markets, we see relatively fewer cases of those innovations coming back "home" to rich-world mass markets. As we have described in some of the cases, companies must first wrestle with difficult questions of cannibalization, timing, and portfolio-management strategies. And yet, we believe that full-circle migrations will proliferate quickly.

Therefore, we invite you, our readers, to join our developer community that will further refine reverse innovation in what is sure to be a process of continuing discovery. Even as we were starting to write this book, that process of collaborative discovery revealed its remarkable potential when we heard, out of the blue, from Harman International's Sachin Lawande— whom you met in chapter 9. Lawande had read our first article about reverse innovation in the October 2009 issue of *Harvard Business Review*. He sent us an e-mail saying that what we had described in *HBR* sounded very much like a project he had just completed at Harman. We got in touch with him and were instantly impressed by what Harman had accomplished. Lawande kindly agreed to share with us the fascinating story of Project SARAS.

We very much hope we will hear from you, too, as you apply the principles of reverse innovation in your own enterprises. Even with all of the guidance we have supplied here, we understand that succeeding will always be a difficult undertaking and there is plenty still to learn.

We wish you good fortune, and we look forward to hearing from you at vg@dartmouth.edu and chris.trimble@dartmouth.edu.

Reverse Innovation Toolkit

You can use several practical diagnostics and templates to move your reverse innovation efforts forward.

Reverse Innovation Discussion Guide

To guide a useful managerial discussion in your company about reverse innovation, consider the following topics and questions:

1. Reverse Innovation Strategy

1. Which emerging economies are strategic for your company? Out of the 150 poor countries, which ones have the following important elements?
   - The bulk of future customers
   - Potential for future growth
   - Talented, low-cost skill base
   - Manufacturing capabilities
   - Physical infrastructure
   - Institutional infrastructure

- Social infrastructure

- Foundation to build R&D know-how

- Potential new competitors

2. Other than price sensitivity, what are the starkest differences between the needs of your customers in poor countries and the needs of your customers in rich countries? Consider differences in performance expectations, the availability and reliability of infrastructure, environmental pressures, regulation, and preferences.

3. Can you meet the needs of your customers in poor countries simply by customizing your existing offerings? Or, is clean-slate innovation needed?

4. Have you so far seen examples of reverse innovation in your own industry or an adjacent one?

5. What trends might eventually make these innovations attractive to mainstream customers in rich countries?

6. Which emerging giants are on your company's radar screen? What innovations have they brought to market? Might they enter your home market soon?

7. Does your capital budget show how capital is divided between poor countries and rich ones? Is the capital flowing to the greatest growth opportunities?

2. Reverse Innovation Mind-Set

1. Which of the following assumptions are commonplace in your company? (These assumptions are *inhibitors* of reverse innovation.)

- Emerging markets are irrelevant.

- Rich countries are the most technologically advanced, so innovation and learning will move from rich countries to poor countries.

- Sales of our existing products and services will gradually increase as emerging economies grow. Therefore, we just need to be patient.

- Existing products and services can be readily customized so that they will succeed in emerging markets.

- The best approach to emerging markets is to lower price by stripping down our existing products and services.

- The bulk of the customers in poor countries have low per-capita incomes, low sophistication, and low affordability. Their needs can be met by cheap products based on older technology.

- Once per-capita income reaches a threshold in poor countries, consumers will buy rich-world products.

- Poor countries today are where the rich countries were in their infancy. Poor countries will evolve in the same way that wealthy economies did. As they develop, poor countries will catch up with rich ones.

- Winning in emerging markets is almost entirely about achieving a very low price.

- Only *product* innovation is necessary to win in emerging markets.

- Our major competitors are other multinationals.

- We can neutralize local players by outspending them or by simply acquiring them.

- Products that address poor countries' special needs can't be sold in rich countries, because these products are not good enough to compete there.

- It is impossible to earn healthy profits in emerging markets.

- We cannot make the same high contribution-margin percentage in poor countries that we make in rich countries.

- We excel in product leadership and technological leadership. These are inconsistent with the ultra-low-cost products needed in poor countries.

- Global brands stand for premium products and high quality. We run the risk of diluting our global brands by competing in a low-cost market.

- We will cannibalize sales of premium offerings if we compete in a low-cost market.

- The role of our employees in emerging markets is to reduce the cost of our operations.

- The role of our employees in emerging markets is to sell and distribute our global products.

2. How widely held are the following assumptions among key decision makers? (These assumptions acknowledge the full power of the reverse innovation phenomenon.)

- To succeed in emerging markets, we must build new products and services, starting from scratch.

- Innovations in poor countries can transform global markets.

- The emerging giants might threaten us in our home markets.

3. People Development

1. Does your senior leadership team have the right skill sets for driving innovation in poor countries? If not, whom do you need to hire?

2. Does your company send its next generation of senior leaders on expat assignments in poor countries?

3. How often does your senior team travel to poor countries? When did your company last hold an important internal event in a poor country?

4. Shifting Power and Authority to Emerging Markets

1. Does your company have a CEO of India and a CEO of China who report directly to the CEO? Is there a CEO of emerging economies that coordinates the development of products for all emerging economies?

2. To what extent are your company's leaders in emerging markets empowered to launch innovation initiatives? How daunting is the approval process they would face?

3. Where are your top fifty leaders located geographically? Does this geographic distribution match the geographic distribution of growth opportunities for your company?

4. Given the demands of running the existing business, how much time can your senior leaders in rich countries spend thinking about growth opportunities in poor countries?

5. How many directors with deep experience in emerging economies are on your company's board?

5. Project Initiation

1. How heavily has your company invested in rigorously diagnosing customer needs in emerging markets?

2. How likely is it that your R&D teams located in the rich world will recognize an innovation opportunity in poor countries and develop a solution?

3. How extensive is the interaction between your emerging-markets people who understand customer problems (e.g., sales, marketing, market research) and those who are able to develop solutions (e.g., research, development, engineering)?

4. Are your R&D centers in emerging economies chartered to develop new products for their own countries? For other poor countries around the world?

6. Project Implementation

1. Has your company ever commissioned a local growth team (LGT) with full business capabilities in a poor country?

2. Consider a specific reverse innovation project or potential project. How will you build the LGT? How would it look different from the rest of the company?

3. In your company, what global assets would be most valuable to an LGT? How easy would it be for an LGT to leverage these assets?

4. How can you guard against cannibalization when ultra-low-cost products are brought from poor countries into rich countries?

5. How does your company evaluate leaders of reverse innovation projects?

Application Exercises

To move from conversations to projects, the following exercises and templates may be very helpful.

1. Clean-Slate Customer Needs Assessment

A solid reverse innovation endeavor begins with a *clean-slate* needs assessment. Your company's knowledge about rich-world customer needs must be thoroughly questioned.

This is best accomplished through in-depth market research. To be sure to establish the right mind-set in advance, however, try the following simple exercises:

1. *Gaps analysis:* In your industry, what are the *needs gaps* between developed and developing economies? Can you identify any trends

TABLE A-1

Gaps analysis worksheet

Type of gap	Is there a gap?	If yes, describe.	Describe any trends that may close the gap.
Performance			
Infrastructure			
Sustainability			
Regulatory			
Preferences			
Other:			

TABLE A-2

Clean-slate market assessment worksheet

Dimension of value	Rank importance in rich world	Rank importance in developing world
Price		
Performance		
Quality		
Reliability		
Service		
Other:		
Other:		
Other:		

that will close these gaps over the next few years? (Refer to chapter 2 for descriptions of the generic gaps and trends). Table A-1 is a worksheet you can fill out to help you with your needs assessment.

2. *Customer priorities:* Consider the dimensions of value that your product or service delivers to your customers in the rich world, and rank-order the importance of each. How do the priorities of your customers in poor countries compare? Use these priority rankings to fill in the worksheet in table A-2.

3. *Future growth opportunities:* Looking ahead a bit, the trends that you identified in question 1 above will help you anticipate opportunities to eventually bring your innovation into mainstream markets in the rich world. Of course, there may also be opportunities to move the innovation into broadly similar markets right away—either in marginalized rich-world markets or in other emerging markets. With each move, you should reconsider customer needs, though not from scratch. Use the worksheet presented in table A-3 to catalog these opportunities.

TABLE A-3

Near-term global expansion worksheet

Growth opportunities	Most significant difference in needs, if any
Marginalized rich-world market 1	
Marginalized rich-world market 2	
Developing nation 1	
Developing nation 2	
Developing nation 3	

TABLE A-4

Clean-slate product innovation worksheet

	Component	Reuse rich-country component	Custom redesign in-house	Buy off the shelf from a third party
#1				
#2				
#3				
#4				
#5				
#6				

2. Clean-Slate Solution Design

Once you thoroughly understand customer needs, it is time to develop the solution. Again, do not assume that what works in the rich world will also work in developing nations.

1. *Innovations in the product:* For tangible products, especially those made up of several distinct components, the worksheet presented in table A-4 may help you establish the right mind-set.

2. *Innovations in the business model:* In many cases, a clean-slate solution design implies rethinking not just the product, but also the

TABLE A-5

Clean-slate business model innovation worksheet

Link in value chain	Leverage rich-country processes	Build from scratch in-country	Partner in-country
Manufacturing			
Sales			
Marketing			
Customer service			
Other:			
Other:			

value chain through which you deliver the product. Reverse innovation is often also business model innovation. Where will you leverage what already exists in your global organization? Build from scratch? Develop new partnerships? Use table A-5 to help lay out the value chain.

3. Clean-Slate Organizational Design

Building a well-functioning LGT can be one of the most challenging aspects of reverse innovation. To get off to a fast start, consider carefully the following two exercises:

1. What skill sets does the LGT need to succeed? Which are available in-house? For which will you have to make external hires? Table A-6 will help you answer these questions.

2. Now, thinking through the same skill sets, indicate which should be the most influential on the LGT, compared with who is the most influential in your rich-world organization. Note: significant shifts in power are often necessary, and they can be tricky to manage. Use the worksheet in table A-7 to see where these imbalances lie.

TABLE A-6

Clean-slate organizational design worksheet

	Skill	Available in-house	Must make outside hires
#1			
#2			
#3			
#4			

TABLE A-7

LGT power and influence worksheet

	Skill	Rank appropriate level of influence in LGT	Rank level of influence in your existing organization
#1			
#2			
#3			
#4			

4. Run a Disciplined Experiment

There are two types of acceptable outcomes in an innovation effort: a success, and a failure that comes as quickly and inexpensively as possible. The most undesirable outcome is a long, expensive, and painful failure.

Therefore, as a reverse innovation initiative moves forward, you want to be sure that you spend a little to learn a lot. To accomplish this, you must test the most critical unknowns as early and inexpensively as possible.

Use table A-8 to list the unknowns your project faces. Be as specific as possible. Consider the following generic types of unknowns:

1. Have you correctly understood the customer problem?

2. Will your solution address the customer problem?

3. How many units will your customers demand at your target price?

TABLE A-8

Critical unknowns worksheet

	Unknowns	Degree of uncertainty (scale of 1 to 5)	Degree of consequentiality (scale of 1 to 5)	Total
#1				
#2				
#3				
#4				
#5				
#6				
#7				
#8				
#9				
#10				

4. How well have you estimated your costs?

5. Do you have the capabilities to execute?

6. Have you planned the right tactics for going to market?

7. Who are your competitors today? Who will enter the market? How will competition affect demand for your products?

Now, using a scale of 1 to 5, rate each of the unknowns on its degree of uncertainty and the degree of consequentiality if you are wrong. The unknowns with the highest total score are the most critical—the ones you should try to test first, if possible.

A Research Agenda

There is still a great deal to learn about
reverse innovation.

Reverse innovation is a recent phenomenon about which relatively little is known.[1] Therefore, we chose grounded theory building as our methodology—a qualitative, clinical, and longitudinal approach based on field studies. This was the appropriate choice because theory in this area is only just emerging; it is best advanced by uncovering new concepts rather than by testing hypotheses. Also, reverse innovation is a dynamic and complex phenomenon. It requires data spanning several years, not just a snapshot. For this reason, we drew on several methodological guideposts for our research.[2]

Though our research was exploratory, we built upon the pioneering and fundamental work of several international business and strategy scholars. Of particular note is the work of Ray Vernon.[3] Vernon developed the product-cycle theory of international expansion based on the experience of American multinationals. He saw the United States as the center of breakthrough innovation in the immediate postwar period, because the nation had a significant lead in technology and per-capita income over the rest of the world. Innovations, Vernon argued, were spread by American multinationals to Western Europe and Japan and finally to developing countries.

Vernon later extended the product-cycle hypothesis as Europe and Japan closed their technology and income gaps with the United States, and he showed how innovations flowed in multiple directions between the triad (the United States, Europe, and Japan) of markets.[4] Our intent was to extend Vernon's product-cycle theory again, this time by postulating that innovations can flow in a new direction: from poor countries to rich ones.

We also drew upon the work of several scholars who have studied developed-world multinationals and who showed how these companies balance competing needs for global scale and local responsiveness by developing global offerings and then customizing them for local markets.[5] Although reverse innovation may appear to be a special case of this familiar problem, the amount of local responsiveness required in poor countries is considerably larger. It requires a clean-slate approach to innovation, as opposed to the simpler method of making adaptations to existing offerings.

Give its "next practice" nature, our book opens doors for new research, including additional efforts to develop theory and endeavors to test the many hypotheses implied by our work. We organize potential avenues for research under three headings: research on innovation, developed-world multinationals, and emerging-market competitors. In 2011, Vijay Govindarajan and Ravi Ramamurti published a comprehensive discussion about these research possibilities.[6]

Innovation

Reverse innovation is a special category of innovation. As such, the general research on innovation has direct applicability. New research could explore the connections in at least the following three ways.

1. How Can the Theory of Disruptive Innovation Be Applied in Emerging Markets?

Clay Christensen's 1997 work on disruptive innovation has intriguing connections with reverse innovation.[7] There is an overlap between reverse innovation and disruptive innovation, though not a one-to-one relationship. Some, but not all, illustrations of reverse innovation are also illustrations of disruptive innovation.

A disruptive innovation has a particular dynamic that endangers incumbents. The incumbent's product has two primary dimensions of merit, A and B. (For example, A could be quality and B could be speed of delivery.) Mainstream customers are mostly interested in A, but there is a minority customer set that values B more than A. The disruptive innovation, at launch, is weak on A but strong on B. As a result, it attracts only the minority. Because mainstream customers don't want the innovation, incumbents tend to ignore the innovation while new entrants exploit the opportunity. Over time, however, technology improves, and the innovation gets better and better at A. Eventually, it meets the needs of mainstream customers on dimension A, and since they also place at least some value on B, they start choosing the innovation. The incumbent is suddenly disrupted; it has ignored the new technology all along.

In Christensen's famous study of the disk-drive industry, dimension A was the capacity of the disk drive, and B was the size of the disk drive. Christensen showed that new entrants repeatedly disrupted incumbents by introducing smaller disk drives with lower capacity. Initially, mainstream customers were uninterested. They needed more memory, not less. But over time, the capacity of the smaller drives went up and up until mainstream customers were interested.

In chapter 2, we identified five gaps that create the possibility of reverse innovation: the performance gap, infrastructure gap, sustainability gap, regulatory gap, and preferences gap. Only the performance gap is a clear illustration of disruptive innovation. Dimension A is performance; dimension B is price. A new technology that offers low performance at an ultralow price is immediately attractive in poor countries but not in rich ones. Over time, however, the technology improves, its performance improves, and eventually the innovation becomes attractive to mainstream customers in rich countries. Future research could fully explore the application of the theory of disruptive innovation to the specific case of reverse innovations created by performance gaps.

2. How Can Bottom-of-the-Pyramid Innovations Migrate from Poor to Rich Countries?

C. K. Prahalad's work on bottom-of-the-pyramid innovations has been extended by other scholars.[8] Future research could examine what types of bottom-of-the-pyramid innovations are most likely to migrate from poor countries to rich countries, and what processes enable such migration.

The reverse innovations that we have profiled tend to target the emerging middle class in developing countries, or the middle of the pyramid. For instance, the Tata Nano, the $2,000 car, targets the middle of the pyramid, not the bottom.

3. What Processes and Mechanisms Enable Poor-World Innovations to Trickle Up to Rich-World Countries?

Pankaj Ghemawat has argued that there is a large distance between rich and poor countries.[9] In fact, it is this large distance that makes clean-slate innovations in poor countries a necessity. Won't that same distance prevent the migration of innovations from poor to rich countries?

We have offered a theory of gaps and trends that might explain why innovations can defy gravity and flow uphill. Our arguments and hypotheses need to be tested rigorously to determine the contingencies. Are they industry-specific? Product-specific? Also, more research is needed on the organizational mechanisms and incentive structures that can facilitate the trickle-up process.

Developed-World Multinationals

There is a rich history of research on Western multinationals. This literature can be extended in three ways.

4. What Can Western Multinationals Learn from the Emerging Giants?

Prior literature has much to say about what Western multinationals can teach local firms in poor countries. Some spillovers from Western multinationals are good, such as improvements to the local supplier base, and others are not so good, such as the suffocation of the development of indigenous technologies.[10]

We have argued that one of the triggers of reverse innovation is the rise of such emerging giants as Tata and Lenovo. A fruitful research inquiry could focus on *reverse spillovers,* or movements of knowledge from developing countries to the rich world. What can Western multinationals learn from emerging giants? What incentive mechanisms are needed to facilitate such learning processes?

5. How Should Multinationals Structure and Manage Local Growth Teams to Execute a Reverse Innovation Initiative?

Many researchers have developed general theories about innovation execution.[11] Such theories can be extended and refined for the specific context of executing reverse innovation projects, while simultaneously maintaining excellence in glocalization.

6. How Can a Western Multinational Overcome Its Dominant Logic?

Developed-world multinationals, especially winners, struggle in emerging markets. Why? Success creates a dominant logic.[12] As we have argued, business models that lead to success in rich countries do not always work in poor countries. Researchers can examine how CEOs of Western multinationals can become more effective at reverse innovation by defeating the dominant logic built on rich-world success formulas.

Emerging-Market Firms

Academics have recently become interested in the structure and conduct of developing-world firms.[13] Our book is written from the standpoint of rich-world multinationals. The insights, however, can just as well be used by local firms in poor countries to practice reverse innovation. This suggests several promising lines of research inquiry.

7. Which Firms—Western Multinationals or Emerging Giants—Are Better Suited to Unlock Opportunities in Poor Countries?

In chapter 4, under the heading "Creating Links to Global Resources," we listed several strong advantages held by local firms. Future research can build a theory of comparative advantage between local firms and multinationals. Such theories need empirical validation.

8. Which Firms—Western Multinationals or Emerging Giants—Are Better Suited to Migrate Innovations from Poor Countries to Rich Ones?

Western multinationals are likely to have the edge, given their global brand, global presence, and global distribution. This conjecture needs to be evaluated and tested rigorously.

9. How Can the Experiences of the Globalization of Japanese and Korean Firms Inform the Globalization of Emerging Giants from Poor Countries?

Prior research has examined how Japanese and Korean firms entered the U.S. market at the low end in the 1970s and 1980s and subsequently moved up to middle and high-end segments.[14] This literature can help build theories about how firms from India, China, and other poor countries are likely to practice reverse innovation. In making the comparison, however, several important differences must be kept in mind:

1. The 1980s-era economic disparity between Japan or Korea and the United States is not as great as today's economic disparity between poor countries and rich ones.

2. The largest of the poor countries, India and China, are far larger than Japan or Korea.

3. Western multinationals could not compete in Japan and Korea, because of both tariff and nontariff barriers. As a result, local firms in Japan and Korea were able to build profit sanctuaries in their domestic markets and use those profits to subsidize their globalization efforts. India and China do not enjoy such an advantage. They face brutal competition from multinationals in their domestic markets.

4. The context within which emerging giants globalize today is very different. The world itself has dramatically changed in the past four decades. For example, it is flatter today than it was in the 1970s, thereby opening up different globalization paths.[15]

NOTES

Chapter 1

1. All quotes from Mehmood Khan are from telephone interviews with the authors, May and July 2010.

2. For more, see Tarun Khanna, V. Kasturi Rangan, and Merlina Anocaran, "Narayana Hrudayalaya Heart Hospital: Cardiac Care for the Poor," HBS Case 505078-PDF-ENG (Boston: Harvard Business School Publishing, 2011); "The Henry Ford Model of Heart Surgery," *Wall Street Journal*, November 25, 2009.

3. We will use the term *poor country* only in the narrow sense that The World Bank uses it— to describe a nation with a low GDP per capita. We will use *poor people* in the same way—only in the strictest economic meaning of the word *poor.*

4. Jeff Immelt, Vijay Govindarajan, and Chris Trimble, "How GE Is Disrupting Itself," *Harvard Business Review*, October 2009, 56–65.

5. We used the International Monetary Fund's 2010 World Economic Outlook Databases, published in October 2010 and available at www.imf.org.

6. We defined *rich countries* as those with at least $23,500 of income per person per year at purchasing power parity, about one-half of the per-capita income in the United States.

7. We have used GDP data adjusted for purchasing power parity.

8. David C. Everitt, quoted in Pete Engardio, "Emerging Giants: The New Multinationals; They're Smart and Hungry, and They Want Your Customers," *BusinessWeek*, July 31, 2006.

9. All quotes from Anjou Choudhari are from a telephone interview with the authors in April 2010.

Chapter 2

1. Juan Alcacer et al., "Emerging Nokia?" Case 710-429 (Boston: Harvard Business School Publishing, 2011).

2. When an improving technology closes a performance gap, a reverse innovation is also a disruptive innovation. See Clayton M. Christensen, *The Innovator's Dilemma* (Boston: Harvard Business School Press, 1997).

Chapter 3

1. All of the currently dominant ideas fit within the glocalization paradigm, including these: Yves Doz and C. K. Prahalad's "integration-responsiveness" grid, in Yves Doz and C. K. Prahalad, *The Multinational Mission: Balancing Local Demands and Global Vision* (New York: Free Press, 1987); Christopher Bartlett and Sumantra Ghoshal's concept of transnational enterprise in Christopher A. Bartlett and Sumantra Ghoshal, *Managing Across Borders: The Transnational Solution* (Boston: Harvard Business School Press, 1988); and Pankaj Ghemawat's "adaptation-aggregation" trade-off as described in Pankaj Ghemawat, *Redefining Global Strategy* (Boston: Harvard Business School Press, 2007).

2. For more, see Matthew J. Eyring, Mark W. Johnson, and Hari Nair, "New Business Models in Emerging Markets," *Harvard Business Review*, January-February 2011.

3. For an interesting perspective, see Michael Schrage, "The Real Cause of Nokia's Crisis," *HBR Blog Network*, February 15, 2011, http://blogs.hbr.org/schrage/2011/02/the-real-cause-of-nokias-crisi.html.

4. For more, see Vijay Govindarajan and Atanu Ghosh, "Reverse Innovation Success in the Telecom Sector," *HBR Blog Network,* May 12, 2010, http://blogs.hbr.org/cs/2010/05/ reverse_innovation_success_in_the_tele.html.

5. For more, see Vijay Govindarajan and S. Manikutty, "What Poor Countries Can Teach Rich Ones About Health Care," *HBR Blog Network,* April 27, 2010, http://blogs.hbr.org/cs/2010/ 04/how_poor_countries_can_help_so.html.

6. Some of the ideas in this section are discussed in Anil Gupta, Vijay Govindarajan, and Haiyan Wang, *The Quest for Global Dominance* (San Francisco: Jossey-Bass, 2008).

7. Ernst & Young, "Winning in a Polycentric World," March 2011, 15.

8. Ibid., 12.

9. Jeff Immelt, Vijay Govindarajan, and Chris Trimble, "How GE Is Disrupting Itself," *Harvard Business Review,* October 2009, 56–65.

Chapter 5

1. All quotes from Rory Dooley are from telephone interviews with the authors, April 2010.

Chapter 6

1. All quotes from Alvaro Restrepo are from telephone interviews with the authors, October 2010.

2. Robert McDonald, quoted in Jennifer Reingold, "Can P&G Make Money in Places Where People Earn $2 a Day?" *Fortune,* January 6, 2011.

Chapter 7

1. Dylan Tweney, "Apple Takes Aim at Cable with Tiny New Apple TV," *Wired,* September 1, 2010, www.wired.com/gadgetlab/2010/09/apple-tv-introduction/.

2. All quotes from Steve Todd are from telephone interviews with the authors, April 2010.

Chapter 8

1. All quotes from Jeff Benge are from telephone interviews with the authors, December 2010.

Chapter 9

1. All quotes from Sachin Lawande are from telephone interviews with the authors, December 2009.

Chapter 10

1. All quotes from V. Raja are from telephone interviews with the authors, December 2009.

2. All quotes from Oswin Varghese are from telephone interviews with the authors, December 2009.

3. Hospitals determined the charges for each ECG exam. GE did not get to say how much the hospitals charged.

Chapter 11

1. All quotes from Indra Nooyi are from a speech to the Yale School of Management in February 2010.

2. All quotes from Mehmood Khan are from telephone interviews with the authors, May and July 2010.

3. All quotes from Gautham Mukkavilli are from telephone interviews with the authors, May 2010.

4. All quotes from Deepika Warrier are from telephone interviews with the authors, May 2010.

Chapter 12

1. Miguel's story and Bernadette's story have been adapted from J. J. Furin et al., "Expanding Global HIV Treatment: Case Studies from the Field," *Annals of the New York Academy of Sciences* 1136 (2008): 1–9.

2. All quotes from Heidi Behforouz are from telephone interviews with the authors, December 2010.

3. This chapter's depiction of Farmer and of the PIH experience in Haiti and Peru draws gratefully on Tracy Kidder's extraordinary book, *Mountains Beyond Mountains* (New York: Random House, 2004).

4. Furin et al., "Expanding Global HIV Treatment," 4.

5. David Bornstein, "Treating the Cause, Not the Illness," Opinionator series, *New York Times*, July 28, 2011, http://opinionator.blogs.nytimes.com/2011/07/28/treating-the-cause-not-the-illness/.

Appendix B

1. Jeffrey R. Immelt, Vijay Govindarajan, and Chris Trimble, "How GE Is Disrupting Itself," *Harvard Business Review*, October 2009, 56–65.

2. Kathleen M. Eisenhardt and Melissa E. Graebner, "Theory Building from Cases: Opportunities and Challenges," *Academy of Management Journal* 50, no. 1 (2007): 25–32; Barney G. Glaser and Anselm L. Strauss, *The Discovery of Grounded Theory: Strategies for Qualitative Research* (New York: Aldine de Gruyter, 1967); R. K. Yin, *Case Study Research: Design and Methodology* (Newbury Park, CA: Sage, 1994).

3. Raymond Vernon, "International Investment and International Trade in the Product Life Cycle," *Quarterly Journal of Economics* 80 (May 1966): 190–207.

4. Raymond Vernon, "The Product Cycle Hypothesis in a New International Environment," *Oxford Bulletin of Economics and Statistics* 41, no. 4 (1979): 255–267.

5. Christopher A. Bartlett and Sumantra Ghoshal, *Managing Across Borders: The Transnational Solution* (Boston: Harvard Business School Press, 1988); Pankaj Ghemawat, *Redefining Global Strategy* (Boston: Harvard Business School Press, 2007); C. K. Prahalad and Yves L. Doz, *The Multinational Mission: Balancing Local Demands and Global Vision* (New York: Free Press, 1987); Michael E. Porter, "Changing Patterns of International Competition," *California Management Review* 28 (1986): 9–40.

6. Vijay Govindarajan and Ravi Ramamurti, "Reverse Innovation, Emerging Markets, and Global Strategy," *Global Strategy Journal* 1, no. 2 (2011).

7. Clayton M. Christensen, *The Innovator's Dilemma* (Boston: Harvard Business School Press, 1997).

8. C. K. Prahalad, *Fortune at the Bottom of the Pyramid* (Philadelphia: Wharton Publishing, 2009); T. London and S. L. Hart, *Next Generation Business Strategies for the Base of the Pyramid: New Approaches for Building Mutual Value* (Upper Saddle River, NJ: Free Press, 2010).

9. Pankaj Ghemawat, "Distance Still Matters," *Harvard Business Review*, September–October, 2001, 137–147.

10. K. Meyer and E. Sinani, "When and Where Does Foreign Direct Investment Generate Positive Spillovers? A Meta-Analysis," *Journal of International Business Studies* 40 (September 2009): 1075–1094.

11. Paul Lawrence and Jay Lorsch, *Organization and Environment: Managing Differentiation and Integration* (Boston: Harvard Business School Press, 1967); Vijay Govindarajan and Chris Trimble, *Ten Rules for Strategic Innovators: From Idea to Execution* (Boston: Harvard Business

School Press, 2005); Vijay Govindarajan and Chris Trimble, *The Other Side of Innovation: Solving the Execution Challenge* (Boston: Harvard Business School Press, 2010); Charles O'Reilly and Michael Tushman, "The Ambidextrous Organization," *Harvard Business Review,* April 2004, 74–81.

12. Richard Bettis and C. K. Prahalad, "The Dominant Logic: Retrospective and Extension," *Strategic Management Journal* 16 (1995): 5–14.

13. Ravi Ramamurti and Jitendra V. Singh, *Emerging Multinationals in Emerging Markets* (New York: Cambridge University Press, 2009); T. Khanna and K. G. Palepu, *Winning in Emerging Markets: A Road Map for Strategy and Execution* (Boston: Harvard Business Press, 2010).

14. Y. Tsurumi, *The Japanese Are Coming* (Cambridge, MA: Ballinger, 1976); A. Amsden, *Asia's Next Giant: South Korea and Late Industrialization* (New York: Oxford University Press, 1992); Ramamurti and Singh, *Emerging Multinationals in Emerging Markets.*

15. Thomas Friedman, *The World Is Flat: A Brief History of the Twenty-First Century* (New York: Farrar, Straus, and Giroux, 2005).

INDEX

Page numbers with *t* and *f* indicate tables and figures

ABOUT THE AUTHORS

Dr. Vijay Govindarajan

Vijay Govindarajan (www.tuck.dartmouth.edu/people/vg/) is widely regarded as one of the world's leading experts on strategy and innovation. He is the Earl C. Daum 1924 Professor of International Business at the Tuck School of Business at Dartmouth College. He was the first Professor in Residence and Chief Innovation Consultant at General Electric. He worked with GE's CEO Jeff Immelt to write "How GE Is Disrupting Itself," the *Harvard Business Review* article that pioneered the concept of reverse innovation—any innovation that is adopted first in the developing world. *Harvard Business Review* rated reverse innovation as one of the ten big ideas of the decade.

VG writes about innovation and execution on his blog, through his quarterly newsletter, in *Harvard Business Review,* and in *Bloomberg Businessweek.* He is a coleader of a global initiative to design a $300 house for the poor (www.300house.com).

Govindarajan has been identified as a leading management thinker by influential publications, including these: Outstanding Faculty, named by *Businessweek* in its *Guide to the Best B-Schools*; Top Ten Business School Professor in Corporate Executive Education, named by *Businessweek*; Top Five Most Respected Executive Coach on Strategy, rated by *Forbes*; Top 50 Management Thinker, named by the *Times* (London); Rising Super Star, cited by *The Economist*; Outstanding Teacher of the Year, voted by MBA students.

VG has been on the faculties of Harvard Business School, INSEAD (Fontainebleau), and the Indian Institute of Management (Ahmedabad, India).

The recipient of numerous awards for excellence in research, Govindarajan was inducted into the *Academy of Management Journal's* Hall of

Fame and was ranked by *Management International Review* as one of the Top Twenty North American Superstars for research in strategy and organization. One of his papers was recognized as one of the ten most-often cited articles in the entire forty-year history of *Academy of Management Journal*.

VG is a rare faculty member who has published more than ten articles in the top academic journals (*Academy of Management Journal, Academy of Management Review, Strategic Management Journal*) and more than ten articles in prestigious practitioner journals, including several best-selling *Harvard Business Review* articles. He received the McKinsey Award for the best article in the *Harvard Business Review*. He has published ten books, including international best sellers *Ten Rules for Strategic Innovators* and *The Other Side of Innovation*.

VG has worked with CEOs and top management teams in more than 25 percent of the *Fortune* 500 firms to discuss, challenge, and escalate their thinking about strategy. His clients include Boeing, Coca-Cola, Colgate-Palmolive, Deere, FedEx, GE, Hewlett-Packard, IBM, J.P. Morgan Chase, J&J, *New York Times*, P&G, Sony, and Wal-Mart. He is a keynote speaker in CEO forums and major conferences, including the *Businessweek*, CEO Forum, HSM World Business Forum, and World Economic Forum at Davos.

VG received his doctorate from the Harvard Business School and was awarded the Robert Bowne Prize for the best thesis proposal. He also received his MBA with distinction from the Harvard Business School. Prior to this, VG received his chartered accountancy degree in India, where he was awarded the President's Gold Medal for obtaining the first rank nationwide.

Chris Trimble

Chris Trimble (www.chris-trimble.com) has dedicated the past ten years to studying a single challenge that vexes even the best-managed corporations: how to execute an innovation initiative.

His work came to fruition with the 2010 publication of *The Other Side of Innovation: Solving the Execution Challenge*. Chris has also published three lead articles in the *Harvard Business Review,* including "How GE Is Disrupting Itself," in October 2009, with GE chairman and CEO Jeff Immelt and Vijay Govindarajan.

Chris first broke into the forefront of executive consciousness with his December 2005 book *Ten Rules for Strategic Innovators: From Idea to Execution*. In June 2006, the *Wall Street Journal* published a Top Ten Recommended Reading List, which included *Ten Rules* alongside *Freakonomics*, *The Tipping Point*, and *Blink*. *Strategy & Business* magazine recognized *Ten Rules* as the best strategy book of the year.

Chris's career mixes rigorous academic research with hard-nosed practical experience. His interest in innovation within large organizations developed early in his career, when he was a submarine officer in the U.S. Navy.

Chris is currently on the faculty at the Tuck School of Business at Dartmouth. He is a frequent keynote speaker and has spoken all over the world. He has also published in the *MIT Sloan Management Review*, *California Management Review*, *Businessweek*, *Forbes*, *Fast Company*, and the *Financial Times*. He holds an MBA degree with distinction from the Tuck School and a bachelor of science degree with highest distinction from the University of Virginia.